THE BLOOD

AND THE

SWEAT

THE STORY OF

Sick of it all's

KOLLER

BROTHERS

A POST HILL PRESS BOOK
ISBN: 978-1-64293-225-6
ISBN (eBook): 978-1-64293-226-3

The Blood and the Sweat:
The Story of Sick of It All's Koller Brothers
© 2020 by Lou Koller, Pete Koller, and Howie Abrams
All Rights Reserved

Cover and Interior Design by Donna McLeer / Tunnel Vizion Media
Front Cover Photo by Joel Ricard, Back Cover Photo by BJ Papas

Photos Provided by: BJ Papas, Lou, Pete, Mei-Ling Koller, Steven Koller, Laurens Kusters,
Gary Humienny, Joost van Laake, Squirm, Silvy Maatman, Dirk Behlau, Jeff Pliskin,
Rod Orchard, Inti Carboni and Bill Florio

Stick Figure Illustrations by Howie Abrams

Post Hill
PRESS

Post Hill Press
New York · Nashville
posthillpress.com

Published in the United States of America

THE BLOOD AND THE SWEAT

THE STORY OF Sick of it all's KOLLER BROTHERS

LOU KOLLER, PETE KOLLER WITH **HOWIE ABRAMS**

Post Hill
PRESS

—TABLE OF CONTENTS—

——— FOREWORD BY ———
CHRIS CARRABBA

I was in high school and I was super into heavy bands. Of course, this was in the pre-Spotify era, so you had to wait around for somebody to tell you what records to get. I had this friend who worked at our small local record shop, and he hated to clean the store, so, if I came in around closing time and vacuumed, sprayed the counters, and took on his less glamorous duties, he would give me a couple of records as pay. I did the work and got the records, but he insisted on picking them for me. He would play me what he was going to give me while I worked cleaning the shop, and he would play it loud.

I remember him playing this one record and thinking to myself, "I need to hear this whole thing. I just have to hear this." So, I took my sweet time cleaning that place and listened to the whole thing. I was absolutely floored, but played it super cool. My friend handed me my two records when I finished cleaning, but neither was the one he had spun while I was cleaning. I was bummed, but I didn't want to give it away that I was nerding out so hard, so I just let it go. Turns out, it was a pre-release copy of an album he received from one of the record labels. I hounded him for a few weeks until I thought he was tired of the record, and finally, he gave me the promo—without mentioning that it was coming out only a few days later. I could have stopped begging and just waited for the regular copy, but he kept me hanging so I would keep cleaning the bathroom, which was no easy feat in that store. Now I had the record, and I became obsessed with it. It was Sick of it All's *Scratch the Surface*.

At my school, nobody knew about hardcore bands. I didn't know anything either, but I wound up talking to one of the older guys I skated with after school and he told me it was their third album. I went straight to the record shop for the first two.

Fast forward a little bit, and Sick of It All is coming to play in Fort Lauderdale. I have long since forgotten the name of the venue, but it had an upstairs room called "The Attic".

So get this. My band was picked by the local promoter to open for them. The band I was in predated me, but by the time my best friend and I joined, it had evolved, or devolved, depending on your taste, from a prog-rock band into a kind of post-punk thing, and then it became closer to post-hardcore; something like Jimmy Eat World meets Hot Water Music, even though I don't think we'd even heard Jimmy Eat World yet. We were beyond psyched to play the show, and didn't think it was that odd for us to be playing with hardcore bands, because in Florida, there were so few bands to begin with that genre overlap was very common at shows.

Even though we weren't a straight up hardcore band, we had a draw that the promoter thought would work for this show. It was going to be the biggest show our band would play to date, but it wouldn't have mattered if we were going to be playing for two people. All we cared about was that somehow, through some exceptional turn of fate, we were going to be opening for our heroes, Sick of It All. I think it was probably the band's biggest show that we would ever play, and it was sold out in advance of us being asked to be on the bill. The pressure was huge. We practiced our asses off and then we practiced some more.

The day of the show was finally here. The other guitar player and I show up, and then, we wait. We wait for our rhythm section, the Bonebrake brothers (their real last name is Bonebrake). I'm still confused as to why we didn't name the band after them. Anyway, we wait for them to show up...and they never do! The promoter tells us if we don't play, we'll never get another show. Ever! Having no idea what to do, the two of us idiots just go up and play our most rhythm-section based songs. I played guitar and my other guitar player, John, had his guitar in one of the Bonebrake brothers' cars, but he had sombody's bass in his car, so that is what he played. I don't think he'd ever played bass once before that night. We were just terrified, and, I'm going to be real honest here, it wasn't good! Let's just leave it at that. We played just long enough to have not killed ourselves with the promoter, but we'd definitely embarrassed ourselves. We were thinking, *do we even want to stay around and see Sick of it All now that we've had our lowest moment?* So, we're walking off stage and Lou Koller comes over and says, "Hey, what happened?" I said, "The rest of the band didn't show up." He said, "But you played anyway?" I didn't go into it having been do or die for our fledgling band in our fickle and political music scene. I just said, "Well, yeah," and he just replies, "FUCKING AWESOME!" In that moment, it didn't matter that we weren't good, it mattered that we stood up and did what we were there to do. That struck me hard and has stayed with me all these years since. I think Lou saying something positive to some kid he had never met before was one of those moments for me where a seed was planted and a root would soon take hold. Lou let me feel like I was part of it for simply being there and following through. He made sure I felt included, even though I was so aware of how small my part in that evening was.

To this day, I have this relationship with my audience that is based on community. There's no real division between me and the audience. That stems from my experience in the hardcore scene, and is exemplified by this guy I looked up to then and now, who just saw me fail miserably and made me feel part of something anyway. I mean, I can draw a direct line from then to when I began doing, I guess what you could call the singer-songwriter thing that I do. What most people would think to do is go play coffee shops or the like, but that wasn't my network, and those weren't my people. That show opening for Sick of it All was scary. I had to play up there with these heavy bands, to a room of tattooed dudes—and this isn't like tattooed now, this is tattooed THEN. What I was about to embark on as a kid with an acoustic guitar in the hardcore scene wasn't as scary as having to play without a band right before Sick of it All. But, I did just that, and got an attaboy from Lou that night, so I figured, *fuck it, I can do this*. I had to deal with something similar just recently. I was about to do a show, and something about it just didn't sit right with me, but I HAD to do it. I remembered, just be you. Do what you do without compromise, and you'll either sink or float, but it will be uncorrupted. Those are all things I took from that specific instance, and from that scene in general.

Some years later, Dashboard is starting to do well. I had only just stopped playing solo, and began having a band. It was one of our first times playing in the UK, at either Reading or Leeds, and I ended up sitting on a road case somewhere backstage. Pete Koller, who I didn't know, but was still a devoted fan of, just randomly came and sat next to me, and started chatting. I don't think he knew who I was, but I guess I looked like a hardcore kid. So, we're chatting, and I told him, "I would have to kick myself if I didn't tell you how important your band is to me." He was very, very gracious. He began asking me about my band for a really long time. I asked him a few things, and he'd give it some thought, then gave me a little direction here and there. I think back to that conversation now....At that point, I really hadn't ever been in a band that was popular long enough for me to dispense advice to anybody. In the coming years, when I was in that position, I remembered how gracious Pete was with his time, and always tried to make my best effort to talk to whoever the new kid is, and listened to that kid in the same way I was listened to. I don't know that I have great advice to give. I don't know that I have ANY advice to offer, but I can listen the way that he listened to me. I don't know that it will have the same impact that my experience with Pete had on me, but if it can, it's worth doing.

We sat there on that road case for a bit, and one of the Gallagher brothers walked by. I didn't care. They just don't hold that place for me. I was chatting it up with one of my heroes, and I was keenly aware that I was going to remember this moment.

There is a way Lou and Pete carry themselves. It's with a genuine kindness and an inviting manner most wouldn't expect. That scene in New York has this incorrect reputation whereby people are unapproachable: tough, mean, too cool, whatever. That's not real. What's real is that they deserve respect for being pioneers, and building a scene that would spread across the nation and the world. That scene was and is inclusive. In fact what people like me and you really learned from that scene is that you must connect with EVERYBODY to make it work. Then there's the ethos and the dedication of DIY that permeates it. Sick of It All took that ethos and spread it through hard touring and incredible, timeless music.

I appreciate that Lou, Pete and every member of Sick of It All, past and present, have been so good to the fans, to the younger bands, and younger musicians around them. They realize that if they bring about a strong, healthy new generation, it's good for them too. The way that they conduct themselves is beyond reproach. They seem to feel lucky that you like them, and believe me, I know bands that carry themselves as if you're supposed to feel lucky to have ever heard them. I have to believe that it takes a lot of effort to maintain a career the way they have, and they still somehow appreciate every moment. Every moment seems to be: We can't believe we're able to do this, even if it's for the tenth time. They're still surprised by almost everything that happens for them. That's not a PR thing. That's genuine. That's Lou and Pete.

INTRODUCTION BY
HOWIE ABRAMS

Over the last several decades, a number of elite hard-edged bands have featured blood siblings within their ranks—from AC/DC's Angus and Malcolm Young to the Van Halen brothers to Pantera's Darrell and Vinnie Abbott to Max and Iggor Cavalera from Brazil's bludgeoning Sepultura. Then there's Bad Brains' H.R. and Earl Hudson. However, when it comes to New York hardcore, the community proudly boasts the blue-collar-as-fuck Koller brothers, who have dominated the scene worldwide since 1986 with the ferocious quartet Sick of It All as their vehicle.

When youths acquaint themselves with hardcore punk—it doesn't matter which era you look at—they are no doubt in search of a much-needed escape. A place to go and a subculture to immerse themselves in which allows them to discard the frustrations of everyday being. These dissatisfactions often include, but are not limited to: parents, teachers, religious institutions, the high volume of assholes encountered on a daily basis, and, last but not least, bad music.

If we're talking about early to mid-eighties hardcore in New York City, this was most certainly the case, although, much like the Big Apple itself, the movement within the five boroughs had its own rules and ways of operating. The leading New York hardcore bands of the day featured members with colorful nicknames like "Stigma," "Gestapo," and "Bloodclot." The scene was as intimidating as it was attractive. In fact, its sheer volatility was a tremendous component of its allure, alongside the loud, fast tunes. Those who came upon it, whether for the bands, the sense of belonging, or both, became immersed in an extraordinary cult-like escapade. All in all, it was an adventure for all who chose to walk through the gates of hardcore.

For Flushing, Queens, natives Lou and Pete Koller, the adventure began as a lifestyle and gradually became a career. My earliest recollection of the brothers does not involve witnessing the duo and their aurally murderous quartet onstage, simultaneously uniting and demolishing a venue bursting at the seams with angry kids. It was having quietly observed them and their crew from across a Manhattan-bound F-line subway car heading from Queens into the city to catch a show. This occurred a handful of times. Whether it was on the way to see NWOBHM pioneers Raven or a CBGB matinee with Agnostic Front, I never chose to communicate with them, although there may have been the odd "Hey, I know that you know that I know we're headed to the same place" nod of acknowledgement. Incidentally, their entourage included future members of bands the likes of Agnostic Front, Youth of Today, Straight Ahead, Rest in Pieces, Raw Deal, Helmet, and others. Who knew?

The brothers Koller were reared on heavy metal's more fringe outfits of the seventies and eighties. At first, it was Black Sabbath. Then there was Motörhead. Later, acts like Venom, early Metallica, Slayer, and Celtic Frost. Shortly thereafter, NYHC stalwarts Agnostic Front, Murphy's Law, and the Cro-Mags entered their collective consciousness, alongside UK faves GBH, Discharge, and The Exploited. Speed and aggression were the order of those days—the higher the beats per minute the better, and groups such as Negative Approach, D.R.I., NYC Mayhem, and Siege soon began to play a substantial role in Lou and Pete's musical development. By 1986, the Kollers were creating their own brand of noise. Sick of It All was born: without question, one of, if not THE most popular and successful hardcore band in the world. SOIA performs for tens of thousands annually to this day, while nearly thirty-five years along as a group. If Agnostic Front are the godfathers of the NYHC movement, vocalist Lou and guitarist Pete are its grandmasters.

Sonically, Sick of It All puts forth short, two-fisted bursts of tornadic energy, yet their tunes are crafted in a manner any purveyor of fine Euro pub anthems can embrace and retain for a lifetime. As lyricists, the fellas take a bold and powerful stance, and have done so since the earliest days of the band. The subject matter is consistently urgent and representative of life, death, and everything in between, be it literal or emotional. Their words are penetrable by careful yet deliberate design.

Lou and Pete Koller have lugged punk rock's much angrier subgenre on their backs to locales across the globe previously reckoned unfathomable for a collective of their ilk, all the while carrying with them a blazing torch of independence and the vast frustration ingrained in the oft forgotten working class of America. As mid-teens, neither Pete nor big brother Lou could have imagined interest in early NYC hardcore becoming a more than three-decade world tour as ambassadors of a fraternity, which so positively, and drastically, altered their being. While Lou and Pete's story might not read as outrageously as that of Oasis's Gallagher brothers or the Black Crowes' notorious Robinsons, the Koller's collective tale is unlike any other, especially within the universe of aggressive music. Theirs is a relatable narrative for anyone who has ever picked up a guitar or perched themselves behind a microphone with a dream of "making it." With that, fame was never their goal. Serving a purpose and making a living while doing so was what they set out to accomplish, and throughout years of touring and recording, Lou and Pete's perspective remained singular, and their blood bond kept them, as well as their band, together.

When all is said and done, Lou and Pete Koller are living the American dream in the same manner as, say, The Ramones probably did. No one embarks on a career in music expecting it to work out in their favor, regardless of quantitative metrics. What remains important to these brothers is continuing to spread the hardcore reality as they see fit and furthering their kinship with like-minded, disenfranchised young people the world over through hardcore.

PART I
GROWING UP KOLLER

LOUIS PIERRE KOLLER B. JULY 15, 1965
PIERRE MICHEL KOLLER B. AUGUST 5, 1966

LOU KOLLER: Me and Pete are two of four brothers: Matt's a year and a few months older than me, and Steven's a year older than him. Pete's younger than me by a little less than a year. Our parents obviously got busy! They wanted to have kids right away.

PETE KOLLER: Our Dad, Louis, was in the army, and he met my mother, Josette, in France. He was born in Queens, and she was born in Poitiers, pronounced like "Sidney Poitier." My Mom has a twin sister, Genevieve, and she was working in the same place my Dad was. He was doing accounting stuff for the army, and my aunt was working in the office with him. Apparently, there was a party which my Dad and aunt were going to attend, and Aunt Genevieve told my Mom, "Hey, we're going to this party with a bunch of American soldiers," and my Mom didn't want to go. My aunt was like, "Come on, come on, you're going, you've gotta go,"

Easter Sunday at grandma's, still hungover from the night before.

so she went, and our parents met at the party. My Mom didn't speak English, and my Dad didn't speak French, but something set it off, and they went on a whole bunch of dates while he was over there.

LOU: They eventually made their way to Queens and got married. My grandparents, my father's parents, lived there too, right at the border of Bayside. Damn, Queens.... My first memories are just all four brothers hanging out together. We had a house in Bayside. It was a two-family house, and we had the bottom floor with a little yard in the back, and it was always just us four brothers running around together.

PETE: It was like built-in friends. There was always someone to play with. We had a little pool set up in our backyard....

LOUIS KOLLER SENIOR (LOU AND PETE'S FATHER): Their mom, Josette, says that Pete and Louie were normal kids growing up. They started in a Catholic grammar school but were soon transferred to a public school, PS 107, because the St. Kevin school began to charge tuition, which we couldn't afford. Both their older brothers were attending PS 107, so at one time, all four

Koller boys were in the same school. The one thing I remember Pete and Lou being interested in then was soccer. This was a surprise to both their mom and me because the boys' older brothers, Steve and Matt, grew up playing baseball. Lou and Pete played on the same soccer team. I believe the team was named the Rams. No championships, but they had fun and made lots of friends. I believe Louie received a trophy two years in a row for being voted most *liked* by team members, like Mr. Congeniality. After the first couple of practices, the guy that signed up to manage the team, who was a member of St. John's University's soccer team, disappeared, so Louie and Pete's mom and I became trainers and managers and were in charge of transportation. I remember returning from their games with six or seven sweaty soccer players in the back of our station wagon. We had to air out the car when we got home.

LOU: We all tried playing baseball together. My dad was big into baseball, and I remember us just being reckless boys. Whatever our older brothers did, Pete and I wanted to do. Batman was a big TV show at the time, and my brothers would run around playing Batman and Robin, and I wanted to play too. We'd all get towels and tie them around our necks as capes, and Matt and Steve would jump down from the top of the basement steps. I wanted to be part of the game too, so I climbed to the highest step–I'm three years old–and I jump and just fall down the stairs and give myself a hernia at the age of three!

LOU: One thing I remember us both being really into back then was television. I also remember our dad bringing us comic books when we were really young, and for Christmas, I would get an anthology of whatever comics I liked, but I didn't become obsessed with them until later when I was maybe thirteen or so.

PETE: Taking the subway was always an event. My first memory of the subway is our mom taking us into the city, all four boys getting onto the train, and it was covered in graffiti.

LOU: Not big, elaborate pieces, but everyone used to write their name and their street, or their name and the avenue they lived on. You'd see "Fred 49," "Rich 43"–those were the big ones in Flushing. "Disco Dan" was the biggest.

PETE: "Fred 49" was a legend to us.

LOU: My brother Matt wrote "Matt 167" and Steve wrote "Steve 167." I was like, "I wanna do that," and my mother's like, "OH NO!" She got mad at them, but the train car was just covered, all over the seats, the floor, everything. Then people started scratching their names into the windows.

PETE: Scratchiti!

LOU: That was happening more when I started going to high school. But our mom would do really nice things with us. If we had off from school and she had the time, she'd take us all to Rockefeller Center or Central Park.

PETE: Our parents always provided. Even if there wasn't a lot of money, there would always be some sort of vacation. There were always Christmas presents. My dad had to work plenty of overtime, or work weekends just to make it. Both our parents worked super hard. Just think of feeding that many boys. I'm twelve, Lou's thirteen, Matt's fourteen, and Steve's fifteen. My parents would bring home food from the supermarket and I'd eat an entire pack of hot dogs before they got them into the house! Actually, I would wait until everyone went to bed and then do it, but you get the point.

LOU: There was one kid on the block; I don't remember his name, but he was friends with Steve and Matt. His parents owned the funeral parlor that was on the corner, and they always used to go play there. I remember being SO jealous, and one day I got so excited that we got to run around inside this funeral parlor.

I didn't see any dead bodies or anything like that. I didn't even see a coffin, but I did see the table they laid the coffins on for viewings. That was the room we all played in. It had all the chairs set up for funerals and everything.

PETE: It was almost always the four of us brothers together, but as we got older, our brothers began to hang out with their older friends, so it turned into me and Lou always being together.

LOU: Don't ask me how I remember this, but when we were really young, our whole family went to France to meet my mother's side of the family. Somehow, I remember walking down the cobblestone streets and meeting our grandfather for the first time. We went into this room, and there was just a pile of toys laid out for us to play with. I was all excited to dig in, but our parents were like, "No, no, you have to say hello to your grandfather first," so I went over to him. He had Pete in one arm, and he scooped me up. I remember him holding me, and after everyone said hello to him, Steve and Matt started playing with the toys and my grandfather wouldn't let go of me. I remember leaning over and staring at the toys....

PETE: Seriously, how the hell do you remember this?!

LOU: I told this story to my mother once, and she asked, "How do you remember that?" I said, "Maybe I wanted to play with those toys so badly, it was torture, so it's still in my head." I remember the floor being covered with toys, and Steve and Matt with big smiles on their faces, running around and just diving into them. My mom told me that Matt, for some reason, seemed to be jealous of me being one of the new babies at the time. She said, while we were in France, he took a toy plane of mine and threw it off the balcony. He said, "I wanted to see it fly," but supposedly, he did it simply because it was mine. My mom said as soon as he did that, I got all upset and grabbed all of his Silly Putty and flushed it down the toilet!

PETE: I'm always super thankful for growing up in Queens. Or just New York, because we never grew up thinking "Oh, that's a black kid," or "That's a Chinese kid." It was always just "There's my friend Keith, or that's Lee." It's a little weird for my daughter Lucy sometimes growing up here in Florida, not having all of these different types of friends in school. For me and Lou, it was more fun that way. Everybody became your pal.

LOU: We didn't realize it when we were in the midst of it, but thinking back to our neighborhood, it was mostly white people: Germans, Italians, Irish.... I remember the first neighbors we had who weren't yelling at us all the time for playing baseball or football in the street because their car was parked there were part of a Chinese family. They didn't speak English, which might explain why they didn't yell at us, but they were always giving us candy and being cool to us. Every kid in our school was a different ethnicity, but we didn't pay any attention to that because we were all just kids. No one gave a shit about stuff like that then. It wasn't until we got to junior high school that people would say things like, "You need to watch out for those guys," this or that ethnic group, and we were always just like, "Huh?!"

PETE: Our school was right down the block from where we lived, but in the fourth grade, I had to go to a different school. I was getting into too much trouble.

LOU: What kind of trouble could you possibly have been getting into as a fourth grader?!

PETE: It has to do with being shy. In fact, my daughter Lucy is kind of going through this now too. If I wasn't understanding what was being taught, I was too shy to ask for help. I'd just be like, "Fuck it, I'm not doing this." I would take an angry point of view on it, like, "Who cares?! Give me a zero." So then I was labelled a "bad kid" and was sent to PS 193 in Whitestone.

LOU: Overall, school was pretty boring, average, I guess. It's funny, because in other people's books, there are these crazy stories like, "And then, at the age of four, I was in the middle of a drug deal...." Well, in the fourth grade, we were at recess, running around like maniacs, and I slipped and broke my leg!

LOUIS KOLLER SENIOR: Louie broke his leg running in the schoolyard. He tripped over a lunch box.

LOU: My left leg, I couldn't move it, so they took me to the office, had a look at me, and instead of getting the nurse, they called my mom, but they didn't tell her I couldn't walk or put any weight on the leg. So my poor mom carried me down the stairs, out of the school, and then our neighbor saw her and helped her carry me home. When my dad came home, he took me to the hospital, and they took an X-ray. They said that there was nothing wrong, *it must just be muscular blah blah blah*, and they put an ACE bandage around it. When I stood up, my thigh bone snapped in half. It was a fracture that I swear to God I could see on the X-ray from laying on the table, and they just kept telling me, "Oh, there's nothing there." When they called the specialist, he goes, "Yeah, right there, it's a hairline fracture." It was the most painful thing I ever went through.

PETE: But that's no drug deal!

LOU: No, but I remember the doctor saying, "We'll get you a wheelchair," and my dad was like, "He should probably walk on it, right?" and the doctor says, "Yeah, sure, he can stand on it." I stood up and all of a sudden, I just screamed, then I fell. My dad picked me up and put me on the table. The ACE bandage was bulging. They took the metal clasps off, and the bone was pushing up through the muscle. Then, the doctors manually pulled my leg straight. Thankfully, it was only one pull. They said they might have had to do it several times until they got it straight. He pulled it, and the whole thing went right back into place. The bone lined up. They took me right back to X-ray after he did that. My feet were even, but it was clearly still broken.

STEVEN KOLLER (LOU AND PETE'S OLDEST BROTHER): He had a body cast on. It went from his chest down to the one broken leg, and then halfway down the other, so we had to take care of him. He couldn't go to the bathroom. We had to use bedpans and stuff like that, but by the time they were ready to take the cast off, instead of the cast being up to his chest, it was down to his stomach. He'd grown like eight or ten inches while he'd been lying in bed. Lou was around five foot eight when he broke the leg, but then he was over six feet when it healed. It was like, "What the hell?!"

LOUIS KOLLER SENIOR: He was in the cast for at least six months. He had a board of education teacher come to the house and homeschool him for the rest of the year.

PETE: Schools even had their own dentists then. They actually had a dental office. They never used Novocain, and I had cavities, so it sucked, but you had free dental. Everything like that was taken care of. When I mention that to people, they're like, "There was a dentist in your school?" Yes, there was a full-on dentist's office.

LOU: Yeah, New York is such a truly unique place to grow up in.
Pete: True, but somehow New Yorkers have the worst reputation around the world, and I'll never understand it. From living in Manhattan for a really long time, and then travelling the world, the only people that are rude in New York are people from other states who move to New York. I think they believe they're supposed to behave rudely 'cause they saw it in movies. Native New Yorkers are like, "We're just trying to pay the bills. We have to get shit done."

LOU: It's not being rude, it's just being a New Yorker; "I gotta get here, I gotta get there. I gotta get it done." If you're dawdling on the sidewalk in front of me, get the hell out of my way because I've got stuff to do! That's what it is, but that's pretty much the way it is in any big city. You've got to catch the train to make it home so you can get to bed so you can get back on the train to get back to work. The only time I'd say it gets pretty rude is at rush hour, when you're waiting to get on the train. How hard is it to fucking let people OFF the train before trying to get on, you motherfucker?! But so many people have the wrong idea about New York. The first time we went to Croatia, the war was still on and people there would say, "Wow, you're from New York, that must be scary," and I'm looking at them thinking, "Your country's at war! THAT'S SCARY!" That's the kind of stuff that blows me away. I think people who have never been here seem to have this impression that New York City is like a video game: you walk down the streets of Manhattan, dodging knives and guns, or there's always a person that's going to pickpocket you. It's all from TV and movies.

PETE: I met people from Zagreb who told me, "A missile flew over the city last week. It blew up right near my house," and without skipping a beat, they'd say, "WOW, you guys are from Brooklyn?!" Everyone outside of New York thinks all New Yorkers are from Brooklyn. "Damn, Brooklyn must be crazy! How do you live like that?!" Especially when Biohazard was at their biggest in the '90s, there was no New York, it was just Brooklyn.

LOU: And even to this day, some reviews will say, "Sick of It All from Brooklyn," and I'm like, "Yeah, I like Brooklyn. It's nice, but...."

PETE: I wish I could afford to live there these days.

LOU: Of course, though, I always have to proudly chime in with something like, "Well, Queens has tough parts too!" I'm glad I came from Queens. There are dangerous parts of anywhere and everywhere. Go to Cincinnati, Ohio; there are some scary-ass places in Cincinnati, or Baltimore, or Detroit. We used to go into Manhattan with our friend, Tom Farkas, a huge guy, probably six foot three, around two-hundred-something pounds. He looked big and menacing and had an afro. We were all into art, and at that time, everyone had a painted denim jacket with album covers and stuff on the back. Tom painted Black Sabbath's Vol. 4 on my jacket. He made his own design. It was really occult-ish looking. It was all red, and he put a skull on it with curly horns and a pentagram and candles and, for some reason, wrote "Crimson Cult" on it. He just came up with that idea.

PETE: Tom also painted a jacket for me, a Harley-Davidson jacket.

LOUIS KOLLER SENIOR: Their mother remembers sewing the KISS logo, along with a number of other band names and logos, onto their denim jackets. Big fad at that time.

LOU: So we go to the city, and we're all excited: "Yeah, we're gonna go buy records at Bleecker Bob's, and we're gonna go here and there." There was a store back then called the Pit. It was a biker store. We get out of the train at Astor Place, and we're walking up to the Pit, which was on St. Mark's Place. A bunch of Hells Angels come roaring down the street on their motorcycles, and they park in front of the Pit.

PETE: Now, mind you, Lou was maybe just into high school, and I was in junior high. We were kids.

LOU: We're all wearing our painted denim jackets and I was feeling "Yeah, I like Black Sabbath and the world is gonna know!" We go into the store and the guy behind the counter is loving us. We're hanging out talking and all of a sudden, three giant Hells Angels, the biggest people I've ever seen in my life, come walking into the store and go, "Give us your jackets," and I'm like, "What?" One of them says, "Who the fuck are you to walk through our 'hood with your colors on?!" I go, "Colors?" And he loudly says, "Gimme your fucking jacket!" I say, "It's just a Black Sabbath jacket," and he proceeds to cut the back out of the jacket with a knife! He cut all of the backs of our jackets out with a knife! We were terrified. They probably took the parts they cut out to hang in their clubhouse on Third Street. Thinking back, they must have looked pretty silly to the other Hells Angels when they got back there and told the rest of them, "Yeah, these guys were rolling through the 'hood, blah blah blah...." Those guys had to be like, "Dude that's a Black Sabbath logo, what's wrong with you?"

PETE: And then they probably looked at the tag, "That says 'extra small' on that denim jacket. How big were these guys? Did you steal these from children???"

LOU: That was like our fourth or fifth time hanging out in the city. The HA guys started yelling at the guy who owned the store too: "...and we don't like some of this other shit you're selling in here either!" The guy behind the counter said, "Just tell me what offends you guys, and I'll take it down right now!" That was a weird experience back then. I thought, "Welp, this isn't Queens, that's for sure!" I guess I understood it more when I learned about the biker mentality, but it was so weird to me when they came in all angry because of a Black Sabbath and Harley-Davidson painted jacket. I mean, "Crimson Cult" meant nothing, and they were painted, they weren't patches. I guess it was Pete's Harley jacket. Thanks a lot, Pete! I lost my Vol. 4 painted jacket because of you! We didn't tell our parents anything about this incident.

PETE: We wouldn't have been allowed to leave the house or do anything ever again.

LOU: It would be years before they even knew we had been going downtown. We'd just tell them, "I'm going out." Back then, no one had cell phones or pagers or anything. They'd ask where we were going, and I'd just answer, "I'm going to Tom's." Then we'd go to Tom's, walk to the subway, get on the subway, and go into Manhattan.

PETE: Sometimes, we would hang out in Times Square, 42nd Street, when it was crazy with bums and hookers and just nutty people.

LOU: They had the best arcades over there, even though it was dangerous as fuck at those arcades. Shady characters everywhere, but there were always teenagers from all over at those arcades.

PETE: Part of the appeal WAS the danger though. We'd get on the bus, go down Main Street, get on the 7 train, exit at Times Square, and start drinking. On one trip, it was me, Lou, our older brother Matt, and Tom Farkas. There was a homeless dude sitting there drinking a bottle of whiskey, and my brother Matt was ripped. He's like, "Yo man, lemme get some," and Matt just takes this disgusting guy's bottle and drinks straight from it! Disgusting but hysterical.

LOU: It was fucking gross! When I was going to Art and Design High School in Manhattan, after a while, we'd cut out and go to Times Square because there was one theatre there where for three dollars you could watch kung fu movies all day. I think one time they had three *Godzilla* movies back-to-back-to back, and we were like, "FUCK YEAH," so we blew off school.

PETE: We'd gotten really into watching *Kung Fu Theatre* on TV on Saturdays by then.

LOU: Yeah, they had *Kung Fu Theatre* on Channel 5, I think it was, every Saturday. That and *Godzilla* movies, horror movies, anything that would get our attention, *Creature Features*.... I used to love how badly they were dubbed. You know, their mouths had stopped moving, but you kept hearing them talking.

PETE: Ultimately, we were just rebelling against the norm of our neighborhood, even with TV. Most people would be like, "Oh, you watch THOSE shows and THOSE movies?" The norm around us was defined by Guidos. We were surrounded all the time by Guidos.

LOU: That's the weird thing though. When we were younger, our older brothers and their friends had long hair and were listening to what we thought was crazy music like Sabbath and Deep Purple. You might hear those groups once in a while on the radio, but the radio back then was dominated by Paul McCartney and Wings, and Boston, which was okay, but our brothers were into great music that wasn't mainstream at that time. But at some point, most of the people in the neighborhood became Guidos.

PETE: Probably because that's how they thought they'd meet girls.

'80s SONGS QUEENS GUIDOS LOVED

"LET THE MUSIC PLAY"
(SHANNON)

"TELL IT TO MY HEART"
(TAYLOR DAYNE)

"DIAMOND GIRL"
(NICE & WILD)

"WHEN I HEAR MUSIC"
(DEBBIE DEB)

"ONE WAY LOVE"
(TKA)

"POINT OF NO RETURN"
(EXPOSÉ)

"I WONDER IF I TAKE YOU HOME"
(LISA LISA & CULT JAM FEAT. FULL FORCE)

"TOGETHER FOREVER"
(LISETTE MELENDEZ)

"DON'T STOP THE ROCK"
(FREESTYLE)

"SHOW ME"
(THE COVER GIRLS)

ANYTHING BY MADONNA

LOU: All these guys had this attitude that *anything that isn't "normal" is bad*. To them, "normal" was this very formulaic, force-fed, bullshit music and lifestyle. It dumbfounded me. You had these guys hating everyone that wasn't them. They were racist too. I had this friend named Rita, a black girl, and she and I were walking to my parents' house one day. We were passing the park where all my brothers' friends hung out. They've known us since we were little, and they all stopped and stared at me and Rita from inside the park. One guy came running over to see who these two people were, you know, this black and white couple walking down the street. When he got up to us, he says, "Oh shit, Lou. Hey, what's up, man? I didn't know it was you." In my head, I was thinking, "What the fuck was this guy gonna do if he DIDN'T recognize me?!" It wasn't even as if we were holding hands or kissing. It was just me and my friend, walking next to each other, talking about the Dead Kennedys. It's crazy how that mentality became so prominent around us. When we were in grammar school, nobody gave a shit about your friend's background and all that, but when we got older, people started dividing things up. In junior high school, it would be great all year, then at the end of the year, there'd be a race riot for NO reason! It's just the way some kids were raised.

PETE: Part of rebelling against this crap was wanting to find our own thing, because we couldn't stand what everyone else was doing, and the other part of it was boredom. I mean, we liked the music our brothers were listening to, but it was always the more aggressive stuff that we would end up liking. I do have to credit our brother Matt. He was into it really early on. He was going to clubs like Great Gildersleeves to see Agnostic Front play with GBH, the Anti-Nowhere League, shows like that.

LOU: Also, there were so many great bands from Queens. Shit, I didn't know Reagan Youth was from Queens until we met our friend Vic Venom. I remember going to a club on Queens Boulevard called the Subway. We saw Reagan Youth there. Then I got a flyer for a Gilligan's Revenge show before they changed their name to Token Entry. We realized Murphy's Law was from Queens. I got the Leeway demo and found out they're from Astoria. There was a brief period when I would jump on the train just to go to Astoria because I loved all these Astoria bands.

PETE: Punk started in Queens. I love all of our English friends, and our friends in UK bands, but—and I have to remind people of this all the time—the Sex Pistols walked into the studio with their manager, held up the first Ramones album, and said, "We want to sound like THIS!" The Ramones were the first punk band! When the Ramones went over there for the first time, they said the whole audience was basically the Sex Pistols, the Clash and all their friends.

LOU: When we met Perry Farrell from Jane's Addiction on that Bad Brains tour we did, he told us, "Yeah, I'm from Queens. My grandmother's from Flushing." I was walking down Northern Boulevard once and DJ Muggs from Cypress Hill was walking towards me. I introduced myself: "I'm Lou from Sick of It All; what are you doing in Flushing?" Muggs says, "Oh, my grandmother lives right there," and points up the block. Seattle had its grunge, and Chicago may have been the spot for industrial, but Queens definitely had it for early '80s and '90s hardcore and hip-hop.

PETE: Then there are all the metal bands: Anthrax....

LOU: Nuclear Assault.

PETE: I think Twisted Sister had some Queens roots. KISS, of course, was from Queens.

LOU: They sold their house and moved to South Carolina right before the real estate market crashed. Damn, if they'd held onto it, they'd be sitting pretty. Imagine if they could have sold it now? Queens is where we established ourselves. There was a little park not far from where we grew up, and there were these guys, even older than our brothers, who called themselves the "Triangle Gang." In the seventies, everybody had a gang. Their symbol was a skull with a top hat, but you couldn't really spray-paint that in Triangle Park because it was just this little triangle off of Northern Boulevard. They'd also hang out in the schoolyard of PS 107. Our brothers eventually hung out there at the Triangle.

STEVEN KOLLER: Triangle Park was like a rite of passage in our neighborhood. There were different generations all the time. Before Matt and I hung out there, we used to hang out down at the corner, because in the park were the older guys. When they got older, they began to hang out at the bar, so my friends and I came into the park. Louie and Pete were younger than us and came around a little later.

LOU: We went there a couple of times. I guess they were tolerant of us to a certain degree. They didn't mind us coming to Triangle Park every once in a while, but we mostly hung out in this alley that led into the schoolyard. Over by the basketball courts were the hip-hop kids, and in the inner courtyard were the stoners. You had this mixed bag of people hanging out in the same area. What was funny for us was that, on our boombox, we would play early hardcore like Reagan Youth and Negative Approach, but we would also play stuff like Kurtis Blow. Rap was just becoming prominent, and you could hear it on some of the New York radio stations.

PETE: Our brothers' friends liked Rush, Jethro Tull, Black Sabbath, Frank Zappa....

LOU: They were total "Rock #1" guys, if you know what I mean. Pete: Yeah, they were the MOST "Rock #1"! But we liked metal, hardcore, AND KRS-One.

LOU: It's similar to how it is now. The younger generations all have their own form of rebellion, their own musical rebellion. I mean, I understand some of the new bands, but not many are really saying anything with their lyrics. For instance, eventually I realized that Sabbath's "War Pigs" was actually a protest song.

PETE: Music today—it's just not that scary.

LOU: We'd hang out in the alleyway, but there were some other places too. We went in the main entrance some nights, and would just hang out and bullshit there, drink and stuff. Across the street was an apartment building so we weren't really disturbing anyone. We could get as loud and as stupid as we wanted to be. One time we heard this screaming and yelling coming from an apartment window across the street. We were all looking up, wondering what was going on. This guy is screaming in Spanish, and we heard a woman crying. The guy starts yelling, "You dirty whore! Fuck you! I'm gonna show the world what a whore you are!" He turned the lights on and threw his wife out onto the fire escape, naked! We were fourteen or fifteen years old at the time, so we were shocked that there was a naked woman up there. We weren't even mature enough to think, we're watching domestic abuse.

PETE: Needless to say, we hadn't seen many naked ladies at that point in our lives.

LOU: There were some other weird incidents. One time we were all standing in the alley talking, and these two kids walked to the entrance of the alley, looked at us, and shot us with pellet guns.

PETE: We chased them to a building, and then when they saw our friend Tom Farkas, who was this very scary-looking guy, they were begging us for forgiveness and to leave them alone. It was all just total stupidity. We did a lot of dumb stuff, but it was always fun. During the summertime just before I started going to Francis Lewis High School, Lou and I got into a really bad car accident. I was in the hospital. I was hit in the head so hard I woke up in the hospital not realizing what had happened.

LOU: It was the weekend. Our brother Steve had just gotten out of the Air Force and had come home. He drove from New Mexico all the way back to New York, and there was a party at our house. Our relatives were there, but Pete and I had plans to go out.
Steven Koller: I must have seen them for maybe ten minutes, and they were going out with their friends. A couple of hours later, we were at the hospital.

PETE: We were really into street racing, but none of us had driver's licenses. It was our friends who had the cars.

LOU: We had two friends who had muscle cars. Pete and I got into one of the cars, and we were just driving around, being goofy. It was misting out, not fully raining, and we're driving along the service road of the Long Island Expressway in Queens, heading towards Long Island. We're driving and driving, and we hit a raised manhole, so we bounce up, and now we're hydroplaning. The driver looks at me and says, "There's no brakes and no steering!" We gradually start to spin to the right while we're still going forward, and the road starts to curve to the left. We shot up, back end first, toward a fire hydrant. The car hit these two concrete posts surrounding the hydrant, completely spun around, and ended up hitting some trees that crushed the back of the car. Now, being teenagers who thought they'd live forever, we weren't wearing seat belts. When the back of the car was crushed in, it came down on Pete and snapped his sternum in half. I was in the front, and bounced around so much, I flew into the windshield. I went shoulder first into the windshield and got cut, and when I came down, I landed on the gearshift. It went under my ribs and burst my spleen. I remember laying there and slowly opening my eyes. There were no windows left in the car. We're shimmering because we were covered in shattered glass. Tom Farkas ran over to our car to see if we were okay. I said, "Get me out of here." I tried to move, and I guess because of the shock and my busted spleen, I couldn't move. He picked me up and dragged me out of the window and stood me up. Then he went into the back and got Pete out. The driver was okay because he was able to hold onto the steering wheel when we crashed. The ambulance came and we went to the hospital. They looked at me and at first said, "He's got a cut on his shoulder and a bruise on his back." Then they took Pete into surgery. While I sat there, my bruise started getting bigger and bigger, and I started getting paler and paler. I told my brother, "Man, my back is killing me," and he told me that my bruise was giant now. I was bleeding internally. They took my blood pressure, and I think it was almost zero. They took three bags of my blood type, wrapped a blood pressure gauge around them, stuck a needle in my arm, and began to squeeze the blood in with the blood pressure gauge. It was like a horror movie. Every vein in my body swelled up, and it was SO painful, but they said they had to do it.

PETE: It's amazing that neither of us have any long-term issues from that accident. I did have some memory loss. One thing I remember is that my brother Steve paid for the rest of a guitar I'd been paying off in installments and brought it to me while I was in the hospital. It was the white Gibson SG I used all the time early on.

LOU: In the end, the doctor looked at me and said," We're not going to remove your spleen, we're going to sew it back together and see how it heals." He told me, "You're so skinny, without your spleen, you'll die," so that's what they did. They repaired it.
Pete: It was around that time that we started REALLY getting into our music.

LOU: I was going to Art and Design High School in Manhattan, but then suddenly the school changed its curriculum, and I was forced to take classes I didn't want, so I quit and went to Francis Lewis back in Queens.

PETE: That day you quit, I remember Dad came flying into the driveway and said, "YOU BETTER NOT BE THINKING OF QUITTING SCHOOL," and just walked into the house. He was SO PISSED!

LOU: But when I sat down and explained to him, while being yelled at, that the school had gotten rid of every class I was enrolled in, he was like, "You are going to finish fucking high school and get a job!" That was all he wanted.

PETE: He still wants us to get jobs!

LOU: But I'm glad our parents are the way they are. Our dad instilled a work ethic in us that we still apply to everything we do.

PETE: It has helped with the longevity of the band. Every show we put on, we're not half-assing it. You're getting 110 percent from us every time!

PART II

DISCO SUCKS, FUCK EVERYTHING

Lou vs. Samhain 1984

PETE: My dad and mom would save up every summer and take us on a trip somewhere. It wouldn't always be somewhere spectacular, but it was always super fun. There was usually a long drive involved, and my dad would have doo-wop music playing, or some kind of fifties music, or Neil Diamond. There was always music playing in the car on those trips.

LOU: In the fall, they'd make us get in the car and tell us, "All right, we're gonna go look at the leaves changing colors upstate."

Those trips are where we first heard music and loved it. My parents got our brothers one of those little record players, and our aunt would give us 45s. "Bad, Bad Leroy Brown"—that was one of our favorites. We'd play it over and over. I don't know how old we were, Pete, but mom and dad got us AM/FM radios with cassette players in them, and we would sit there at night and tape songs off the radio. I remember getting excited because I taped Donna Summer's "Last Dance," and then the next song was Steve Martin's "King Tut." I was like, "I got it! I got it! I taped it!" All different types of music. And then later, I remember hearing The Supremes. I would get goosebumps. I remember sitting in the back of dad's big convertible Impala and hearing The Supremes. I thought, oh my god, this is beautiful. Then we really got into our dad's record collection. He had this record, I'll never forget, called Two Great *Guitars*. It was Chuck Berry and Bo Diddley. Fucking great!

PETE: I would stare at the cover of that album because it had both of their guitars on it. But also, when my mom would be cleaning the house, she'd put on her French music like Edith Piaf.

LOU: She dug Charles Aznavour, and she liked Roy Clark. I remember that because I went out and got her a Roy Clark "Best of" album and she was really appreciative.

PETE: One year my parents bought me an acoustic guitar. At the time, I didn't give a shit about learning anything: schoolwork or guitar. Then they gave me Roy Clark's Big Note Book, which turned me off even more, because it would have had something to do with learning! (Laughs) So I was like, "Fuck this. I don't wanna fucking do this." It's like going to school! But then, later on in life.... Just recently, we used one of Edith Piaf's songs as an intro at one of our shows in France and it was fucking great. The audience was all swaying back and forth.\Louis Koller Senior: They were in grammar school when they got their first record player, a small portable one. No one will believe this, but the first record they bought was, "You're So Vain" by Carly Simon.

PETE: When it came to music, I would always follow what Lou did because for some reason he always bought records, and I never had ANY money.

LOU: It's because I had a paper route!

PETE: And you would use that money to buy records. I don't have any money right now either, so I don't know what the fuck is going on! (Laughs)

LOU: Our older brothers liked some heavy shit. They turned us on to bands like Deep Purple and Rainbow.

PETE: Hells yeah!

LOU: I really only liked the more up-tempo stuff. I loved Rainbow songs like "Long Live Rock and Roll," and "Kill the King." I wasn't so much into "Man on the Silver Mountain." It's a good song, but I dug the other stuff more. They were also into shit like Frank Zappa. We'd listen to that too, and I'd like the funny lyrics, but I gravitated more so to aggressive music, much more high-energy. Pete: There's the Beatles song "Revolution" that begins with a scream. We'd play that scream over and over again, as loud as the stereo could go, just the scream! We didn't really care about the rest of the song. I remember our mom coming down and SCREAMING at us, "Turn that down!" I wasn't the biggest Beatles fan, but I didn't hate them either. I keep going back to something Jimmy Gestapo said on the In-Effect home video. He said something to the effect of "Everybody around us in our neighborhood was listening to dead people and we weren't into dead people." Eventually, Lou and I found something that was alive and made you feel alive. Something you could touch and totally be a part of. When we first went to see Ozzy Osbourne on the Blizzard of Ozz Tour, it was like, *FUCK, that's Randy Rhoads up there*, but you'd never get to meet him or anything like that. Then later, I'd say, "Fuck! That's fucking Vinnie Stigma! He's right next to me!" Yup, Randy Rhoads and Stigma, my two favorite guitar players!

LOU: YES! We went to that Ozzy show, and we were psyched because we got floor seats, but people from the upper tiers were constantly whipping fireworks down at you! It was fucked up but kind of exciting too.

PETE: Plus, it was like a fucking smoke screen of weed!

LOU: The first big arena show we went to together was Black Sabbath and Blue Oyster Cult on the Black and Blue Tour, and it was amazing. We were in Madison Square Garden, and it was huge and crazy. Those first few arena shows were funny, because people would have these little leather wine sacks with them that they'd bring into the venue because you couldn't bring in bottles.

PETE: Bota bags!

LOU: Yes! That's what they were called. But this whole crazy journey started when our brother Matt first played us a Black Sabbath album.

PETE: I distinctly remember being in our basement one night, I don't remember how old we were, maybe twelve or thirteen, and my brother Matt says, "Oh, you gotta listen to this." He shut out all the lights in the basement, and we had one of those grim reaper blacklight posters. The grim reaper's face was glowing in the dark, and he put on "Iron Man" from Black Sabbath, and we were just like "THIS IS FUCKING GREAT!" I was like, "This is the greatest shit ever!" It was heavy, and I always loved spooky, horror stuff. Lou would collect comic books like *Iron Man*; I would collect *The Witching Hour* and more scary comic books. This was the perfect music for me—heavy AND scary—so I was super into it.

LOU: It wasn't "Iron Man" that scared me; it was when he played the song "Black Sabbath." That intro, and then, "What is this that stands before me..."

PETE: Plus, the creepy lady on the cover!

LOU: I was never much of a ballad guy. I wasn't an Eagles guy or whatever. Our brother Matt played those albums, and we were scared to death but also felt, "This is SO good!"

PETE: Basically, we were kids. We'd listen to Black Sabbath, go out and buy beer, and get fucking wrecked in the park! Then listen to it even more, and start to think, "I wish I was in a band! Imagine if we were in a band!"

LOU: Along with Sabbath, I got into Ted Nugent. *Double Live Gonzo!* was a great album, but I would buy some other Ted Nugent albums and be sorely disappointed at how bluesy rock it was. I wasn't into that. I think one of the turning points was when Matt brought home the first Plasmatics album. We were getting deep into metal, Judas Priest and stuff, then all of a sudden, he brings home *New Hope for the Wretched* and I'm like, "Holy shit!" One day I walked into Jimmy's Music World on Roosevelt Avenue and Main Street in Flushing, Queens. On the "new releases" wall was Priest's British Steel and all their other records. They had *Stained Class, Hell Bent for Leather*.... I looked at the cover of British Steel and I'm like, "What is THIS?" I picked it up and turned it over to see the picture on the back and was like, "Woah!"

PETE: It wasn't until we were maybe thirteen or fourteen that we started going to record stores by ourselves. We went to a few in Flushing, but when we began heading into Manhattan, we'd go to J&R Music World down by City Hall. They sold imports of albums which hadn't been released in America.

LOU: I also remember going to Bleecker Bob's when it was actually on Bleecker Street before it moved around the corner. We went there and one of my older brothers' friends told us, "You gotta see this poster." It was when Motörhead was huge in Europe, and Motörhead was headlining with special guests Ozzy Osbourne's Blizzard of Ozz and all the other bands underneath, most of them being New Wave of British Heavy Metal bands. I stared up at this poster like, "Oh my god, that is the coolest thing I've ever fucking seen!" That was my first trip there. But it was at J&R that I bought Accept's *Restless and Wild and Breaker*.

PETE: I was just along for the ride with these guys, you know? But it was always a fun adventure. A little scary, riding the trains for the first time by ourselves.

LOU: I think it was a bit more wild-west down there back then. Not like, gunshots, but it was not as safe as it is today. It was just different. I was so used to Queens. Anyway, when I picked up *British Steel* at that record store, I looked at the back and saw the pictures of the guys, and I'd never seen guys dressed like that, probably because I hadn't been to the West Side of Manhattan yet, but it was the coolest shit to me. I thought, *Look at these badass guys*, and then I read the song titles like "Grinder" and "Metal Gods," and I was like, "I gotta get this!" Going home and putting it on was just incredible. I didn't even know it at the time, but my best friend who lived around the block, Peter, his older brother was deeply into Twisted Sister and said, "Oh, you like Judas Priest," and I told him, "Yeah, I just got British Steel," and he goes, "You should check out this one, and he played us *Hell Bent for Leather*. Again, we were blown away by that. Then his brother played us the Twisted Sister single and I was like, "Holy shit!" He told us how they played all the area clubs. I hadn't even realized that KISS was from Queens, and then it turned out later that our older cousin had been Ace Frehley's babysitter back when he was a kid. We found out years later. She told us, "I used to babysit Paul." I asked, "Paul Stanley?" She said, "No, Paul Frehley," which is his real name. Going to the record stores then, mostly because of KISS's *Alive!*, I would start to look for live albums because they usually had a band's best shit on it. I remember buying Scorpions' *Tokyo Tapes* and only liking one song on it. I was really disappointed. It wasn't until a friend of ours, this kid who lived around the block from us, went away on vacation to Scotland for the whole summer and came back with gifts for us. He had an Iron Maiden patch on his jacket and said in this heavy Scottish accent, "This is what's happening in England right now." He gave us the first Def Leppard album and Iron Maiden's first album. That's how we first learned about the New Wave of British Heavy Metal. I liked the Def Leppard album, but LOVED the Iron Maiden record. It was probably 1980. We had only seen the Iron Maiden album cover and some Motörhead stuff, but we didn't have any of the music. We went on a search for that Twisted Sister single we'd heard. I'd look in phone books for independent record stores and then people would tell us, "You can get it at this place in Brooklyn called Zig Zag," and we would travel on the train all the way to Brooklyn. We got there, and the guy told us, "No, man, that single is all sold out," but then we saw the Motörhead albums and all that. Maiden's *Killers* had just come out when I was searching for Twister Sister, so we got *Killers*. I mean, just that cover, holy shit! Then we found out there was this store in Long Island called Slipped Disc, so we went out there to try and get shit. At the same time though, I remember our brothers playing us the Plasmatics. I got into the Sex Pistols at the same time, and I remember buying an Exploited live album. At first, I was like, "Wow, this is just too much," then I gradually got more and more into it. We eventually heard about a record store in Queens called Ken's Music Box.

PETE: Later on we rehearsed in the basement of the store, but before we'd heard about it, a friend told us there was a great import record store on Union Turnpike near St. John's University.

LOU: You would have to take two buses to get there, which was better than going all the way out to Long Island. That's when I first got a copy of *Kerrang!* magazine from the UK. The issue had Bon Scott on the cover, and all the New Wave of British Heavy Metal stuff in it. It also had a demo section with bands like Angel Witch and this and that. We became friends with the guy from the store. He was always cool because he'd play you stuff once in a while. I liked the adventure of looking at the album covers and thinking, what does this sound like? Just reading *Kerrang!* and finding out about all these bands, thinking you were going to love them just because they were in the magazine. But then you'd come across the ones where the reviews were like, "You have to listen to these bands called Heavy Pettin' and Mama's Boys, they're so brutal" So, you get these albums, and what a fucking disappointment! I wanted to write to Kerrang! and get my money back! That store had rows and rows of records in the middle. I would always go to that section, the new releases, but it was mostly metal stuff, and some punk and hardcore. We'd get those *Metal Massacre* compilations from Metal Blade. The first one had Metallica's "Hit the Lights" on it. You'd hear a song like that and of course you'd want to search that out further. Then Slayer had a song on one, and it just snowballed from there. It was more aggressive. It wasn't just the speed; it had this grittiness to it. Even before that, the first Anvil record had some faster stuff on it which was great.

PETE: There was Accept's "Fast as a Shark." Great song!

LOU: At the time that seemed really fast.

PETE: And it was very, very aggressive. If you listen to it now, you're like, "It's really not that fast."

LOU: But when Udo screams in the beginning.... Plus the double bass makes it seem faster.

PETE: We thought Motörhead's "Overkill" was a fast song too, but compared to what came after it.... Wait, let me stop this for a second. We are skipping over how much we loved KISS!

LOU: You're right! We had this friend who was really into KISS. He lived around the corner, and we'd go to his house and listen to records. We came back one day and told our Mom, "You gotta see this band, mom! The guy spits blood!" and this and that. It was almost summertime, so the school year was ending. We walked into our house, and my mom says, "I went shopping today and I got you guys a present." She'd bought us a copy of KISS's *Alive!* That's where it REALLY started! We have to give it to our mom. She set us on the road. She gave us Alive! as an end-of-school present, and we played that fucking record FOREVER!

PETE: And we'd just stare at the album.... I would STARE, even at the back cover of the people just sitting there in the arena.

LOU: And then *Destroyer* came out, and we were like, "Oh my god, this is even better!" It was funny being a KISS fan back then. You'd walk through the neighborhood with your KISS belt buckle, and all the older guys would be like, "KISS, that's fucking garbage music," with their Allman Brothers shirts on, and you'd be like, "FUCK the Allman Brothers!" Everyone would say that. Everyone would be like, "Oh, you like that stuff? They suck!" We'd be wondering, *Who the fuck was buying their records then?* They were so big. When I listen to them now, they're not particularly up-tempo or high-energy, but for me, it was songs like "Detroit Rock City" and "Shout It Out Loud." Those had this energy to them.

PETE: "Love Gun," great song! We had one stereo in the house, and we all liked music. Even with KISS, we had one copy, like a house copy. You have to understand, this was the seventies. My dad was a bank teller with four preteen and teenage boys that ate everything in sight and were always getting into trouble. We were always growing out of our clothes, so there wasn't much money to go around, but they always did their best. I remember bringing our copy of *Alive!* to elementary school for show-and-tell. My mom had actually written "Koller" on the cover in pen, so no one would steal it. I was ready to play it, and my friend Jerry Cooney, not the boxer, says, "Play 'Black Diamond.'" So, I played it, and Jerry got up on a desk and just threw a fucking chair across the room because it made him go crazy! I vividly remember this. I was laughing so hard, but I was also in awe of the power of that music, thinking, *Wow! This music is driving people crazy!* Our teacher made me shut it off, screaming, "Don't you ever bring that back to school ever again!" I was like, "Wow, music is fucking crazy!"

LOU: Well, your friend threw a chair! No wonder she made you leave it at home from then on. There would be times where my parents would be in the living room watching TV, and the stereo was in there too, so you'd have to sit there with your headphones on listening to the radio or your albums. I'd sit there and have one leg up on my knee listening away, and my dad would come over and kick my foot off my knee just to fuck with me. He'd kick you out of your trance. I remember him coming downstairs one day, and he was like, "Yeah, I listened to your KISS record, and what's with that song, "...and she took off her clothes?" I was like, "Uh, I have no idea what you're talking about, dad. It's just a record."

PETE: He did always have good one-liners! When we got into the shaved head phase, he was like, "What is this? Is this the new uniform the kids are wearing?" At the time, I had Doc Martens on and my head was shaved and all that. I'd gone from the long hair costume to the shaved head costume.

LOU: Yeah, I thought I had cool spiky hair, but when I saw a picture of myself, I looked more like Robert Smith from The Cure than Sid Vicious, and I was like, "WOW, I look like fucking Robert Smith." Once we were into the hardcore scene for a while and had been going to shows for a number of years, I started to see a hypocrisy in punk kids as far as image goes. They all wanted to be different, but they would all dress the same and wouldn't like your band unless you looked "punk" or "hardcore," so we were like, let's just look like fucking Queens Guidos and see what happens. That's where our rattails came in. They're famous now.

PETE: Yeah, hardcore had become a very big thing for us, obviously. I think what really got us going was meeting Armand at Francis Lewis High School. We were kind of long-haired guys with Iron Maiden patches and Motörhead patches, and this guy comes into school with his hair down to his waist, wearing an upside-down cross, and we were like, *This guy's gotta be down with us!*

LOU: And he was! Through him we met Vic Venom from Reagan Youth, and they turned us onto Venom. I also remember Armand playing bands like Negative Approach for us, and I was like, "Fucking amazing!" They introduced us to all these great bands from England and told us about this great scene going on in New York. We discovered the New York hardcore scene from that.

ARMAND MAJIDI (SICK OF IT ALL DRUMMER): There were two guys who introduced me to tons of metal and hardcore punk stuff: one was Ricky Boeckel, who later played in E-X-E and Bile, and the other was Dan Monaghan who went to my high school. Dan was full-on into metal and took me to my first shows. Ricky played me the first hardcore record I'd really heard, which was the first Necros 7-inch. Hearing that made me realize that hardcore was even more aggressive than metal. It wasn't as heavy or full sounding, and the production was raw, but I loved it. I mean, back then there were no well-produced hardcore records. Then I met Vic Venom and a guy named Bill Hepper. There was a whole cast of characters at Francis Lewis into aggressive music.

PETE: The only people we hung out with were people who were into Motörhead and stuff like that, and it was a progression to faster, heavier stuff. Then it became tangible stuff, bands we could actually go see. We went to L'Amour in Brooklyn, and L'Amour East in Queens. Of course, we couldn't get in because we were too young, but when we did eventually get in, it was like, "Wow, there's a band onstage," but somehow, the bands still felt untouchable. Metal shows were always different that way.

LOU: Although, when we first went to see Motörhead at L'Amour East, Lemmy was just walking down the street by himself and then hanging out at the bar. Not that you could really bother him, but he was so cool all the time. Back then, we would hang out after the shows by the backstage door to try to meet the bands. When Venom first played in Staten Island in 1983, we went right to the backstage door and just hung out there. We were sitting there, and this guy sits next to me and goes, "So, you like Venom..." and it was Cliff Burton from Metallica, because they had opened up. I said, "Yeah, I fucking love them, and I thought you guys were great too." He was disappointed because, when Metallica was onstage, the crowd basically just stared at them. We had all been right up front.

PETE: We were always into it, and it didn't matter if anyone else was. We knew this was great music, and we didn't give a fuck if the crowd was kinda just hanging around or super into it.

LOU: I remember back when Maiden was opening for Priest at the Palladium with Paul Di'Anno on the *Killers* Tour, we were yelling, cheering for Maiden, and this guy behind us goes, "Sit the fuck down! They're the opening act," and our Scottish friend yelled, "It's fucking MAIDEN," and we turned back around and banged our heads. We just loved the energy of live shows, but like Pete said, metal shows had a very specific vibe as far as the bands feeling untouchable and far away. It got stale after a while.

PETE: Very stale, but also, we wanted to go see these bands on a more regular basis. Punk bands and hardcore bands seemed to be playing all the time.

LOU: Early on, we got into a lot of the English stuff: GBH, The Exploited.... Then Armand brought us some Discharge and then the American bands, especially the New York bands. I kinda liked Black Flag, but I didn't worship them like everyone else seemed to.

PETE: A lot of people will bring up a band like Black Flag. You know what? I don't really care for them at all. I'd rather listen to Discharge, Anti-Nowhere League... I like that sound over the Dead Kennedys or anything like that. It sounded too thin, and sort of jokey. The New York stuff was really different. First of all, there were shows every weekend, so it was closer to me than what I liked from California, even though, to this day, I love Suicidal Tendencies. They had a little bit of that urban angst to them. There were characters in New York like Stigma, and Jimmy and Billy Psycho. Even though The Psychos weren't the greatest band, they were still fun to watch. Ultra-Violence also wasn't the greatest band, but they were still fun to watch, and you knew the guys and you talked to them every weekend. It was as much about friendship as it was about the bands. The only guy in high school that was into what we were was Armand. Lou had already left high school, then Armand moved away, then all of our friends who were into the scene went to John Bowne High School; Richie and Rob and many of them went to that school, so Sunday was the day you got to hang out with everyone, and we did that at CBGB matinees. It was more of a family thing, and that's what kept driving me to more New York bands. We'd get into our friend Devil's car, and drive for God knows how long, and there'd be nine people in a car that fits five, just to go see NYC Mayhem play somewhere or hit up a CB's matinee. Technically, these bands weren't perfect, but that's one of the things I liked, because I am not a great musician. Just knowing these guys, although they don't really play that great and their guitars aren't really in tune, made me feel more comfortable trying to play, just by liking these bands and these people. It made me realize, *I can do this.*

LOU: Like Pete said, we loved Suicidal, but they didn't have the same grittiness that was coming out of bands like Murphy's Law or Agnostic Front or Warzone and all the other New York bands. Agnostic Front just sounded like New York City. When I hear Agnostic Front, I picture riding the fucking subway.

PETE: Yeah, a dirty, graffiti-covered subway train. I'd rather listen to AF over the Dead Kennedys or Circle Jerks any day. It's serious business when you're listening to AF! Then there's one of the best hardcore bands ever, Murphy's Law, who has a sound that is totally different but still VERY New York.

LOU: I was talking to Joe from the Vandals, and we were discussing hardcore, and he goes, "When The Vandals came out, we were hardcore compared to the other bands in our scene. We were like, 'Yeah, Vandals are hardcore! We're hardcore punk!' And then we played a show at Fender's in Long Beach with Agnostic Front from New York, and we just looked at each other and said, 'THAT'S hardcore! We are NOT hardcore.'"

PETE: Everyone says, "This is hardcore, and that is hardcore," but Agnostic Front is NEW YORK Hardcore, and there is a difference.

LOU: As far as the New York stuff we liked, Agnostic Front's *United Blood* was one of the first, and Reagan Youth too. We dug Cause for Alarm and the Misfits who were technically from New Jersey, but the Misfits were always in there for us. When *Walk Among Us* was out, we played that to death. But I remember, when *Earth A.D.* came out, Armand was going, "I don't like it," and I'm sitting there going, "This is such a great progression." I love *Earth A.D.* Talk about aggression and energy. The way that album opens, it's just great. It still had that sing-along Misfits catchiness, but it was faster and heavier.

PETE: Our older brothers' friends would say, "Yeah, I can see why you like THEM, because their style is sort of like KISS."

LOU: We kept listening to more of the American stuff, and the New York stuff. I loved Urban Waste, and I remember getting that first D.R.I. 7-inch. It had, I think, fourteen songs on it. Then we met Tommy Carroll, and Tommy was always into finding the fastest band. He'd play us some demo and be like, "No one's faster than this!" That was a really fun time because, while we loved the speed, there were bands like the Offenders from Texas who had fast songs but weren't as fast as, say, D.R.I., but they were great. D.R.I. were at the top of their game at that point; they were fucking great. I loved "Violent Pacification," and that's not even a fast song, but it had such a good rhythm. Then there was Corrosion of Conformity. I remember getting *Eye for an Eye.* That was the first show I decided to go to at CBGB. I got the record, and there was an address on the back, so I wrote to them, and Woody, their guitar player, wrote back to me. The Cro-Mags' demo had just come out around then too. I was at a GBH show, and Harley and John were walking around selling shirts and demos, and I bought the demo. I wrote to Woody about that and he was like, "Hey, we're playing CBGB soon." Truthfully, I had already gone to CB's, but hadn't gone inside. I don't remember who was playing, but I saw the crowd, and I just kept going.

PETE: The week after the COC show, Agnostic Front was playing. We got the flyer and it said Agnostic Front and the Psychos, and we had just gotten *Victim in Pain*, which absolutely changed my life. We listened to it the first time, and the second it ended, we turned it over and listened to it again, and we just kept playing it and playing it and playing it. It was something that really hit a primal chord.

LOU: It took what a band like GBH was doing and made it more raw and powerful. Like I said, it sounded like New York City. *Age of Quarrel* is probably the greatest NYHC album to me, but *Victim in Pain* is my favorite because it put New York on the map, and it sounds just like New York at that time. I remember getting the flyer and we were like, "We have to go to this," and the whole thing snowballed. I'm trying to remember the timeline, but before we went down to CB's, we'd gone to see Dead Kennedys at a place on Avenue C called The World. We saw DKs three times, but the first time, they had DOA, Reagan Youth, and a whole bunch of other bands opening up. I remember going to those shows and just being blown away. We eventually go to see Agnostic Front at CB's. I've got long hair and my painted Motörhead vest, and this guy comes up to me and asks, "You like AF?" and I'm like, "Yeah, *Victim in Pain* is such an amazing album, blah blah blah," and the guy is like, "Okay, cool, enjoy the show." It was fucking Vinnie Stigma! Minutes later, he gets up onstage, and he's in the band. I flash back to going to see Black Sabbath and I think, "Wow, Tony Iommi would never have walked up to me before the show and said, "Hey, enjoy the show." That sold me. I loved it. Even the New York crossover stuff, which a lot of old hardcore people considered controversial—it's what kept hardcore fresh. Hardcore could have just died after a while. I loved it when hardcore bands were like, "Let's play in a more metal style, and then in the breakdown do the chugging instead of a box riff or whatever."

PETE: Even the sounds of the guitars, I think that's something which helped Sick of It All become more popular. I would try to emulate a more metal sound while keeping my playing style punk. It wasn't just a squeaky, thin sound; it was bigger and thicker.

LOU: Those early crossover type shows were strange though, because a lot of the metal people that came down to CBGB were more open-minded than the supposedly open-minded hardcore people who'd been there for years. I mean, the first Agnostic Front show we all went to, we had long hair; I had a freaking Motörhead vest on, and we were accepted right away. Fast-forward not even two or three years later when the crossover was in full swing, and people started with, "Hey, that guy with long hair is wearing Doc Martens," and they'd actually steal their Doc Martens. They'd cut the fucking laces off with a boxcutter and just take them.

PETE: I always thought the punk and hardcore scene was supposed to be "Who gives a fuck what you look like?! Who gives a fuck about this or that, as long as we're all here together," and sometimes, it was the complete opposite. With the whole crossover thing, the metal people weren't taking anything away from hardcore; they were just enjoying the music. One thing about the CB's matinees versus L'Amour: at CB's I always felt safe. You didn't even think about it. But any time I was over at L'Amour, I'd be on edge. The people who worked at that club would physically harass and fuck with people who paid to get in. I remember, and I don't mean to sound like a tough guy, but I beat up a bouncer at L'Amour, and then I had to hide from the rest of them because they literally wanted to KILL me. They were just Guido dicks working at events they didn't understand. At CB's, Big Charlie Hankins and Wrecking Machine were the bouncers. It was completely different. At L'Amour, we were always waiting for some bad shit to happen.

LOU: Agnostic Front genuinely embraced the crossover. They had metalheads coming around and telling them how amazing Victim in Pain is and what a great band they were, and of course, they wanted to expand on that. But hardcore was trying to keep itself all to itself, and you can understand that to an extent because hardcore was theirs, untainted by commercialism, even though the minute you're selling your demo, you're participating in commercialism. The hardcore matinees at CBGB didn't have the typical "rock and roll vibe," if you know what I mean. When you'd go to L'Amour in Brooklyn, there'd still be a lot of that hair-metal mentality. Even if you'd go to see Slayer, or even the Cro-Mags there, the bar would have all the metal girls dressed really sexy, which is great on one level, but you wouldn't see that at a hardcore matinee. When we first started going to the matinees, one of my favorite things was checking out all of the hot Goth girls that would show up. I'd be like, "Where do THEY live?!" They were probably coming home from Danceteria and were like, "Let's stop by CBGB before we go home."

PETE: At a lot of the shows we've been doing lately, especially over the past few years, there are a lot of women there, up front, but in the early days, they were mostly standing at the bar, away from all the jumping-around business.

LOU: Lots of people have fought to have more women be part of the scene. You had 7 Seconds with "Not Just Boys Fun," and other bands with other songs, but I think it's come to the forefront in recent years. I think women have much more of a voice in underground music, even in metal.

PETE: If you're going to a show for a release, the ladies gotta release it too. They'll scream and shout, or maybe the lyrics truly mean something to them and they want to sing it.

LOU: Let's not forget the people who got carried away trying to figure out what was punk versus what was metal. People became obsessed with that whole thing. There were even bands that got confused. I mean, Sid Vicious wore swastikas. Then there are songs like Slayer's "Angel of Death," although I think Slayer was just trying to be brutal and shocking. I remember this metal band from New Jersey called Blessed Death. They played one of the rare Monday nights that Agnostic Front played and had this song called "Into the Ovens." I imagine they wrote that song thinking, "Yeah, this is what punk people want to hear." I don't even think they were really Nazis or anything, but they probably looked at some old World War II imagery and thought that was somehow a good idea. The cover of *Victim in Pain* was one thing. There was a message attached to that. Then you have a band like Blessed Death.... What the fuck was that about?! They didn't do too well with the AF crowd. After they played "Into the Ovens," AF's fans didn't want to hear any more of them and were terrorizing their fans. They had to stop playing.

PETE: Yeah, definitely NOT punk! Later, we started to see a lot of the phony tough-guy bullshit. When Sick of It All started touring, I remember going overseas and seeing these bands with tough-guy images, and lyrics that are all about living on the street and fighting.

LOU: Then you find out they're from a farm town in the middle of the Netherlands. What streets are you fighting on exactly?!

PETE: Survival of the fucking cow-milkers!

LOU: It sounded like such a pale copy. We talk a lot about how the scene around the world changed once people actually *saw* AF and the Cro-Mags, whether in photos or live. It was visually striking. I'm not going to say I didn't look at a picture of the Cro-Mags and say, "Holy shit, I want to be cool like that." I did, but I'm just not built for it. If I went up onstage and acted tough, it would be like a comedy act, but other people around the world bought into it a little too much. I remember how many bands adopted that look: no shirts, chest tattoos, name tattooed across your stomach in old English, blah blah blah....

PETE: We never tried to play it up like we had a tough upbringing, came from broken homes, or were living on the street. That's Cro-Mags stuff, that's AF stuff. We all have great families and loving, caring parents, so we never jumped on the bandwagon of "Yeah, I'm from the streets" and stuff like that, which I'm proud of. When people say, "I hear growing up on the streets of New York is rough," I'm like, "Well, I was at my parents' house." Thank God for my parents!

PART III

SICK OF IT ALL: THAT'S THE NAME!

LOU: The way Sick of It All started was very informal. Pete and I began to skip those summer family vacation trips with our parents. We would stay home because we were a little older and didn't want to go anymore. I had a paper route or whatever the hell job I had, and Pete had stuff to do too. We'd invite our friends over and just play music in the basement for hours on end. It was insane. Just shitty songs that we would make up on the spot. It was so much fun. We would do songs like "Life of Riley," stuff like that. Then Richie Cipriano came up with this song called "Jamming on the G," which was really just "Life of Riley," but we were yelling, "JAMMING ON THE G." Then we'd go crazy, starting it with a slow mosh style, then going fast, then back to yelling "Jamming on the G." Somehow though, it just kind of fell together. It became, "Hey, we should start a band."

PETE: Lou and I basically said, "Okay, you're gonna sing and I'm gonna play guitar," and we just began doing it. The way I learned to play guitar wasn't by learning to play Slayer or Metallica songs, I sat down and wrote "Friends like You," and then I wrote "My Life."

That's how I learned to play. There was this kid with a red Mohawk from Francis Lewis, and he started coming over too. I think I was playing guitar, he was playing guitar, and Lou was playing bass. Then we got another kid, Jorge, who also went to Francis Lewis and was straight from Colombia, and he played drums. He was a Colombian punk. We were just trying to make songs. We were trying to get something going, but then those other guys started doing something else. That's when Mark McNeely came in, who was in Francis Lewis high school too and was getting into the scene a little bit after us. Then David Lamb, the original drummer for Sick of It All, who was part of Richie and Rob Echeverria's Corona crew, said he could kind of play drums, so we started doing shit with him and Mark in the basement. Basically, everyone we knew who could play something would come over and make tons of noise in our basement. Plus, we were drinking a lot.

LOUIS KOLLER SENIOR: I think their mother and I were just glad to know where they were, and that they were not getting into any trouble somewhere. There were times when I thought I could see dust rising from the floorboards when they were playing down in the basement.

LOU: One time we were down there for like six hours, and one of our friends went upstairs and then came down yelling, "Yo, your whole house is surrounded by all your neighbors." We looked out the window and every one of our neighbors was staring at the house, talking to each other like, "What the fuck are they doing in there?!"

LOUIS KOLLER SENIOR: I personally don't remember our neighbors complaining, although there was one instance when their mom and I came back from France to find out that our "lovely" neighbor had called the police about the noise.

PETE: Little did they know, we were creating history, those motherfuckers! I had just bought my first guitar, a Hondo Flying V that never stayed in tune. I didn't know anything about intonation. I didn't know what the fucking bridge would do, so it was always out of tune. Then I saved a lot of money and put a down payment on my first real guitar, a Gibson SG Special. To this day, Craig will be like, "Play me the A on the high...," and I'm like, "Just show me the fucking dot! What dot is it? Is it number six? Is it on the dot, or beyond the dot? Which one?" I can hit that dot while doing a spinning, flying kick, so fuck it!

LOU: You want to know why I wanted to be the vocalist? Because I fucking sucked at the bass so bad, and as we started writing songs, I realized, "Shit, I can't change my fingers as fast as these guys, so I'll just sing, if you want to call what I do singing." We began going to Giant Studios in Manhattan to rehearse because that's where Straight Ahead rehearsed. They'd just gone from being in NYC Mayhem to becoming Straight Ahead. Craig and Armand would come to the rehearsals too, and we'd have so much fun.

PETE: When we went to rehearse back then, we would bring fucking everybody from Queens, and everyone from Manhattan, and there'd be tons of beer and everyone would just have fun. It was all about laughing. After rehearsal we'd go play pool or some shit.

LOU: We realized we needed a name, so Pete and I came up with the idea for the name "Sick of It All." We were basically fed up, angry kids. We were frustrated and young and didn't like the Guidos and jocks in our neighborhood. I'm sure people still get harassed for being metalheads or punks these days. There was that meme going around that says, "I was into punk when it was still called 'Hey faggot,'" which is so true. You'd get fucked with because you had a different haircut or different clothes. We eventually decided on "Sick of It All." What's funny is our drummer at the time, who was Asian, said, "No, let's just be "Sick OF All."

PETE: Of course, the Asian kid says, "No, no, no—Sick OF ALL!" (Laughs) Total cliché.

LOU: He liked the three-letter thing, S.O.A., and I was like, "There already IS an S.O.A.! Ever hear of Henry Rollins?! Sick of It All, that's the name!" I love it still. There were people at the time who were like, "Your name is too long, you should just call yourselves SOIA," and I was like, "That's just like saying 'Sick of It All." I love doing interviews on live radio and they mistakenly say, "Sick IT of All is here." It happens ALL the time. We even do it sometimes, putting the "it" ahead of the "of." Even to this day in ads and flyers and stuff, we get called "For the Sake of it All." We always play the Underworld in London. We sell out two nights in a row every time we're there, and the last time we played, on the marquee it said, "Sold out tonight—Sick Off It All." It's just ridiculous.

PETE: The name was perfect, especially at that time because, growing up, we were just pissed off at normal, average kid stuff, teenage stuff, our neighborhood, the assholes we had to deal with....

LOU: The closed-mindedness of the people around us. It's weird, we hadn't traveled anywhere at that point, but I guess our mother being from France and having lived through World War II, having seen what happened to her neighbors and her friends, affected our mindset. She'd tell us these stories about her friends who would just disappear. Her older sister and her best friend were coming home from work, and German soldiers were whistling at them. They said something back to them and were thrown in jail.

PETE: I think she said she gave them the finger, and they threw her in prison.

LOU: She told us there was a Jewish woman in there with them who got taken away and that was it. She was gone. Our mom telling us all this shitty stuff, combined with how closed-minded these idiots in our neighborhood were.... We were always getting into scuffles and altercations with these morons.

PETE: At one of those early rehearsals, Craig came and told us that Straight Ahead was doing a show with Youth of Today and Crippled Youth in Long Island at the Right Track Inn in Freeport. Lou: Craig said we should play that show too because he needed another band that would play for no money, but we didn't think we were ready, and he said, "If you're not ready now, you're never gonna be ready," and he just put us on the flyer.

CRAIG SETARI (SICK OF IT ALL BASSIST): I totally forced them to play that show. When they told me they didn't think they were ready, I put "special guests" on the flyer, so in case they didn't wind up playing, it didn't look like they canceled. I kept on nagging them for like two weeks, to the point where they said, "But you didn't put our name on the flyer," so I put it on the next version of the flyer so they HAD to play. I actually think Armand got up onstage with them that night and sang "My Revenge," which he wrote.

LOU: That was our first show. That's when it became serious. I mean, if it wasn't for Craig forcing the issue, we probably would have just kept playing in the rehearsal studio. That would have been it. The lineup for that first show was me, Pete, Mark McNeely on bass, and Dave Lamb on drums. The only songs we still have from that time are "My Life" and "G.I. Joe Headstomp." I remember people watching us, like the guys from Token Entry and Mark from Supertouch, and I distinctly remember we made sure to do a cover song at that show and learned a Cause for Alarm song. We played our set, and people politely applauded, but when we played that Cause for Alarm song, everybody went fucking crazy! It was the hardest thing we ever did.

PETE: Then Dave quit because he didn't want to do it anymore, and we kind of kicked Mark out because he was more into telling people he was in a band than actually being in one. He was WAY more into just hanging out. He wouldn't even know the songs—he would just ride the open E—and Dave, well, he was Chinese and somehow got into white power. We found out that he actually had a poster of Hitler on his wall at his house!

LOU: It was that side of being a skinhead that we couldn't believe or understand. This was before the internet, and he would write letters to these people at Aryan newspapers. I asked him, "Don't your parents see this?!" He was like, "They don't read English." I said, "What happens if these guys come to visit you and find out you're Asian?!" He would just get mad at us.

PETE: Yeah, for some reason, he went from being just a regular guy from Queens to doing THAT, hating himself obviously.

LOU: Years later, on our first California tour with Bad Brains, we did a headline show at Spanky's Cafe. We hadn't had any contact with Dave in years, and all of a sudden, he shows up at the show with six Marines, all black guys, and we were like, "What the hell is going on?!"

PETE: Anyway, now it's just after our first ever show, and we have no bass player and no drummer.

RICH CIPRIANO (FORMER SICK OF IT ALL BASSIST): I was at their first gig. I turn to our friend Mike and I go, "Um, wow. Mark's not even playing the bass parts." Mike says, "Yeah, that's probably why they're going to ask you to play their next show." I'm like, "Oh great. I'm going to be in a band."

LOU: Richie and Rob from Rest in Pieces had a band with Craig—I think Chuck Valle from Ludichrist, later Murphy's Law, was involved too—called Smegma. It never really went anywhere because they never had a drummer, so we asked Richie to play bass in Sick of It All. He was into it but told us we had to get him a bass. He had only played guitar, and then we asked Armand, who was doing Rest in Pieces at the time, to do us a favor and be our drummer for a demo and he just ended up staying. That's when we started writing more songs. I think Pete wrote all the music, and I wrote 99 percent of the lyrics, but then Armand and Richie began writing parts.

RICH CIPRIANO: Believe it or not, when Dave was in the band, he whistled some of the songs to the other guys. If he had an idea in his head, he would whistle it. He whistled "No Labels, No Lies." There were two or three songs that he just whistled, and those turned into real songs. I think before I even started jamming with those guys, I wrote a few bits and pieces that they heard which later became "G.I. Joe Headstomp."

PETE: First thing we did with those early songs was record them for our demo, and we started selling copies at Some Records, which was only a few blocks from CB's. Everyone would go there between bands on Sundays. That was THE place. At first, we would bring ten demos, and a minute into the matinee, they'd be all gone. Duane would ask us to bring more, so every weekend we'd bring more and more until we were bringing fifty, then a hundred, and they would always sell out. It was at the height, when the scene started getting really big. For the newer people just getting into it, we were the new band, and they latched onto us as if we were theirs.

LOU: Yeah, people seemed excited. It's not just that we were the fresh, new band; we were playing music that was kind of a new version of what people in New York already liked. We'd listen to songs like "Victim in Pain" and want to have our own song like that. That's how "My Life" came about. It doesn't sound like "Victim in Pain," but that's what we were trying to emulate. We took the hardcore that we loved and went in a little bit of a different direction with it. I think that's what excited people about it. People seemed to like the demo cover too. I loved *Calvin and Hobbes*, and I hated the world. I saw a picture of Calvin swinging a bat, and I thought, *I wish I could take a bat to the world*, so I drew the world, and I drew Calvin next to it with the bat!

PETE: I think it helped that since we were coming from a middle-class family, that image wasn't trying to represent being all street-tough. Our fans were coming from places like us. They didn't relate as much to, say, "Survival of the Streets." I think they related more to a kid being pissed off at the world. It's funny; while all this stuff was going on, I graduated from the Center for the Media Arts. I got my degree in graphic arts, and my dad was like, "Hey, I circled all these job openings for you; I'm gonna take you to the interviews." He would take me to these interviews and I'd be like, "Well, I'm kind of in a band, so I really don't care if I get this job." I would put the kibosh on the interview as soon as I got there. I didn't give a fuck about what I'd just gotten out of going to school. I didn't want to draw album covers; I wanted to play on fucking albums. I remember my dad driving me all the way out to somewhere in Long Island, and he goes, "THAT'S what you're gonna wear?!" I had on red Doc Martens and tight jeans, and I kind of had a skinhead look to me. But hey, I went. My dad wanted me to go, so I went. I didn't lie to him; I went.

LOU: Then things began to fall into place with the band. We were all working our shitty day jobs, but still going to lots of shows.

PETE: Back then, we paid our rent with stolen records from various mailrooms. There was a whole system. We got paid for working at these places, but then we'd swipe a Motörhead box set and sell it to Bleecker Bob's for fifty dollars!

LOU: I got a job at a company called Concrete Marketing, and I got everybody else in the scene jobs in their mailroom, but I would tell them, "Don't go crazy taking everything. We can take these and sell them downtown if you're smart about it." It covered my lunch and travel expenses, maybe for a few days, but not for a whole week. There was a certain ex-roadie of ours, who now sings for a band that begins with "H," who went hog-wild and couldn't resist stealing beyond stealing.

PETE: Ruined it for everybody!

LOU: Fucking ruined it! But those were the fun times. I remember going to the Anthrax in Connecticut to see Token Entry, and Ernie told us that we should come up during their set and do a song. It was only me, Pete, and Richie there. We didn't have Armand, but Ernie told us he could play "Friends like You," so at the end of their set, for the encore, the four of us played "Friends like You." That was a big boost because Token Entry was a big band at the time. Other bands began seeing us and started asking, "Hey, you wanna go to Washington, D.C., with us? Want to play with us at this VFW hall in New Jersey?" It just started snowballing. We didn't consciously say, "All right, let's go and be a real band and do this or that."

PETE: Everything we did was still based around just having fun. For instance, instead of getting a van that was comfortable to drive to shows in, where you could fit the equipment and everything, we'd get a cargo van and fill it with a bunch of NUTS from Queens, without ANY equipment. We'd just borrow shit when we got there. Armand didn't have a drum set for probably the first seven years of the band, maybe more.
Lou: We thought it was more important to bring our friends than any equipment.

PETE: It was non-stop, hysterical laughter. Then we'd remember we had to play a show.

LOU: Eventually, we were asked to do the 7-inch for Revelation. I remember exactly when they asked. I was standing on the steps outside the Anthrax, and Ray Cappo and Jordan Cooper approached me saying, "We want to do a Sick of It All 7-inch," and I was like, "Uh, alright." They also asked us to do that 7-inch compilation, Together, and they wanted us on the 12-inch *The Way* It Is compilation too. We recorded just those two songs for the 7-inch comp, and for the 12-inch, again, we just did two songs, and then we went and re-recorded everything for our 7-inch. At first, I was excited about recording, but when we got into the studio, I was so nervous. I was like, *we don't know what to do. I don't know how to sing....* We asked Armand, "What's that cheap place on Long Island where Rest in Pieces recorded?" I don't even remember the name. The guy wasn't into hardcore at all, so I'd go in there and start screaming my head off, and the guy's like, "Whoa, whoa, whoa—you gotta calm down! The mic picks up everything, so you should do it like this." That's why when people talk about the early recordings, I'm like, "Yeah, musically, the songs are good, but I fucking hate my performances." We were kids and didn't know what we were doing.

ARMAND MAJIDI (SICK OF IT ALL DRUMMER): Even if you ask Lou and Pete now, they'll say they're not musicians. They'll call themselves entertainers. They love the term entertainers. It's almost a shame because I know they're more capable than they think. Pete can actually sing too. Onstage, when you put a mic in front of him, he gets all Cookie Monster, but he can really sing. I wish he had more confidence in his voice.

LOU: Something important that helped get our name out there was when Pushead reviewed the *Together* comp for *Thrasher* magazine. He sang for Septic Death and loved fast, crazy hardcore. He mentioned all the bands and wrote something like, "but Sick of It All steals the show with their two tracks." *Thrasher* was super influential at that time. It was one of the only non-music magazines that really turned people on to new, aggressive music. Pushead started the ball rolling for us. Later he reviewed the 12-inch comp, and I think we did our first interview for *Thrasher* with Mike Gitter. When I finally got to meet Pushead, he was cool as shit. He turned me on to all sorts of weird shit: art, anime.... He was a champion of ours from the beginning.

PETE: With our 7-inch, we were like, "Fuck, we've gotta glue all these things together! Quick, we gotta fold these things and get to a show." We'd sell them all when we went to Boston, or D.C., or

Connecticut; we'd come back and have to ask Ray and Jordan for more. I remember gluing the sleeves together in my bedroom in the first Alleyway house. I fucking loved it! I loved it because we handled every aspect: "Let's put the collage together for the lyric sheet; we'll do it ourselves." I was really proud. Revelation had to keep repressing it due to demand. I loved staring at the stack of them. I swear, I would just sit there and stare at them just like I did with the stack of demo tapes we would bring to Some Records.

LOU: We had taken the band pictures in the alleyway where we hung out with everybody, which was done pretty much to show where we came from. There was the Lower East Side Crew, the Sunset Skins, the Astoria Boys, and we were known as the Alleyway Crew. People lumped us and all of our friends together as the Alleyway Crew because Tommy Carroll dubbed us that at our first show while thanking us from the stage during Straight Ahead's set.

PETE: I think Tommy said, "Thanks to the Alleyway Boys or the Alleyway Crew for coming down and playing with us."

LOU: That 7-inch image has become a pretty cool, iconic shot in hardcore. We've even used some of the outtakes for ads; we've made flyers with them. There's one of Pete hanging upside down on the fence while Richie's doing some weird thing. That shows there's a sense of humor there too. But the one we chose for the cover...to be honest, when I saw that photo, I knew that was THE one because we looked like a hardcore band. That's all we wanted. It was our version of AF or the Cro-Mags or whoever. No one really ever gave us individual nicknames like "Stigma" or "Bloodclot." I guess we have "Craig Ahead," and we do call Armand "Armand Hammer," from the brand Arm & Hammer. We just used our given names.

PETE: Then, at some point, the dragon pretty much became our logo.

LOU: A friend of ours was going into the Marines, and he went and got what became known as the Alleyway dragon tattooed behind his ear. After that, we were like, "Let's all get 'em." The original dragon image, which differs slightly from the one we use today, was done by legendary tattooist Greg Irons. It was on one of his flash sheets. Greg was a big deal in the seventies and early eighties. When we did the first 7-inch, they had a photo of my Alleyway tattoo in the lyric sheet, and then it just became associated with Sick of It All from that.

PETE: There are so many people all over the world who have that dragon tattoo; it's insane. I saw a picture of this guy with his entire head tattooed with the dragon and the words "Just Look Around."

LOU: That's devotion. When people first started getting the tattoo, somebody asked us how we felt about it, and I replied, "Well, I guess we better not suck or start turning out crap records." Some people misunderstood the Alleyway concept and made it into a thing that it wasn't, like a gang. I've heard people ask, "If I get the Alleyway tattoo, is that a bad thing? Is something going to happen to me?"

PETE: It's people just showing how much they like our band.

LOU: It started to get silly after a while. In California, this guy came up to us and was showing us his Alleyway dragon tattoo. He said, "I hope you guys aren't going to jump me or anything." I was like, "What?! You tattooed our band's symbol on your arm." After a while, when people would ask "Hey, is it cool if I get the dragon tattoo?" we would jokingly tell them they had to go talk to our friend Devil first because he was the sheriff of the Alleyway. It was great. We'd send people over to him, and in a very serious tone, he'd pause and be like, "Yeah, I guess it's okay." He loved fucking with everyone.

PETE: At one point, people tried to create a beef between us and Mobb Deep, because they started to use the same dragon.

LOU: We had a friend, Lisa Rowe, who worked in the hip-hop industry. One day, she walked past the Loud Records graphic artist guy's desk and saw the new Mobb Deep album, and she asked, "Why do you have a drawing of Sick of It All's dragon on there?" and he said, "That's the new Mobb Deep album that's coming out soon." She said, "But that's Sick of It All's dragon," and he said, "No, that's Mobb Deep's," and she showed him a necklace Pete made and gave to her back in 1987 and said, "See this?! I've had this for over ten years. You're gonna have to talk to someone about that." Prodigy and Havoc got them tattooed on their hands. They said they got it off a tattoo flash sheet, but they were working with the Beatnuts guys at the time, and if you went to the Beatnuts' production spot, they had all these different stickers on the door. One of them was a Sick of It All sticker with the dragon on it, so apparently they saw that shit every day for a while.

PETE: Oh yeah, they'd seen it.

LOU: But there was never any beef. If this happened to any other band, as opposed to us, that band would have said, "Hey, that's our symbol. Give us a hundred fucking grand!" But with us, it's like, "Hey, that's our symbol. All right, cool, we'll compromise."

PETE: Damn it! Why couldn't we just cash in like every other scumbag band?!

LOU: Another misconception that followed us for a while, because of the association with Revelation Records, was that we were a straight edge band. It's hysterical because we used to get drunk in that very alleyway on the Rev. 7-inch cover. But actually, not long after, I gave up drinking. Pete too. Not because of choosing to be straight edge; we just didn't want to do it anymore. But we weren't militant about it. We weren't extremists about it. So many people were fucking hypocrites. That's why we wrote "No Labels, No Lies"—because there were all these kids who were supposedly super straight edge, but then you'd come across these photographs of certain "straight edge heroes," at the height of their, um, "edge," smoking a joint. It was all fucking lies!

PETE: When I was living on the Lower East Side, I remember the singer of a VERY straight edge band going down to Avenue D to sell his records so he could buy heroin.

LOU: Youth of Today was super popular at the time, and Bold was coming up. I remember Ray Cappo telling us, "We're going to do an East Coast run, and we want you guys on it." He asked, "What other bands do you think we should get?" We told him they should get Sheer Terror and he was like, "But, you know, their attitude..." and it was the same thing on the other side. Paul Bearer would make fun of us for "always hanging around with those goody-two-shoes boys," and I would be like, "I don't give a shit. I like you guys and I like Youth of Today." I wasn't going to sit there and choose a side.

PETE: I think that is one of the biggest pluses for us; we didn't care about stuff like that at all. We like metal, we like Youth of Today, and we like Sheer Terror, and we'll play with anyone. I think that attitude reached people in the crowd. We never wanted to be labeled; we're just playing music we love.

LOU: But we still had to deal with all of these misconceptions. It was weird to me that people would take a song like "Pushed Too Far" as if it was about being tough guys. I wrote it about ALL of us: the freaks, the punks, fighting the outside world, because we used to get harassed all the time. We'd walk through our neighborhood and Guidos would drive by and throw a beer can at us, screaming, "You fucking freak!" It was us fighting back, and that's what we did. After a while, we would carry these things we called "fight rocks," or we'd carry D batteries inside our denim jacket pockets, because you could either throw them or hold one in your hand when you hit somebody.

PETE: That could be a new merch item: Sick of It All fight rocks. Seriously though, they'd throw beer cans from their cars and we'd hurl fight rocks or batteries back at them. They'd be devastated because it would fuck up their life, I mean, their CAR! It was such a fucking outer-borough thing.

LOU: We did a show at the University of Connecticut. I forget who all of the bands were, but John Brannon's band, Laughing Hyenas, was one, and Screeching Weasel played too. Then there was us and Raw Deal. A month or so after that show, the guy from Screeching Weasel had written a review of his own show in *Jersey Beat* fanzine. Naturally, he praised his band, applauding Laughing Hyenas for being "innovative," and then he writes, "Up next were Raw Deal and Sick of It All. They're interchangeable. They looked like they came to play basketball, not play a hardcore punk show." That was his review. Why? Why don't you open your mind, you know?

PETE: Then we have to deal with, whether it be my dad or one of my friends, "How long do you guys think you're gonna do this for? How long can this last?" It's not like a job where there's the goal of the gold watch and retiring. Why the fuck would I ever want to retire? I'm doing something that I absolutely love. In all sincerity, if I don't hear music all day, I feel like something's missing.

LOU: I mean, what else are we going to do? Even if I went back twenty years to when I was in my thirties, what was I going to do, quit?! And do what? Get a JOB?!

PETE: Yeah, I'm going to quit now and get an entry-level job with a twenty-year-old boss.

LOU. I could go to school and do what? Become an accountant? If I loved math, I would have done that, but I love this!

PETE: Physically, if I had a desk job, which I'm not putting down at all, I'm just saying for myself, I'd be sitting all day, doing my work, and obviously hating it. What I do now is train every single day so I can give it 100 percent onstage every night. That's keeping me healthy and young. I don't ever want to let anyone down with our performances. That's always in my head. I don't want anyone to come back like, "Yeah, they kind of sucked tonight. They looked like they were just going through the motions." When I'm up onstage losing my shit, it's because I'm feeling the music. When someone tells me "I love this song" or "This song got me through a tough time in my life," and one of us wrote that song, that's the best feeling.

LOU: Yeah, it's amazing. One minute, you're in your teenage years, screaming along to Judas Priest records, pretending you're at a big rock concert, and suddenly, you're actually playing in front of thousands of people. I've never thought, *Wow, I'm some sort of a rock star*. I just enjoy each moment.

PETE: Our mentality is totally different than what most bands seem to have. You definitely have to feel it. You have to feel music, and all through this book I'm going to be saying that, because I truly feel music. Sometimes, if I'm listening to certain bands, I still think, *imagine if I got to play with these guys*. I imagined being in those bands when I was younger, and then I remember, Shit, *I AM in a fucking band*, but sometimes I still imagine it: *Wouldn't it be cool if I was onstage with that band playing?* This is how I still think, because music gets me so jazzed up, any kind of music really. Two years ago, we played Hellfest in France with Foreigner. Fucking Foreigner! When they were playing, we thought they were playing the fucking CD over the PA system. This was Foreigner going on BEFORE us! We were like, these guys are fucking legends, and Sick of It All from Queens is going on AFTER them. But that's the beauty of music; there's THAT music, where people just stand there watching and are like, *Wow, these guys are great,* and then there's us, throwing flaming garbage cans at them, shitloads of noise and feedback. People were super psyched that WE were playing AND Foreigner.

LOU: It was fun, because while our crew was setting up, we were watching Foreigner and they were perfect, like a recording, the vocals and everything, and then we come out and there's feedback, distortion....

PETE: We were out of tune!

LOU: Squealing! And we weren't standing still like Foreigner was; we were jumping around like crazy! We got the whole place to bounce up and down for almost every song. I don't know what Foreigner thought of it, but I fucking loved it! We've had a number of experiences like that, and it's crazy because I can still remember the first "big" show we ever played. It was at Irving Plaza, and it was a huge bill. AF, Murphy's Law, Leeway...all the best New York bands, and I remember we were going on first, and there was some band called Gore, like a metal band or whatever. This was 1988. It was the big New Music Seminar show. I remember Chris Williamson telling us, "You guys get fifteen minutes, Gore gets fifteen minutes, Rest in Pieces gets twenty..." and the guys in Gore were like, "We're not going up there and playing for only fifteen minutes," so they left. Chris Williamson looks at us and says, "Well, they're gone so you guys get TWENTY minutes," and we played our entire first album's worth of material. He saw us get up there and do our full set in twenty minutes without complaining. When we went on, there were maybe twenty-five people there, but by the time we finished, the floor was completely full and everybody was going crazy. From then on, every once in a while, he would say, "I want you guys to play this show or that show," and we'd be were like, 'OK sure.'"

PETE: It wasn't called the Superbowl of Hardcore yet. The second big show we played was at The Ritz. I think that one was the first Superbowl. I don't remember much about the first one. I remember the whole getting-extra-time business, but I remember the second one more so, because we were like, "WOW, we're gonna play The Ritz!" To me it was like playing Madison Square Garden.

LOU: That's the show where we got the wall of death photo that was inside of *Blood, Sweat and No Tear*s. Warzone headlined.

PETE: And they paid for all this extra lighting and put it all over the stage.

LOU: And I fucking tripped over it because the lighting guy at The Ritz, in the middle of one of our songs, pulled the lights down to be fancy, made it dark, and shot them back up. I was running across the stage at the time, and when it went dark, I tripped over the damn Warzone lights.

PETE: I remember you turned to me before soundcheck and said, "I can't remember any of the words to our songs."

LOU: Because I was so nervous.

PETE: I said, "Let's do 'Alone,'" but I couldn't remember how to play it. I was like, "Shit!" But as soon as we kicked into it, it turned back on.

LOU: We were going up to do our soundcheck, and I was like, "Holy shit, look at the size of this place! Twisted Sister played here with Queensrÿche, for God's sake!

PETE: We'd seen Motörhead there; we saw Slayer there.

LOU: Man, it was intimidating. I think this is the same show where, after we did our soundcheck, we were all relaxing, sitting where they had that VIP section, and they were announcing what times the bands were going on. They said, "Sick of It All, you're going on first at 9:00," and we all went, "YEAH, WE'RE NUMBER ONE!" We were just joking around, and the guys in Warzone got so pissed because we were going, "Yeah, we're number one." I still have no idea why that bothered them.

PETE: I noticed at that show there seemed to be such a weird feeling of competition on Warzone's part. They were like, "Yeah, we're going on last, we're the HEADLINER," and we were just like, "Who cares?" It was really strange. I think it was because, music industry-wise, they're always looking for the next big thing and the spotlight was beginning to be on hardcore at that point.

LOU: Even though these bigger shows weren't the most ideal thing for hardcore, they kind of worked. But then as the shows got even bigger, every show would have to be stopped because of fighting, which gave the entire genre a bad name.

PETE: I remember people from the CB's scene would try to keep that under control as much as possible. If you saw a big doofus from somewhere else, and he thought it was about, "OK, let me go and attack the smallest guy dancing who's actually feeling the music," people would kind of rat-pack him, you know?

LOU: That's when the downfall started. This crew mentality set in with kids wanting to be like the Cro-Mags and AF. "Oh my God, look at these tough guys covered in tattoos." Not long afterward, CBGB stopped doing matinees because it became too much. That kid pulling a gun out, that was just stupid. There was no reason to pull that gun out except to show off and show everybody, "Yo, I'm gangsta. Look, I got a gun." We were like, "Why the fuck is there a gun at CBGB?!"

PETE: It started long before the gun incident, when one of the people we know started dancing with a hammer in his hand. Everybody was really young, trying to get a tough-guy rep, or a crazy one, like "Yo, that guy's fucking crazy." Now, thinking about it, my God, how stupid. It's a show where they're playing music that you want to hear. Go fight in a fucking ring! Fight somebody in the street, but don't do it at our show! The scene started killing itself with this, *Yeah, we're a tough-guy band and these are our tough-guy fans, and they're going to beat up the other fans who paid to get in!* And then those fans don't show up anymore, and the guys who got in for free are the only people there to watch the show. It was a tough time. The scene was also becoming more mainstream, I guess. The shows were bigger, and it had begun to spread.

LOU: Yeah, when CB's was ending the matinees, they were packing them in like crazy. CBGB only held, I think, 350 people legally, but you'd step into the doorway and it would take you a good fifteen minutes just to get past the bar to the dance floor, which would be packed. Look at the Agnostic Front "Anthem" video; it's just insane. People can't even dance, they're packed in so much.

PETE: When they showed that AF video in the lobby of the main hotel at CMJ that year—they had that HUGE screen—every single person was like, "WHAT THE FUCK IS THAT?!" I was standing there all proud, because those are my friends. Even the hip-hop artists were like, "Wow, look at that shit!" I'm like, "Yeah, that happens every weekend in my world!" Whenever we would play a show, we wanted to show everybody, this is what we do. That's why we've always talked shit about barricades and how bigger venues have a negative effect on hardcore shows. How can you have a hardcore punk show with a barricade? I get it to some degree, especially at clubs that don't have hardcore shows very often, but it's like Lou said on the In-Effect video with us, AF, and GB, and it's exactly what happened in the end; kids fucked things up and a lot of the hardcore is now gone from hardcore.

LOU: I will say though, now that we go all over the world, people look at that video and say, "Wow, look at that scene." It helped solidify not just punk or hardcore from America but NEW YORK hardcore. Sure, there are great bands from Texas and Florida and California, but this is OUR sound. This is OUR scene. If a kid from Belgium is watching it, they see fucking three thousand people at this show, blown away by the scene that was originally this tiny little thing. It's amazing if you think about it.

PART IV
ROAD LESS TRAVELED

1. SO, WHAT ARE YOU GOING TO DO?

PETE: When we started Sick of It All, we never thought about there being a beginning or an end to the band. It kind of just kept happening.

LOU: Around 1989 when *Blood, Sweat and No Tears* was coming out, we were offered a West Coast tour with Bad Brains. Just before that, my mom came to me and said, "Your uncle George called. He has a farm in France and needs some help. He has a deal for you guys: you can go to France for the summer and work four days on the farm. He has an apartment in the heart of Paris where you can go live on the weekends." What more could a young man want? Me and Pete were like, "Whoa, that's crazy." I remember thinking, *Holy shit, that would be cool. We should really think about it,* and then we got the offer from Bad Brains to do two weeks of shows with them and Leeway out west. I remember thinking, *What the fuck?* Why is this happening now? We wound up saying yes to the Bad Brains, and I remember my dad being kind of disappointed. I said to him, "Dad, it's as if you were in a band in the fifties and Elvis said, 'I want you guys to open up for me.' That's how much Bad Brains mean to us."

PETE: When the first record was coming out, I had just graduated from the Center for the Media Arts, and my dad kept pressuring me to get a job. Some of the want ads would say, "twenty years' experience minimum." My dad would say, "Well, you could try."

LOU: I remember going into my supervisor's office. I worked in the art department in this rich guy's carpet factory. We made rugs for the super-rich—Michael Jackson, Peter Frampton, the State Department. We did rugs for the richest man in the world. All of his rugs were silk for his yacht. I asked the supervisor if I could have the two weeks off for the tour, and he said, "Yeah, that's cool. Your band's going to California. That's awesome. Take two weeks off." And then this other guy goes, "Well, we've got to ask the manager, but he shouldn't have a problem with it. We've got plenty of guys to cover for you." So, he fucking talked to the big boss guy, not even the boss of the company, just the manager of the factory. He was this fucking super-rich, rude asshole. The second supervisor comes back. "What's up?" I asked. He goes, "He wants to talk to you." He'd said something to him like, "Oh, he wants to go out to California with his little band? Good. He should get a new job when he comes back." The supervisor told me again, "But he wants to talk to you." I thought, *does he want to belittle me or something?* He's like, "Just go talk to him." So, I walk in and he's just like, "They told me what you want to do, so here's your choice: choose your band or stay here and work." I was like, "All right, goodbye!" I just got up and left and that was it. Never went back. Not that it was a cool thing to do. I was just like, *I don't want to be talked to like this by this fucking asshole.* I could have stayed in that art department for another God knows how many years until one of the other guys retired or died. There was a guy there who was one of the most talented artists I'd ever seen. He was from Russia, where he had been an art director of some huge company. He had books out in Russia. Here, he was making two dollars more than me. I basically HAD to say, "Fuck this!" I was sweating because I had to pay $700 a month for rent. I had a three-bedroom apartment in Queens on top of a house, and I was like, *oh my God, how am I going to afford this?*

PETE: I know our parents are proud of what we've done, but they're still always super worried. My dad still says, "So, what are you going to do?" Then he wonders why we don't call him as often as we used to. The conversation usually starts, "Hey, how's the road? The weather's great over here. What are you going to do when this is all over?" That's always slipped in there. I always respond with "Aren't I getting an inheritance?" and he just laughs. We always had jobs early on: mailroom jobs, construction, demolition, all that stuff. But when we started going to Europe, I remember we made three thousand bucks each! We were all like, "Holy shit!" Not complaining, but it was brutal, brutal touring as far as travel and lack of sleep. Then I got home and paid my Manhattan rent, and had nothing left. Then I went back to work. I worked at the Palladium then. It took a long time before we were able to actually make money.

LOU: Not until later in my life did I ever think, *God. Why didn't I fucking finish college, or do this or that?* But back then, it was just the norm to struggle. It was going on tour, coming home, going right back to your shitty job, and not having a career because you were leaving all the time. But back then, we would go to work until Friday; Friday night we'd load the van up and go play a show. We'd do Baltimore, D.C., and somewhere else over a weekend and be back by Sunday night/Monday morning. We didn't have driver's licenses. We'd drop Armand off, then we'd drop Richie off, or Craig, whichever one was in the band at the time, go park the van at the rental place, drop the keys in the slot, and walk home. Then we'd have to be up at 6:00 a.m., or not sleep, and go right to work. We did that for years, and it became the norm because we loved playing in the band so much.

PETE: There were definitely times when we had to ask ourselves if what we were doing was realistic.

LOU: A perfect example was those Amnesty International benefits we would do in New York from time to time. We would play for two or three thousand people and not get paid. We committed to doing those benefits, so I understand playing for free, but sometimes, across the street, there would be some metal show with fewer people and these guys in tour buses who had fucking gear endorsements, and we're sitting there going, "We just played to three thousand people, and I gotta get up in fucking four hours to go to work. What am I doing wrong?" I'm not saying that those bands didn't struggle, but I never understood why the music industry took metal so seriously and ignored hardcore for so long. Later on, I realized that it's all about generating money. That music generates income for the record labels, and hardcore is not "supposed" to do that. Unfortunately, it shot itself in the foot with that attitude.

**An Amnesty International
Benefit Concert**
at the
𝕽cademy
with

SICK OF IT ALL
BLACK TRAIN JACK
ORANGE 9mm
debut performance - with members of BURN

ENDPOINT

$12 TICKET INCLUDES
1 RAFFLE ENTRY FOR
HARDCORE MUSIC PRIZES
PLUS POSTERS & T-SHIRTS
ADDITIONAL RAFFLE TICKETS
ARE $2 EACH.

plus Spoken Word by
RAY CAPPO of SHELTER
WALTER SCHREIFELS of QUICKSAND
and more...

All tickets $12   SATURDAY JUNE 12TH
DOORS OPEN 7:00 pm   SHOW STARTS 8:00 pm

THE ACADEMY 234 West 43rd Street (Between 7th and 8th Ave.) TICKETS AVAILABLE NIGHT OF THE
SHOW AT THE ACADEMY OR AT TICKET MASTER LOCATIONS AND BY PHONE CHARGE (212) 307-7171

PETE: This is fast-forwarding several years, but we know the guy who started the Full Force Festival in Germany. We were looking for a raise one year, a higher guarantee because we'd done really well there in previous years, and I remember the guy was like, "No way! They're a hardcore band, they don't expect to be paid." It's like, "No, we're men with families and fucking bills." People depend on us just like anyone else who works to pay the bills and keep their house. How dare someone say that! He would have never said that to even a lesser metal band.

LOU: People need to quantify success. One time, our parents came to my house, and I have this plaque up on the wall from Fat Wreck Chords for 250,000 records sold or whatever. My mom was all excited like, "When did you get that?" I said, "I don't know, they sent it to us around Christmas time," and then she made my father take pictures of it. I was like, "You can have it if you want. You can take it home." That's the kind of stuff that legitimizes what we do for them. I remember when we did that huge show at 1018 (The Roxy) in New York with VOD, Snapcase, AFI, and Ensign. My dad came backstage and goes, "There's people out there selling your tickets for seventy-five bucks." In his mind, he was thinking, Wow, you guys made it, but I had to remind him, "We ain't getting a cut of that!"

2. IT'S AN ONGOING GIVE-AND-TAKE THING

LOU: I think the most important reason there's been longevity for us is we found something we all love and want to keep doing. We try hard to keep our egos out of it. There are definitely arguments. There are times when money becomes involved, and with this band, we split everything four ways. Sometimes that sucks, because some people do more than others at certain times, but the four-way split is the only way to keep it going and keep the egos in check.

ARMAND MAJIDI: I handle the band business because no one in the band is business-minded other than me. I just sort of fell into it. They have no interest in doing it, and I have a good handle on it. I can create a budget; I can keep our tours within budget. Luckily, I haven't had any real issues discussing money with those guys. It's great that they just trust me, 'cause it would suck if they didn't.

LOU: No one should "claim" anything in this band, because we all love this. Sometimes there's a weird dynamic within the band. If Armand has something that he wants to discuss with Pete, he goes through me, or he might go through Pete to talk to me, because we don't want to have fights. Plenty of times, it's me and Pete on one side and Craig and Armand on the other. A perfect example is the latest album, *Wake the Sleeping Dragon!* with the track sequencing. We had very different opinions on what it should be.

PETE: Lou and I definitely let them win that argument; we let it slide. I do not like the sequencing of the new album AT ALL, but I love the new album.

LOU: It's an ongoing give-and-take thing, and it's funny how we have that dynamic where there are filters, where Armand will go through me to talk to Pete to test the waters, or he'll go to Pete to test the waters with me. I do think it's that way because we're brothers. Otherwise, you end up like Oasis or The Black Crowes, where the brothers get into fistfights and their relationship falls apart. I guess everyone has an ego no matter what they say. We're a very humble band. Craig likes to remind us all that we've got to be humble. We could brag about a lot of shit, but we don't.

PETE: And Craig is an insane narcissist!

LOU: But we all are.

CRAIG SETARI: When it comes down to it, those two get along with one another pretty well. Their personalities are very different, but like the rest of us, they understand that we have one objective, which is to continue this band. We don't sweat that objective; it's just something we all understand. All the drama you see with these other bands who've been doing it for a long time, we don't get into that. It's pointless. Even though we have conflicts, we just keep going. Those guys might kick and scream once in a while, but they're still always going to get in the van and play the show. The objective is the bottom line.

LOU: Going onstage and having people sing back words you wrote or go wild when you go into a song or a riff, and watching people's faces light up and they scream.... Even now, I get excited when we go into a song like "Death or Jail," where it starts with the guitars, and all of a sudden, the crowd just cheers, and you're like, *Holy shit, they love our song!* I feel so alive. Time doesn't matter; my age doesn't matter. People say things like, "You guys look so young, how do you stay so young?" It's because we're doing this! Look at bands like Aerosmith or whatever; no matter what you think of them, they've been doing this for decades and they still get up and give it their all. I remember seeing an interview with Steven Tyler—this is going back years—saying that he still gets excited about every show, and I'm glad to hear that, because at most arena shows, in my head, I'm like, *These fucking guys don't give a shit. This is just a paycheck for them.* I will say I'm pleasantly surprised sometimes. I went to the farewell Black Sabbath show at the Garden and they all looked like they were having a great time. Geezer Butler was fucking going wild, and they looked like they still loved it. It keeps you young. I recently got an email from our friend Mike Sentkewitz. He was around us all the time when we were going to shows and forming the band, but we'd lost touch for years. He wrote, "Wow, you guys are doing exactly what we wanted to do as teenagers. I'm so proud of you," and that made me feel amazing.

PETE: The four of us are a family now, whether we like it or not. We're stuck with each other. When Richie was in the band, it was great, but when Richie left, we tried other bass players, and when Armand left for a little bit, we tried playing with other drummers, but there was just no chemistry. Bringing Craig in, there was a chemistry again.

CRAIG SETARI: I was kind of half an Alleyway guy. We'd known each other for years because of the bands I played in, going to shows and just hanging out. By the time Sick of It All got rolling, I was in AF, but when that was done, they asked me to do a tour with them and then join the band. That was twenty-seven years ago. It's the four of us or bust.

LOU: I know if Pete had left the band, we probably would not have lasted this long. He's my brother, he looks out for me, and I look out for him. That's just the way it is. There have been times when it's like, "I really don't want to do this tour, but we're all hurting for money, so all right, let's do it," or when Pete's daughter was born, and we had to go on tour. Pete used to be the guy who was like, "Let's tour for eight weeks at a time; I don't give a shit." Then when his daughter Lucy was born, he was like, "I can only go out for maybe two to three weeks," and we had to say, "Wait Pete, you gotta understand...." He was great about it, and he compromised. Believe me, I understood as a father.

PETE: But now Lucy's old enough to come out with us, so that's all right.

LOU: There are plenty of times where something delicate has to be handled. The guys would be like, "Hey, can you talk to Pete, your brother," but I don't think there was ever a situation where I was like, "Hey, YOU have to go talk to him about whatever the issue is, he's MY brother."

PETE: I think that's the way I feel about all the guys. Sometimes it's like, We gotta do this because, *all right, Craig or someone in the band needs money right now.* Obviously, we always need money, but if something (unforeseen) happens, we'll all agree, let's do these shows, let's make the tour a little bit longer than we wanted.

LOU: Around 1990 or early '91, both Armand and Richie decided they wanted to leave the band. It sucked!

PETE: That was just before we had that AF tour.

LOU: Yes, but that tour wasn't Armand's motivation for leaving. Armand wanted to get a regular job. I remember we did the We Stand Alone EP. We were like, *this will show that our intention is to keep going.* That's why the EP had pictures of the old band and me and Pete with the new guys.

PETE: Lou and I did not want to stop at all, and I remember we were like, *no matter who leaves the band, we're gonna keep doing the band.* I remember being very adamant about making sure the new guys, EK and Eddie, were in the photos.

LOU: That's a period of Sick of It All that I don't really remember because I didn't like it. I especially hated trying out bass players. Eddie only did the AF tour with us and then he left to play with Cycle Sluts from Hell because he said they would pay him two hundred bucks a week, and they were opening for Motörhead. He came back and was talking about how great it was, saying, "Yeah, we had our own catering truck following the tour, and every morning I'd get up and they'd make me whatever I want," and "This is how it is in the big leagues," and I'm like, "OK, whatever." At the time I had an OK job, but it was at a place where I had gotten as high as I could. Sure, I could still get an annual 5-10 percent raise every year—I definitely wasn't going to be super rich—but I couldn't get any further with it. There were two guys above me, and it took them years to get to their positions. They were like, "Someday, YOU could be the head of this department," and I'd be like, "Oh cool," and they'd be like, "Yeah, it only took me sixteen years, and I've been here since I was twenty." I'm thinking, *THIS is what you've accomplished in THIRTY-SIX years?!*

PETE: Like that movie Coming to America with Eddie Murphy: next year you'll be on FRIES, and after fries comes assistant manager! Fucking McDowell's!

LOU: I was thinking, *Wow, I'm just gonna go to the bathroom and hang myself at work!*

PETE: That's why no matter what, we kept the band going. Even if it wasn't the most fun, because Richie and Armand weren't there anymore, we still kept the name going and we did really well at the shows we played.

LOU: We did have fun, and Sick of It All was becoming a hot band at the time. There was that big Superbowl where the In-Effect *Live in NYC '91* home video was filmed. It still irks me that Sick of It All was documented at that period. I'm not saying anything against EK or Eddie's playing abilities, but we just never gelled. We got along well enough and we played well together, but it didn't feel like a BAND.

PETE: Eddie though—and I'm not talking shit—was always like, "Yeah, I'm a star, I'm a great bass player," and I'm like, "Oh yeah, who gives a fuck?!"

ARMAND MAJIDI: Watching the band when I went on my musical hiatus was really disappointing. I like Max and EK, they're good guys, but I wasn't a big fan of their drumming. Their styles didn't match the impact or the energy of the Koller brothers. You had Lou and Pete who were explosive, and with EK, you had a drummer trying to lay into a pocket. Plus, Lou and EK's personalities were like oil and water back then.

LOU: There was one weekend when we rented a van and told EK, "All right, we'll meet you on Houston Street." He was staying over there with his girlfriend at the time. "You've got to be there at one o'clock," we told him. He waited until three o'clock to show up.

PETE: We called him probably a hundred and fifty times. He would never give us her address, so we wouldn't know where they were. We were just waiting there for him. Then he just comes walking up the block with ice cream in his hand. He was super arrogant, almost like, Yeah, you wait for me, because you can't do anything without me. Then Lou attacked him.

LOU: I didn't attack him. I walked up to him, angrily asking, "Where the fuck were you? We were supposed to leave hours ago." He goes, "Yeah, so what do you want me to do, yo? I'm here now." And I just slapped the ice cream out of his hand, and grabbed him.

PETE: Let's just say EK had some bad habits. In my mind, I always thought, *EK's a cool guy, but hopefully Armand will come back.* Not too long after that, we had rehearsal, and I was on the phone with

Armand. He told me, "Yeah, I can play again if you guys want." I called EK right away and said, "Don't come to fucking practice." That was that.

3. THE ASSHOLE BROTHERS

LOU: We were playing Buffalo, during that run with Agnostic Front, and it was freezing cold. I remember Eddie had this thing where he'd jump out of the van when we'd arrive at the club and he'd go run and find wherever the heater was and just sit by it, never touching any equipment, not doing anything. He'd be all miserable and grumpy. We pulled up to the club and the driveway was just a sheet of ice, so we were being really careful. As soon as we stop, we go, "Wait. Before we get out of the van, don't run inside and go hide by a heater. We were careful not to direct it at anybody in particular. I was just saying out loud that everybody had to grab equipment and the merch, and we all had to load in. And Eddie goes, "So say the Asshole brothers!" And I go, "Oh, we're assholes?!" I open the side door of the van, grab Eddie's bass, and yell, "Go get your bass," and I shove it out the van. It slid down the driveway on the ice, all the way to the street and he had to go and chase his fucking bass!

PETE: They always called us "the Asshole brothers" because we had to be stern, we had to be the bosses. When it was Armand and Richie, we knew that we had to load in, that we had to drive all night, but everything got done. Eddie and EK were thinking, *Hey these guys are getting big; this is like a big money-making machine and everyone does everything for us,* which did not happen.

LOU: And I don't know where they got that idea from. They hung around with some of the bigger bands like the Cro-Mags, who were getting huge at that time They were like their pals, especially Eddie; he was always jocking them hard, but I don't remember the Cro-Mags having people waiting on them hand and foot.

4. THE SHITBOX

LOU: We were on tour a while back and had this van we called "the Shitbox." The Shitbox was an airport transport bus that Armand and Craig convinced me and Pete we needed. The idea was that, for support slots and tours that didn't pay us very much, we could skip renting a vehicle and go do these dates anyway because we'd have our own vehicle, which would eventually pay for itself. They thought it would be awesome.

PETE: In theory, that should have worked, but we weren't in THEORY, we were in the Shitbox!

LOU: The tour wasn't a particularly long one, but it was rough. I was an asshole on that tour. Every time I stepped into the Shitbox, I was like, "Oh, this piece of shit," and every time it broke down, I said, "What a piece of shit!" We were driving late one night....

PETE: We had just played Rhode Island and were headed to Canada....

LOU: The Shitbox broke down AGAIN and I just started going off on a tirade. I was really angry and didn't want to be there. It was fucking cold. We finally got the Shitbox started again, and I couldn't stop saying bad shit about it, which I shouldn't have. Armand lost it and was yelling, "Your fucking negativity isn't helping at all, what the fuck?!" We had a really big argument in the van. I end up getting out of the Shitbox and said, "I quit!" I started walking and saw a hotel. I headed up to the hotel, and Pete comes up behind me and asks, "What's wrong?" There had been a lot of shit going on. I felt like I wasn't being listened to in the band, among other things, and I said, "I quit. I'm fucking done!" Pete, without missing a beat, says, "If you're done, I'm done." That's my brother. He knew that by saying that, I would calm down, and then Armand and Craig walked in, and we sat down and talked.

ARMAND MAJIDI: If one of those guys left the band, I just don't think we could continue. I don't think our audience would want Sick of It All without one or both of them. It's been the four of us nonstop since 1993. It's such a unit. I've always thought it was cheap when bands continued after losing a key member. I mean, it depends on the member, but it's especially bad when it's the singer.

PETE: Wait, we skipped the best part, when you kicked the window of the Shitbox and ALL the fucking windows and the door exploded! (Laughs)

LOU: I went to kick the door open, and as I kicked the panel, all the glass shattered.

PETE: It was one of those school bus doors, so it's all glass. The whole fucking thing exploded, and it's fucking freezing, and we have to head to Canada in the middle of winter.

LOU: We had to tape it up with cardboard and drive to the hotel to rent vehicles.

PETE: So, me and Louie drove in one car, and everyone else drove in another car.

LOU: It was so messed up.

PETE: But the crazy thing is that, no matter how many times the Shitbox broke down, we made really good money on the Shitbox tours, because we didn't have to rent a van or anything. It was really crazy. It turns out the Shitbox was worth it, and there are great stories. Craig eventually sold it to a church group.

LOU: Craig was like, "I feel guilty, but I had to get rid of that thing."

PETE: The guy was telling Craig, "I want to take my family down to Disney in this thing," and he's like, "Yeah that'll be great!"

LOU: The Shitbox stranded us in so many places, oh my God!
Pete: We were stuck in the Florida panhandle for three fucking days!

LOU: It was the middle of nowhere. Everybody who called us was like, "Oh my God, what are you doing in THAT town?"

PETE: The only thing in that town was a prison, and the only reason there was a hotel there was because people visiting prisoners stayed at the hotel.

LOU: We were on tour with Negative Approach for those dates. We told John Brannon that the Shitbox finally died, and he, from the stage, announced, "We lost a member of the tour family. This goes out to the Shitbox!"

PART V

HOW CAN THEY BE OFFENDED BY THAT?! (SONGWRITING)

1. NOT OPENING THE FLOOR TO POLITICAL DISCUSSION...

LOU: I think our lyrics reflect the way we are as people. Why can't people just be cool?! Just live your life, and let everyone live theirs. We probably lean more towards the left, but we make it a point not to come out and blatantly yell at people no matter what. One of the ways I learned to do this was when I became a vegetarian. I had never been a vegetarian but hung out a lot with Civ and Gorilla Biscuits, all those people. I learned something from them because I liked the way they went about being vegetarians themselves. They didn't sit there and go, "How can you eat meat?!" and freak out on people who did. They would just make their own food and not force it down anyone's throat. They would never tell you about how evil it was to eat animals. That was better for me than having somebody scream at me about how shitty it is to eat meat. If you want to know why I'm a vegetarian now, it's because I didn't get yelled at about it. I think that's the way we are with our political beliefs. We lean towards a lot of what we've learned from our parents. The best thing is to be kind and open-minded to every race, lifestyle, and anything else.

PETE: It does get a little complicated sometimes when you're getting into *I'm a left-handed Trans, vegan....* (Laughs)

LOU: Cherokee, something, something.... You have to make things easy for me, although I respect the complexity of diversity. There are some subjects where you have to be straightforward though. Going back to the *Just Look Around* album and the song "Indust.," we knew when we were writing a song about AIDS that we should use the slogan "Silence Equals Death," because at that time, the straight community and the music scene we were a part of still thought that AIDS only happens to gay people. It's like, no, it doesn't. When we were writing that, it wasn't even aimed specifically at the hardcore scene. It was mainly inspired by the people in our neighborhoods, the guys who weren't really into punk who we hung out with. They'd say things like, "That's a gay disease." We're like, "Dude, what if you're going to have sex with somebody who shoots up? That's even more of a risk."

PETE: It gets weird sometimes when you're taking a position while in a band though. You have to be smart about how you speak to your audience. People who don't necessarily agree with you just want to argue, and we don't think alienating them makes sense.

LOU: Especially because we have fans that are, I don't like to use the term "regular guys," but that's kind of what they are. They're working-class people, and you have to understand their values. You can't just beat them over the head with your opinions because their reaction is going to be "I have to fight back" if they feel differently. But if you just slip it in there like, *Hey, I don't need to know how you feel about the war, but we have a lot of our friends and families going over there.* The people involved, the civilians there.... How can they be offended by that, no matter what their politics are? Online it's the worst though. I posted something on Facebook recently, helping to promote a show benefiting organizations assisting immigrants. What did I get? Tons of comments about "fucking illegal immigrants."

PETE It's just so easy now to be an asshole.

LOU: Trump's just divided everyone and made them choose sides, right or left. He says, "It's going to take a huge incident to make the country united again," alluding to another 9/11. Are you saying that that's what unites us, a tragedy, or are you saying that we're going to have to make one? What?! That guy who shot up the mosques in New Zealand—he was quoting Trump—and said, "I wanted to stir up a problem with the Second Amendment stuff in America," and, "We finally have a white president for the white people." He put some fucking manifesto up on Facebook. I mean, I understand why some people flock to Trump. The older generation especially was like, "Oh my God, a black president; he's going to give all our money away to black people. Obama was trying to create all these programs to help people, and certain sects of white people felt like they were being ignored and treated like shit. He was trying to raise everybody up to a certain level, so that there's a level playing field. Now, when all of Trump's supporters are doing their taxes, they're like, *How the fuck do I have to pay thousands of dollars more this year?!* Then, "Obamacare...." Most didn't even realize that "Obamacare" WAS the Affordable Care Act. You can't win.

PETE: People seem to only care about themselves more than ever.

LOU: There's no empathy. I was having a discussion with someone about the border wall. He spewed all these "facts" and numbers about what the government supposedly estimates as far as illegal aliens on welfare. I responded, "Yeah, but there are more poor white people in Pennsylvania who voted the president in, who are on welfare, than illegals." He goes, "Doesn't matter. They're not illegal." That just hit me. It's twisted. Then he mentioned the poor baby that died coming across the border. He says, "Nobody asked them to come across the border." I'm like, "You don't understand. They're not running from Mexico. They're coming from South America and Central America where these regimes were screwed up by American intervention. Most don't understand all this shit. They have no empathy. Then there's Black Lives Matter....

PETE: People just want to be treated fairly, whether it's looking for a house or whatever else. That's what it's about. Yes, there will be some bad apples in any large group, whether it's a religious group, or Black Lives Matter, or whatever it is.

LOU: People must understand that we're not the same. I know that we've all been taught growing up that we're all the same.... No! We're all supposed to be the same, but we're not, and that's the whole point. For how many decades has society corralled poor people, black people, and Latinos into these housing projects? Then a new economy based on criminal activity is created, and the people outside of that say, "Just keep them there. Just stay the fuck in there."

PETE: Lou can get all riled up!

LOU: 90 percent of the time, we try to get our message across without triggering something. I heard from a friend that Paul from Sheer Terror once said onstage, "I don't know about anybody else, but I got into hardcore and punk to offend people. When was the last time Sick of It All offended anybody?" I wish I would have been there because I would have yelled out, "We must be offending you, fatso!"

PETE: You're never going to make everyone happy. We play benefits, and people complain that it's aligned with the wrong charity. "How much of the money REALLY went there?"

LOU: I posted something on Facebook once about St. Jude Children's Hospital. They provide free housing and care for families whose kids are going through cancer treatment and chemo. Somebody was like, "But that's a Christian charity." I was like, "Are you fucking kidding me?! Who gives a shit?!" You could be Muslim; you could be an atheist. If your kid's going through chemo at their hospital, they give you free care and a place to stay so that you can be near your fucking kid.

2. INJUSTICE SYSTEM

LOU: I wrote songs like "Pushed Too Far" and "World Full of Hate" about the overall shit going on in the world. "Bullshit Justice" was written because I watched a TV crime show where a murderer got off on some technicalities, even though it was clear he was guilty. I was sitting there thinking, *How can they do that?!* Especially as a kid, you're like, *There's right and there's wrong and that's it!*

PETE: We grew up being taught "Don't worry, the police are good and they're always going to help you," which brings us to "Injustice System." We played a show at Streets in New Rochelle, New York. They started having a lot of hardcore shows up there because New York hardcore was getting big. It was Murphy's Law, us, and I forget who else, but we played our set, which went great. The thing about Streets was, the hardcore kids would travel from the Bronx, or other parts of New York City, but then there were these local kids....

LOU: VERY white trash! So, during Murphy's Law's set, all of a sudden a riot breaks out between the locals and the hardcore kids, and fights are going on everywhere: inside the club, outside…. Everybody was involved in this shit—me, my older brother—and we're all just hitting people. Pete had been outside putting his equipment away, not bothering anybody. Out of nowhere, a cop comes running over….

PETE: First, the cop attacked our friend Minus, so Jason Krakdown tells the cops, "Hey, c'mon, that's my friend," and then they go after him. I turned around and saw everyone getting beat up by the police and asked, "Hey, what's going on?" Then a cop swung at me. I ducked, and he swung again, so I ducked again. He was mad that I wasn't getting hit, so then someone grabbed me from behind and flipped me over onto the ground. They're all trying to cuff me. One guy is pulling me to the right; the other guy is pulling me to the left. So then this one cop, the one who wound up pressing all these charges against me, grabs me and puts his fingers in my mouth to try to pull and break my jaw, so I bit his fingers really fucking hard! I was arrested for that.

LOU: They took Pete for three days. They wouldn't let us see him, so we went and got a lawyer and they wouldn't let the lawyer see him either. My parents weren't allowed to see him; nobody was allowed to call him—it was all illegal. They did this to everybody who wasn't from New Rochelle.

PETE: There was one kid standing there with no shirt on and a knife, and the cop was just like, "Go on, get out of here," simply because he was a local.

LOU: So, we had to go through that and then go through a trial, which they delayed, and in the end, the charges were dropped. I wrote the lyrics to "Injustice System" about that.

PETE: The cop never showed up to any of the hearings….

LOU: Because he knew the whole thing was bullshit.

PETE: We later heard he got six months paid leave, and there was nothing else done to him. They were going to keep Minus longer than the rest of us because they were like, "He doesn't have a father; no one's gonna come and get him," so my parents drove him home when we were finally able to leave. The cop who I supposedly assaulted said to Jason, "There's no bail for you!" He was acting as if he was the judge. I had all the show money, and I gave it to Jason and said, "Here, now you can get out," and of course, the cops were pissed at that too.

LOU: Eventually, all of this crap settled down. The scene even threw a benefit show for Pete at CBGB.

PETE: It was amazing and showed me that I actually had great friends.

LOU: When we first headlined CB's, there was a line outside, and I thought, *They're obviously here to see the WHOLE show, not just us,* but when so many people showed up to the Pete's Sake benefit, we realized, *Wow, these people are here to support us, to support Pete,* so it was really amazing to me. I remember when we played the Chuck Valle benefit at the Wetlands after he was killed. We started with "Clobberin' Time," and it was like an explosion happened with people flying everywhere. It was a benefit for a friend who was murdered, and that's how we thought we should pay tribute to him. Chuck would have been laughing his head off watching that.

PETE: Sometimes, I think the fact that it's a benefit for a cause makes people go crazier, because while everyone paid their money to get in, at some point, their feelings and emotions about the benefit take over. They realize why they're there.

LOU: That's true. At that Pete's benefit, there was that impromptu Straight Ahead reunion, a moment which can never be duplicated. It wasn't planned; everybody in the band was just there, so they were like, "Let's just get up and do it," and it was fucking amazing! They did three or four songs and it was just pure energy. It was the highlight of the whole show, and they basically did it for their friend.

3. ALLEYWAY STYLE

LOU: We started out playing that old hardcore style because we didn't know how to play very well. With each album, we learned how to play our instruments, how to sing, how to write songs. We grew, and as we grew, our songs got a little more sophisticated, as far as hardcore goes anyway.

PETE: Plus, we like, and are influenced by, all kinds of music, not just hardcore. I think being into Motörhead, for me, as far as playing and writing, helped me come into my own sound and style.

LOU: We began to write heavier groove songs, which we referred to as "Jackson Heights groove metal" because between us and Leeway and a few other bands, that's where it came from and that's what it sounded like. We liked that heavy stuff, but then we'd be in the van playing the 4-Skins and Sham 69. We'd be like, "Damn, listen to that singalong." That's the kind of shit that we wanted.

PETE: We'd always write stuff that we would want to dance to and sing along to. With "Good Lookin' Out," I was like, "What would really get everyone to go nuts as an opening song?" I was thinking about how it would go over live. That's how I write; if I was in the crowd, I wouldn't be able to wait for this part or this song to come up.

LOU: We just write what we like to play. There are people who say stuff like, "Why don't you guys just write a hit song already," like it's so easy. "Why don't you write a pop tune?" I go, "We don't play pop music." I remember talking to Mike Ness once about writing songs. I think it was about Social D's *Between Heaven and Hell* album, and he said, "We got a producer who knew commercial music, and I'd bring him songs. He'd be like, 'This is great. Now go home and write me ten different choruses.'" Mike's like, "What do you mean ten different choruses?" Turns out he wanted different melodies, different words. I'm sitting there like, "I can barely finish one song, and you had to write ten choruses for the same song?" That's a lot of pressure, and some bands can't handle it. After we did *Blood, Sweat and No Tears*, we started getting ready to write for *Just Look Around*, and our friend Brian Freeman turns around and goes, "Oh man, you've got the sophomore pressure to nail that second album." I was like, "What pressure? We'll just write another record. Let's write a second." It didn't hit me at first, but all of a sudden I was like, "Holy shit, he's right. We had our whole lives to make the first record. Now we have to write this one within a year. What the fuck are we going to do?!" It's a challenge for every band. The last time I saw Killing Time, when they did their anniversary show, Carl and Drago came up to me and asked, "What number album is this for you guys?" I said, "I don't know, I think it's number ten or eleven." They were like, "How the fuck do you keep writing albums that are all good? We wrote one good album, then we struggled with the rest." There's no formula. Like Pete said, we write what we love and understand. A lot of bands think too much. If we did that, we would have sounded like Hatebreed on the last three records. I'm not putting down Hatebreed at all by saying that. I'm saying that's what the sound is now. It seems like all the newer bands have directly or indirectly been influenced by them. Look at Knocked Loose. I mean, more power to them, it's just not us. Then you'll have the bands that, to this day, play that super retro, generic, straight edge style. I'm like, "How is that exciting to you? I could just put on a Youth of Today record. Why do I need your version of those songs? You might as well just cover that album." It doesn't excite me.

PETE: When Craig writes, he doesn't sit there and think, "Oh man, kids like The Bronx, or kids like Knocked Loose. I have to write something like that." He thinks, "I like Malignant Tumor, that's hardcore." Shit, I just write what would make me go crazy on the dance floor, a song that would give me chills when played. Something that would get me fucking psyched out of my mind.

LOU: Who the fuck actually likes Malignant Tumor? Nobody! (Laughs) But one of us writes a song, brings it to practice, and then when you add the rest of us, BOOM, it's Sick of It All! All of a sudden, you'll have "Inner Vision," which has the flavor of old school hardcore but with a modern spin on it. Some people are like, "You guys are geniuses," and we're like, "No, this is hard." Sure, we're worried about our mortgages. We're worried about paying taxes. We're worried about whether or not our kids are going to the right schools. But when it comes to music, it's never like, "Oh, I've got to write an album that can pay my mortgage. I want to write an album that's going to make me want to fucking smash a cop car window!"

1. HARDER THAN YOU

PETE: We met Howie Abrams through Danny Lilker because they were at all the CB's matinees. Danny was friends with Craig and his older brother Scott. We'd see them every weekend.

LOU: I remember Howie and Steve Martin talking to me. It was at a show somewhere, and Howie asked, "Hey, are you guys doing anything new? Are you still dealing with Revelation?" and I told him we wanted to do an album. Revelation had just told us that they wanted to do our album but asked if we could wait a year because they were going to do a Gorilla Biscuits album. Howie told us, "Well, we want to talk to you about that. There's going to be a new label." That was In-Effect Records. We didn't have any qualms about it. We thought, "This is great. It's Steve and Howie. They know the scene, and we're gonna get better distribution." Of course, later on, there were certain people who kept saying things like, "You're going to be on a major label." We'd tell them, "No, it's not a major label," and they'd respond, "Well, it's THIS label,

which is owned by THIS label, which is owned by Sony, which has investments...." They went through this long conspiracy route, which I think ended with missiles blowing up children!
Pete: I think we were even running guns to South America!

LOU: Somewhere into our discussions, somebody asked, "Who would you guys want to produce your album?" and we just looked at each other. We thought, "What do producers do?" We had no idea.

PETE: But we knew we loved the sound of that first Leeway album. That's how we decided on Tom Soares and going to Normandy Sound in Rhode Island. There was this huge, sloppy guy up there who owned the studio, Phil Greene. He worked with New Kids on the Block and Marky Mark. He worked with Brad Whitford from Aerosmith on his solo stuff too.

LOU: He said something when we were about to begin recording *Blood, Sweat and No Tears*, which almost fucked everything up.

HOWIE ABRAMS (IN-EFFECT RECORDS): We'd all just driven from New York to Rhode Island. The gear was loaded in, and you were basically ready to record your debut album. You had to record and mix twenty-one songs in three days. Phil was in the control room with his disgusting, bare feet, chain-smoking and dropping his ashes all over the board. He was nowhere near done with whatever mix he was working on. Tom Soares was pissed and kept asking him, "How much longer, Phil?" Phil wasn't even answering him. At some point, Phil asks Tom, "What do you have coming in, another shitty hardcore band?!" I was like, "What the fuck?!" For the next thirty minutes, Tom and I basically tried to make sure we kept you guys away from him in that room. I was just glad no one heard him say that except me and Tom.

PETE: Jamie Locke, one of the assistant engineers, was helping out, centering the studio speakers, and Phil says, "Wait a minute, I gotta go to the bathroom." Phil fell asleep in the bathroom for seven hours! Jamie was like, "What the fuck?!" It was pretty intimidating going into that studio though. Instead of it being just the Alleyway guys coming to rehearse or record, now people were depending on us to get this shit done. But that board they had in there was fucking cool. One thing I'll always remember is how Tom was always like, at the end of the song, "Don't even breathe because these mics pick up everything," so we'd sit there in silence after a take. Now we're like, "Who gives a shit? Just shut the fucking machine off!"

LOU: Plus, it was reel-to-reel tape. It wasn't digital like now, where you can just cut out any sound you don't like. But, Tom helped us a lot on that first album. He gave me ideas, telling me, "You don't just have to yell all monotone." I said to him, "But I don't know how to sing," and he said, "You don't even have to sing, just change your tone here or there." He was actually showing me how to sing.

PETE: I always felt pressure when recording back then, because when I'd fuck up, you'd have to do it over again and again, and if you kept fucking up in that same spot, you'd start feeling very self-conscious about that spot coming up, and then you'd fuck up again.

LOU: Punching in was very different then. You had to time it just right. Tom would sit there and go, "OK, you start singing before the part we need; just keep going." He had the quickest finger. He'd go BAP BAP and he would catch one WORD, without even looking at the button. I loved asking him stuff like, "When you did the Leeway record, what's that part where Eddie's going, 'Let's get this tight, so you can eat...'" and he goes, "Oh, I kept making him do a part over and over because he kept messing up. He was really hungry, so he's in the bathroom, where we tracked the vocals, yelling 'Let's get this tight, so you can eat....'" I thought that was cool. He told us stories about the Cro-Mags too.

PETE: You know what album I really liked from there? Meliah Rage. It has that Normandy sound.

LOU: Our record differs from those bands in that we had to squeeze *everything*–recording, mixing, vocals, back-ups, everything–into three fucking days. When people tell us that's their favorite Sick of It All album, I say, "No, you probably just like that era; you don't like that album." There are good songs on it, but we redid them in 2010. People should listen to that because those versions actually sound how they SHOULD sound. There are songs that I feel I did really well, like "Alone." I thought I sang well on that. "Injustice System" too, but there are other songs where I'm just yelling monotone. Tom would be like, "I wish we had more time, but we don't. We've gotta move on. We got a good take."

PETE: And the mix for the whole album was like a twelve-hour mix for twenty-one songs. I remember sitting there for all twelve hours and Tom was like, "Come on Petey, you're the only one, come on, stay awake with me." Everyone else was sleeping on the floor.

LOU: He was mixing a song an hour. At the end, he laid down behind the board and said, "Wow, we fucking did it, fellas!" He was so happy. On one of the anniversaries of the album, I posted a picture of the cover on Facebook, and he posted the comment "We did it, guys!" He's very proud of it.

PETE: I know some of the last songs we wrote and recorded for *Blood, Sweat and No Tear*s, like "Alone" and "Dissolution," were, to me, the ones which actually started to have the Sick of It All sound that we've carried with us.

LOU: Songs which actually have our own identity.

PETE: They had maybe a little more metal, and a little more groove to them, probably because of what we were listening to at the time, which was a lot of hip-hop and plenty of metal.

LOU: We were trying to take on a hardcore sound, maybe not consciously, but we would listen to how Negative Approach was heavy as fuck but not metal, how the Cro-Mags demo was heavy, but it wasn't metal. That sound, to me, is still the best. It's a perfect combination because it's got punk energy but adds that power metal bands have. If you go to a few generations later, punk disappears from hardcore, especially today. There are still plenty of underground bands that are punk as fuck, but later generations, bands like Snapcase for instance, took more of the metal approach, and got rid of the fast punk style. A song like "Give Respect" was very Oi!-influenced. "Friends like You" was a punk/Oi! song, a style we liked. We loved the heaviness and the power of metal, but we loved the raw power of punk, and the singalongs of Oi! Those styles were what really got us.

PETE: I think most of the metal influence for me was trying to get a metal guitar sound but play it the way we play it. The whole song doesn't have to be down-picked, chugga-chugga stuff with big breakdowns.

LOU: The lyrics were mostly personal. "Pushed Too Far" was written from my perspective about the hardcore scene, us and the New York scene fighting the outside world because of all the times we got fucked with while going to a show or walking through our neighborhood, getting messed with because some people thought we looked weird. When *Maximum RockNRoll* reviewed our first album, they called us "tough guys," and made it as if our songs were about beating people up at shows, but they just weren't. Other songs like "Dissolution" were very personal; "Alone" was a personal song too. We touched on some political stuff because of the English influence of bands like Discharge, Crass, and The Exploited. It's not like we sat down and read the *New York Times* and had discussions about lyrical content based on current events. We'd write what we knew about, and those are the things we knew about at that time. I mean, really, at that time, it was us hanging out in the Alleyway, taking the train to the fucking Lower East Side to go to shows. That's what we knew.

PETE: It was our oldest brother Steve's girlfriend, Patty, who helped us connect with KRS-One for the intro to "Clobberin' Time."

LOU: She was working at a recording studio. One night, she came to our house and told us, "I'm working with this rapper. You wouldn't know him; his name's KRS-One." Pete and I said, "Oh, Boogie Down Productions," and she was surprised that we knew who that was. That night when she went to the studio, she told KRS-One that her boyfriend's little brothers were hardcore punk kids and were fans of his. He was like, "They know my music? I wanna meet them," so we went down to meet him. He was working on a record for his wife, Ms. Melodie, and she was not too happy that he took time out to hang out and talk to us.

PETE: I think she was out to dinner at the time we got there. We were sitting there with Kris, joking around and having a good time, and then she came walking in. He looked really nervous. He was like, "Oh shit, uh, she's back!" She was fucking pissed, but thankfully, he had recorded the intro to "Clobberin' Time" before she'd gotten back.

LOU: It was RIGHT before she got back. Armand had originally asked him to do the intro for us. He did it once and I thought, *that's great*, and then Armand said, "Um, could you do it again?" We were all like, "What does Armand want from him?" Even back then he was a fucking nitpicker. He tells KRS-One, "This time, can you say 'BLAST MASTER KRS-One?' " Kris was like, "Ohhh, you want that old school shit!"

PETE: He's was a super nice guy too.

LOU: I don't have it anymore, but he gave me a BDP patch, which I put on a hat.

PETE: I put mine on my Adidas jacket.

LOU: I was walking out of CBGB one afternoon, and one of those guys from the homeless shelter upstairs yells, "What do YOU know about BDP?!" He was all mad that I had a BDP patch on my hat. Later on, Roree Krevolin approached us about doing a show with Boogie Down Productions to benefit Amnesty International. I remember being all excited about the show. She was saying how KRS-One was really excited about it, but he didn't want to go on last. We were like, "No, he HAS to go on last!" I think he felt that people were gonna leave after us or something.

PETE: He didn't understand that the whole New York hardcore scene was into hip-hop, which everybody pretty much was, especially the real shit like BDP.

LOU: It was us, Burn, and Boogie Down Productions with Heather B., KRS-One, and DJ Kenny Parker. Rest in Pieces played too, but I don't really remember them playing. It was during Burn that a bunch of BDP guys were up front, and whenever anybody started slamming, they got all angry. I had to come out and say to everybody, "No, be cool, this is what happens at hardcore shows." After that, they kind of stepped back and let it happen. I remember going to the back of the club when BDP was on and just watching the whole place, hardcore people and all the hip-hop people just bobbing their heads, thinking, *This is so cool!* I'm glad we got to be a part of that.

ROREE KREVOLIN IN ASSOCIATION WITH THE MARQUEE
PRESENTS

A CONCERT TO BENEFIT AMNESTY INTERNATIONAL
BENEFIT IV
AT THE **marquee**
NEW YORK

WITH
BURN
REST IN PIECES
SICK OF IT ALL
BOOGIE DOWN
PRODUCTIONS
WITH **KRS – ONE**
HEATHER B
DJ KENNY PARKER

ALL TICKETS $9
ON SALE NOW

FRIDAY MARCH 29th
DOORS OPEN 8:00pm
SHOW STARTS 8:30pm

TICKETS AT TICKET MASTER, BLEECKER BOB'S AND AT THE MARQUEE BOX OFFICE
DAY OF SHOW ONLY (547 WEST 21st STREET 212 929-3257) PHONE CHARGE 212 307-7171

1. I DON'T EVEN KNOW HOW ANYONE GOT OUR PHONE NUMBER

LOU: For us, those early appearances on the Revelation comps, plus the 7-inch, changed the game for us. People began to know who we were outside of New York. We started getting offers to come to Washington, D.C., to play the Safari Club, Maryland, Boston. Boston was crazy. I don't even know how anyone got our phone number, but we got a call from someone we didn't know saying, "We have this band called Wrecking Crew, and we wanna bring you guys up to Boston."

PETE: When we got to Boston, I didn't know there had been a beef between Boston and New York. I couldn't have cared less anyway. Lou: We were the first generation of "There is no New York-Boston rivalry" in New York. We just love this music; let's all play together. We'd begun headlining these shows, and they would be packed. We were very surprised. I can't tell you how many times we played the Unisound in Pennsylvania and there'd be three or four hundred kids there to see Sick of It All and Krakdown or us and Raw Deal. We never considered ourselves as leaders of a new wave of hardcore or anything like that, but I guess we kind of were. We were doing so well at that point. I remember a promoter in Bethlehem, Pennsylvania, talking to me after one of the shows. He said, "I'm booking this band from California; they're fucking great. They're gonna be huge, and I want them to play with you." It was Operation Ivy, but they broke up before the tour because they thought they were becoming too popular! THAT'S the reason they broke up. More recently, there was that band G.L.O.S.S. with all transgender members. What a fucking record they put out! I told Craig, "You have to listen to this. This is the best hardcore punk in decades," and then I heard they began to get interest from Epitaph Records, and then major labels started calling, so they were like, "We have to break up." Why would a band break up over that?!

2. IT AIN'T ABOUT NO GOLDFISH...
(Touring with Exodus)

LOU: I saw a flyer for a show back in '85/'86; it was for Slayer with Agnostic Front opening. I remember talking to Roger and saying, "Holy shit, you played a show with fucking Slayer!" Jeff Hanneman had even been wearing an Agnostic Front skinhead shirt on tour. And Roger goes, "Yeah, they offered us a whole fucking tour too, but we could probably make more money headlining, so we passed on it." I just stared at him like, *Are you out of your mind?!* They offered you a fucking tour? How big would Agnostic Front have gotten if they had done that Slayer tour when Slayer was becoming one of the biggest metal bands in the world?! My thinking was, *you've got to play with anybody and everybody. If they're bigger than you are and happen to be a different genre, that's the luck of the draw. That's what you've got to do.* That was our mindset.

PETE: Whenever we were offered some shows or a tour, I always felt, "Cool, more shows!" It didn't really matter to me if it was with a metal band, or any other type of band; I looked at it as "This could be really fun." I never thought, *Wow, this will make us bigger amongst metal people* or anything like that. It was just, *Yeah, more shows.*

LOU: It didn't scare us or intimidate us, but we weren't used to doing big shows. When we were offered Exodus dates, it was simply, "Oh wow, Exodus, a band we love. I can't wait to go."

GARY HOLT (GUITARIST EXODUS, SLAYER): Lou and Pete come from the same place as Exodus. I came from a working-class family as well, and this kind of music is always played better by people who might have to steal their guitars, if you know what I mean. We all know those guys whose dads bought them five Marshall stacks for their very first gig.... Fuck that! It's a street mentality. I go into things like that blind. I wasn't ever like, "Oh, that band's not metal." I didn't see a difference. Maybe it was part of our Ruthie's Inn mentality—because there were already a lot of punks at our shows, and we went to punk shows and listened to punk, although we didn't really know what East Coast hardcore was yet. I was just like, "These guys are hard; this is badass." I didn't know a lot about that New York hardcore movement; I just thought they were killer and later realized that this blend of metal and hardcore was going on on both coasts. It was a lot like the Reese's ad—*Hey, you've got your punk rock in my heavy metal; you've got your heavy metal in my punk rock*—and it tasted hella good.

LOU: I guess those dates with Exodus had been previously advertised with Annihilator as the opening band, before we took their place. We were in D.C. setting up. The lights go down, and as we are walking out to the stage—it's kind of quiet, people are clapping—you hear this guy scream, "ANNIHILATOOOR." I had to say, "No, we're not Annihilator, we're Sick of It All from New

York. We play New York hardcore." We just went into the set and it was great. At first, people stood to the back, but we won a lot of people over.

PETE: The cool thing was, probably 90 percent of the people there were ready to accept us. They probably thought, *this is fast, this is loud, these guys are running around like crazy, awesome.* It's funny because we realized on this tour that being on the road with metal bands was WAY different than what we were used to. Going backstage for the first time with the Exodus guys, there was this huge pile of coke on a mirror, and I'd never seen that in my life. There were girls waiting at the backstage door simply because these guys were in a band. Craziest shit ever.

GARY HOLT: I'm honored to have taken those guys out on one of their first tours. For Exodus, those dates were a bit of a downward slide, but for Sick of It All, it was the beginning of an upward trend. We were dealing with infighting and label problems and were maybe going through the motions at times, but then you had those guys who were hungry and just going for it every night and winning people over.

3. OH WELL, WE LOST ONE OF YOUR GUYS
(Touring with D.R.I. and Nasty Savage)

LOU: Through the tour we did with D.R.I. after the Exodus run (and not to insult D.R.I. because I would say this about our band too), we realized you definitely didn't have to be good-looking guys to meet girls. As long as you're in a band, and you have drugs, it seemed you could get any woman you wanted!

KURT BRECHT (D.R.I.): I remember reading an old interview with Lou, and he said something to the effect of "We learned from being on tour with D.R.I. that you can be the ugliest guys in the world and still get girls if you're in a band." I wanted to write to

Lou and say, "So you think you're hotter than me?! You're Mr. Handsome?!" Our drummer at the time I read that was from New York, and he told me it would be a bad idea to tell that to Lou, but I think it's funny.

PETE: It was us, D.R.I., and Nasty Savage on that tour.

LOU: When we were first told about the tour, we knew we were gonna get paid shit money, and they were insisting that Nasty Savage go on second because they were signed to Spike's label. Regardless, we decided to do it, and we got fifty to seventy-five dollars a night to open, except in Canada, where we got one hundred twenty-five bucks. We thought that was the greatest thing in the world.

PETE: That extra money in Canada really helped. It kept us going.

LOU: Our brother Steve volunteered to be the road manager and driver, and he didn't take any money at the end of the tour. We were gonna pay him and he was like, "Nope, that's cool, don't worry about it."

STEVEN KOLLER: It was a good experience. How many people can say they were a tour manager? But I drove A LOT on that tour. The bad part was that the roadie and I would be driving them six hundred miles in one night, from show to show. Then we were up the whole time setting up the show, then breaking it down, and then back to driving again. It was forty-one shows in forty-six days, and the total miles at the end was 13,835 MILES!

Steven Koller's Tour Diary

PETE: At the end, he drove from Salt Lake City all the way to New York nonstop.

LOU: Because he was crazy! He played Guns N' Roses' *Appetite for Destruction* the whole time until we got to a gas station, when I took the tape and threw it in the back of the van somewhere. He was like, "Why'd you fucking do that? I wanted to hear it," and I was like, "Yeah, we've heard it enough!"

PETE: That was a crazy drive. It went from snow into other shitty weather and back to snow, but we got to play all these places we'd never been to. We got down to Florida and it was amazing. There was a huge hardcore scene just waiting. We thought, *Shit, we gotta go on first, who knows what the reaction's gonna be?* but it was great. Those shows were really cool. We played Clemson University, and NOBODY showed up for the show at all.

LOU: That may have been the one in that student center that had all glass walls. They wouldn't let anybody under eighteen in, and there were probably two hundred kids stuck outside who were under eighteen. They watched through the glass as we played to no one. Then Nasty Savage played to no one, and D.R.I. played to maybe fifty people. Raleigh, North Carolina, was a great show for everybody. We went on and it was one of those nights where you had a few Sick of It All fans, and by the end of the set, people were going crazy. It was new to them, it was exciting.

PETE: Touring with Nasty Savage was fun though. Nasty Ronnie.... They were all really good guys.

LOU: Yeah, we all got along with them and laughed every night. Nasty Ronnie was really surprised when we told him we had the band's *Wage of Mayhem* demo. He showed us all these wrestling tricks, like how to smash a TV on your head but not really smash it on your head. He'd say, "What I do is I throw the TV up and I catch it, mostly on my chest, and then I grab my head afterwards and I cut it." He would take five aspirin before the show so his blood would be really thin and run like crazy. He'd lift his hairline up and show us all these scars up there. We just thought, *Oh man, that's fucked up!*

PETE: Their drummer was also in that crust band Assück.

LOU: Yeah, he was the first snooty vegan I ever met. He wasn't snooty when you were hanging around and talking to him, but we were walking somewhere in the Carolinas, behind some barbecue place, and I go, "Oh man, that smells good." I still ate meat back then. He looked at me and said, "Set your own arm on fire and see how good THAT smells!" That definitely DID NOT make me want to become vegan. I guess he was ahead of the vegan curve. Every once in a while, when we'd play Florida, some of those guys would come out. Sadly, one of their guitarists passed away, and one of the guys came to our show to let us know.

PETE: It was a great tour. In Dallas, we were listed as "For the Sake of It All." Denver was the biggest crowd of the whole tour, 2,500 people, and it was a great show for everybody. Spike from D.R.I. was walking into the venue from the bus, and some bouncer said, "You can't come in here," and he told them he was in the band, and the guy just took his pass away from him, so they started fighting. Everyone's like, "Shit, why isn't D.R.I. onstage?" and Spike is smashing the entire backstage up, all the mirrors and windows and all that shit, because the bouncer just tried to beat him up. The promoter told Spike, "OK, I fired him. He's outta here, just go onstage," and he goes, "I'm not going on." D.R.I. waited around forty-five minutes before they went on, but Spike did go up there and play.

LOU: There were some other interesting moments on that tour. Felix, their drummer, and Kurt were not getting along. So, one night in Florida, it was between songs, and I guess Felix threw a drumstick at Kurt's head, and Kurt turned around and spit at him. Felix just smiled and Kurt totally lost it and dove through the drums to get at Felix!

PETE: I was standing on the side of the stage like, "What the fuck is he doing?!" He dove straight through the drum set and they started fist-fighting. Everyone starts freaking out, and the police come running in. They had been standing right outside, and now a huge riot breaks out!

LOU: The bouncers didn't know what was going on, and people start storming the stage to break it up. Then the bouncers started hitting the people coming onstage.

PETE: I remember one of their roadies coming up on the stage and hitting whoever the fuck was in front of him with a weighted mic stand. The police were saying, "We heard that a crazed fan was attacking the band." We said, "No, that's the band fighting each other," and the cop was like, "Sooooo, what are we supposed to do? What the fuck do we do?" That was the end of that show.

LOU: Oh, what a great night that was. We also played at the Kitchen Club. It was outdoors in Miami. When we got onstage, there was a barricade, but between the barricade and the stage, there were two fucking giant palm trees. We were like, "What the hell? This is gonna suck!" But when we started playing, kids would be coming over the barricade, getting onstage, and then grabbing onto the palm tree leaves and swinging out into the crowd like Tarzan. It was the craziest thing.

PETE: Wait, I have another Nasty Ronnie story. The show was at Saint Andrew's in Detroit, and we're all in a shared backstage area. Ronnie brings some girl backstage and says to her, "Hey, why don't you come with me," and she's like, "Oh, you have a bus?" He goes, "Well, we have a VAN, it's kind of like a bus but it's a little bit smaller." It was a total piece of shit. He starts making out with the girl, and everybody's there in the backstage area, all three bands, and he starts getting a blowjob from the girl. He put a towel over her head and just stood there in front of everyone! He was just laughing. Total rock star, Mötley Crüe shit. Richie and I were like, "Um, let's get the fuck out of here!"

LOU: On that tour, we'd all get booked into the same hotel, and all the rooms would be next to each other. I guess they put us all together so we wouldn't disturb anybody else in the hotel. D.R.I.

would be next door to us with all the girls and the drugs. We didn't know what to do, so we'd make these stupid videos on Richie's video camera. We'd get so bored, we would run into D.R.I.'s rooms, just bust through the door, and they'd be like, "What the fuck's going on?!" Eventually, they loved to watch our videos. They would stop everything and be like, "Let's watch Sick of It All's videos." They were just these dumb videos that would make everybody laugh. It was great. Some of them wound up on our home video years later.

PETE: Around the middle of the tour, they would still be picking up girls and bringing them back to the hotel, but by this point, they would want to be IN our videos, acting like total idiots, and the girls would just be sitting there. The girls were probably thinking, "Yeah, drugs and drinking and band guys," and those guys were just acting like total jerks.

KURT BRECHT: I guess they would do all this video stuff in the hotels to cure the boredom of touring. I don't think I made any with them, but I remember seeing them walking around with lampshades over their heads, laughing and stuff.

RICH CIPRIANO: I tried my darndest to be the ringleader of all the insanity, plus I had the video camera. But really, all my goofiness was aimed at Armand. It was my mission to make him laugh. He's so smart and quick-witted, and we both loved Monty Python, so I looked up to him for goofballness! As far as some of the skits we did on that tour, we did one I guess you could call "The Rockers" because we acted like we were on a big ROCK tour. It was basically all of us trashing a hotel as if we were Mötley Crüe. I think their guitar player Spike started with a lampshade on his head, saying something like, "Oh, it's gonna get crazy in here tonight." Their bass player was holding cans of beer, trashed. We basically just destroyed the room and filmed it, but we actually put everything back perfectly before we checked out. No holes in the walls, no TVs out the window. If you watch the video, it looks like we did thousands of dollars of damage, but we couldn't afford to get charged for anything like that. We were making fifty bucks a night.

LOU: In one sketch, I would pretend to fall off the balcony. We'd film me looking like I was going over the side of the balcony, then we'd stop, everyone would run downstairs, and I would find some bush or something to jump into. Richie would say, "GO," and I would jump into the bush as if I'd fallen off the balcony. Just dumb things.

RICH CIPRIANO: We watched some documentary in one of the hotel rooms, and they were talking about peat, you know, as in peat moss. In the documentary, this guy is walking on the peat, so of course, we created "Walking on the PETE." The hotel had a pool, so Pete lays next to the pool, and we walk on his back: walking on the Pete. Pete is on the edge of the pool, so to add to the slapstick of it all, there was the ol' falling-into-the-pool routine. We would rewind that and watch it over and over again.

PETE: The most infamous video idea within our camp was called "You've changed. Have I?" That was the whole premise. It would start with Armand and Richie, and Richie would say, "Hey Armand," and then Armand would respond, "Hey Richie." Then Richie would say, "You've changed," and Armand would respond, "Have I?" and he would have a stupid-looking hat or a lampshade on his head. So stupid!

LOU: Then Armand would take the hat off and Richie would say, "Oh, you've changed AGAIN," and it would go on and on and on. Ridiculous.

PETE: The editing was terrible, which made it great. One of them might have a shoe on their hand or have shaving cream on. I ran into one of D.R.I.'s techs recently and he was STILL talking about that shit. It's moronic but making them helped us pass the time. Now, those videos are legendary.

LOU: That was a tour that really helped us. It exposed us to the crossover crowd, even though we were not very polished. We didn't down-pick everything, but that crowd really loved the energy. It also got us into a bunch of the metal magazines like *Metal Maniacs*. They all loved D.R.I. at that point, and finally got to see us too.

PETE: If we'd done our own headlining tour at that point, we would have only played to smaller groups of hardcore and punk scenes, but this was with the biggest crossover group at that time. Our first times playing in Florida or the Carolinas or Georgia were at some pretty big shows.

LOU: Plus, it showed the show promoters that we could draw. When the tour reached Boston, it was one of those shows where we went on first. For the rest of the show, half the crowd just hung out at our merch booth with us. It was the whole Boston scene hanging out and talking with Sick of It All. They'd watch D.R.I., and when they'd play a song like "Violent Pacification," they'd all run into the pit, then come back out and hang with us.

PETE: We all got really sick on that tour too.

LOU: I got sick first. I had to go see a doctor in Florida, and they gave me antibiotics. He recommended that everyone in the band get a shot to stave it off, so we found a clinic, and everyone went in to get shots. I was in the waiting room, and the nurse comes in and nonchalantly says, "Oh well, we lost one of your guys." I say, "You lost one?!" She told me that one of our guys had fainted. Right at that second, Pete walked in behind her, and I asked, "Pete, you fainted?" The nurse goes, "Not him, the big guy." It turns out, Armand has an aversion to needles, and when she stuck him in the butt, he collapsed onto the gurney. She had to push him out on the gurney. Can you imagine having to pull that guy's pants up and shove him onto a gurney by yourself?!

PETE: Gross!

4. NEW TITANS ON THE BLOC
(Touring with Sepultura, Napalm Death, and Sacred Reich)

LOU: We were doing a College Music Journal (CMJ) show that year. Sepultura played on the Saturday with King Diamond at The Ritz, and that was when Sepultura were THE up-and-coming metal band. I remember watching them and thinking, *Wow, these guys are a great thrash band!* A lot of the crowd left after they played. The next night we were playing at this place called Jammin' in Times Square and those guys came. We had a really good show, but at the end, there was some kind of equipment problem, and Pete took one of his pedals and threw it across the club. It shattered against the wall.

IGGOR CAVALERA (SEPULTURA, CAVALERA CONSPIRACY): Max and I were there when Pete threw his pedal. We looked at one another and thought, *this is the most punk rock thing ever!* He didn't do it to look cool, or for any cameras. He was frustrated and just threw it from the stage.

LOU: Fast-forward to that Monday—Pete was working in the Roadrunner Records mailroom. The guys from Sepultura came in and were talking to Pete, telling him how we were a big influence on them or whatever, so Pete goes, "Oh yeah? If we're such a big influence on you guys, why don't you take us on tour?" half joking. A month later, Sepultura approached the guys at our label about the New Titans on the Bloc tour with Sepultura, Sacred Reich, Napalm Death, and us. We were going to share a vehicle with Napalm Death, who we'd never met, and we're wondering, *Are these guys gonna be rock star assholes?* I didn't know shit about the grindcore scene, but then meeting them was just great. We were all just idiots bonding over stuff like Monty Python and whatever dumb stuff we could come up with. They actually knew all about us. Their original drummer, Mick, had come to one of our rehearsals once with Danny Lilker while he was in the U.S. He was taking pictures of us, which was weird because we were just kids in the basement of a record store.

BARNEY GREENWAY (NAPALM DEATH): I had Sick of It All's Revelation EP, and Shane had even done a cover of "My Life" with Unseen Terror, so when the New Titans thing unfolded and we found out who we were going to be traveling with, you can imagine how excited we were. Honestly, I can name a tour or two where I laughed the whole way through the tour, but nowhere near the extent that I laughed with those guys. Sick of It All and Napalm Death are a perfect fit. We're different, but as touring bands, it's amazing. Pretty immediately, those guys felt like brothers, like we would be friends forever.

IGGOR CAVALERA: It was a cool combination because we were a band that wasn't afraid to take a band that wasn't metal out with us, and they were a hardcore band not afraid to take that step. We just wanted to take out the coolest bands we could think of. Napalm Death had the whole political grindcore attitude. The bill had a lot of different layers musically. We had found out about Sick of It All while we still lived in Brazil through fanzines. It was a cool, naive time when Max and I would listen to bands without knowing what they looked like, whether they had long hair or short hair. We only had the music. Someone would hand us a tape, and we would listen, sometimes for months, without knowing much information about them. Sick of It All was one of those bands. We didn't know for a long time if they were hardcore or metal; we just played their tape on our boombox. They were such an aggressive band, and all we knew was that they seemed to be breaking down barriers.

PETE: It was a cool lineup. Sick of It All was kind of the new name in hardcore, while Napalm Death was the name in grindcore, Sepultura was fucking Sepultura, and then you had Sacred Reich, who had the same manager as Sepultura.

LOU: Napalm Death's manager at that time was trying to make Napalm Death into the next Slayer, which I guess was admirable. I remember a few years later going to see Napalm Death at The Ritz. It was packed and they looked like they were going to be a huge band, but it just never happened on that level, kinda like the rest of us.

PETE: That was the tour that started with a riot and ended with a riot.

LOU: The first show was in Allentown, Pennsylvania, where we'd played before. They had a pretty notorious Nazi-skinhead thing going on there. The first time we played there, out of a crowd of a thousand or so people, there were maybe one hundred skinheads. When they would start to talk their shit, the whole room would boo them and get at them, and they would disappear. The next time we played, there were more of them, but the crowd still handled them. This time we get there and it's 90 percent of the crowd, these Nazi fucking skinheads.

BARNEY GREENWAY: Napalm Death has always been anti-fascist. I understand now that all the right-wing stuff people were attaching themselves to was basically a trend. It was just stupid kids, but there were some serious characters involved in that. I consider myself a bit of a pacifist. I don't care to join in the circle of violence, but back then I wasn't having any of it. In Allentown, even before the gig, you could sense something was going on. When Sick of It All went on, there was a chant in the crowd: "Fuck New York, fuck New York!" The guys kind of brushed that off, but all of Napalm was standing on the side of the stage and you could see these neo-Nazis, or "pretend-Nazis," beginning to stir things up. I realized that things were going to get pretty serious in a minute.

PETE: Historically, that's when the Klan moved their headquarters to, Allentown. I remember seeing that on the History Channel.

LOU: What set things off that night was probably just that we were from New York City, and we walked out onstage!

PETE: They were yelling all kinds of shit at us.

LOU: There were bouncers and there was a barricade, and I came out and said, "Hey everybody, we're Sick of It All from New York City," and they're yelling, "Go back to Jew York you nigger lovers." I think Pete jumped up on the barricade right after that, and started punching some guy in the face, because they started to spit on us. The barricade was chest level, so they would hold themselves up to spit on us. You had no way to defend yourself.

PETE: They were holding themselves up with two hands, with nothing blocking their faces, so I started punching everybody who was standing there.

LOU: It was kind of like a carnival game where you knock down the clowns with a ball. I saw Pete, and then I went up there, and all of a sudden, all over the club, you could hear my microphone smashing people in the face. They started climbing over the barricades. Richie was swinging his Rickenbacker five-string bass, swatting Nazis. EK came flying over; he picked up a cymbal stand and just started hitting people with it.

PETE: He was hitting somebody with the whole hi-hat stand. It was crazy.

BARNEY GREENWAY: I don't want to romanticize it or glorify it, but Mitch jumped in, I jumped in. It was just a free-for-all. There were far less of us than there were of them, so we made sort of a tactical withdrawal back to the dressing rooms. I truly thought someone was going to be killed. Then the police came, and naturally, the bands got the blame. I was like, "Are you fucking serious?!"

LOU: That's when we realized, "Holy shit, this isn't like the old Allentown, this is a new place where 90 percent of the crowd are Nazis." They just came flowing over the barricade, fighting with bouncers, fighting us.

PETE: The police too!

LOU: Out of nowhere, somebody came running in and sprayed mace all over everybody. Luckily, we didn't get hit. He got the bouncers, as well as the whole front row of Nazis, and then we were all dragged off the stage.

PETE: The bouncers were trying to KILL everybody, and all of Sepultura were standing there like, "What the FUCK is going on?! This is how this tour is starting?"

LOU: I remember going upstairs in the backstage room. It was just me and Pete. I don't remember where Richie was. Sepultura's road manager burst into the room and he goes, in this Southern accent, "What the hell was THAT?!"

PETE: He was a fat douche!

LOU: I said, "Did you see what they fucking did? They were spitting at us, they were calling us nigger lovers," and he goes, "I don't care what they said to you. This is a ROCK and ROLL show!" With his twangy accent, it sounded like he said "RACK and roll show!" "You don't do shit to the audience," he continued. Him saying "shit" sounded like "sheet."

PETE: Of course, I was ready to punch this fucking dick in the face.

LOU: So, he leaves, and me and Pete are like, "This sucks, we're going to be sent home." All of a sudden, Iggor and Max come running in, asking, "Are you guys OK?" We're like, "Yeah," and Pete says, "But I guess we're going home because of that fucking dick road manager of yours." We told them exactly what he had said to us, and Iggor immediately goes, "Fuck that guy!" and he runs out of the room, and so does Max. I guess they went to see their manager, Gloria, and then they came back in with Gloria. Iggor says, "He's gone, we fired him!" I felt a little bad; I didn't know if that guy had been a part of their crew for life, or if he was just a guy they hired because he's a good RACK-and-roll tour manager, but Gloria was just like, "Fuck it, I'LL do it. I'll be the tour manager now."

IGGOR CAVALERA: We're from Brazil, so it was quite logical that they would want to stand up and fight against these right-wing people who would sometimes show up at the shows. They were on our side. Maybe that road manager thought we were like other headlining bands who were OK being the soundtrack to jocks beating people up or being racist, but we were different.

Mosh Manor Production

LOU: *Decibel magazine* did an oral history of that tour, and in it, Shane from Napalm Death said, "Sick of It All had to open every night and I'll tell you something, it's not easy going on after Sick of It All. The bar they set, and their energy—we just fucking hated it most nights."

BARNEY GREENWAY: We were just hysterical laughing all day. They made those ludicrous videos all the time, and I remember Glen Benton from Deicide was walking by with that silver inverted cross he had in his forehead. Lou saw him and slapped a quarter onto his forehead and walked in front of Glen for a video. It was absolutely perfect timing, and Pete, Rich, and I were just howling! That was just a foretaste of things to come.

PETE: There were some really wild places, like when we played New Mexico for the first time, in a hockey rink.

LOU: I was told ahead of time, "You shouldn't jump into the crowd," and of course, I was like, "Oh, that's ridiculous, I'm a hardcore guy!"

PETE: So that's the first thing you did!

LOU: I should have listened because they were pulling off my shirt, they stole my necklace, they tried to steal my shoes.... I was like, "What the fuck is going on," but it was because, to this crowd, I was a rock star, and I didn't understand that. Then we played a Native reservation.

PETE: That was the first time we ever encountered religious groups protesting our show. I wish I had kept it, but they made flyers with our name and the other band's names on it. I went outside the venue and got one so I could keep it.

LOU: It was basically a form which had a blank space and they typed in "Sick of It All."

PETE: It said we promoted drug use, promiscuous sex, and, of course, Satanism.

LOU: The sheriffs came to that show and said they had some sort of problem with what was happening, and Gloria was like, "Well, we have permits for this," and the promoter was like, "I have permits for this," but for some reason, the cops didn't want that show to go on. Then Gloria was arguing with the cops and they grabbed her, yelling, "We're taking you downtown," and Gloria was like, "OK," and she started yelling instructions at everybody: "Don't tell Max; the show has to go on." We had to run and hold Max back; Iggor, all of Sepultura, and all of us had to calm him down. Sepultura were fucking great that night too, and she got released later that night.

PETE: I think they were trying to check the bus for drugs or some shit, and she was saying, "You can't go on there without a warrant. Do you have a warrant?" The cops were like, "Well, we have suspicion." She asked, "What suspicion? Because we're a rock band," and they were like, "We don't like your attitude."

LOU: There were other incidents where the bands would get harassed. But we'd also run into cops who were cool. I remember heading to Florida, going through Texas in our van, and we got pulled over for speeding. The cop was really cool with us and said, "Look, there are three more speed traps along this highway before you hit the next state, so just take it easy."

PETE: That was on the Biohazard tour we did. Our road crew was Minus, Ezec, and Toby. What could go wrong? Just a bunch of nuts, and everybody had weapons. The cop was like, "You guys got any weapons in here? I'm gonna find 'em if you don't tell me," and everybody said, "Yeah, we've got this and that," and he gave them all back. He said, "Well, the part of town you're going to, you're gonna need these." This was just a little bit after all that Waco, Texas, shit went down, so they were pulling over anyone they thought was suspicious.

LOU: Sepultura was just one of those bands. They weren't huge yet, but they were on their way, and they treated us and all the bands so fucking well. It was really nice. Our soundman was the same guy who worked for Napalm Death, and he came in one night at First Avenue in Minneapolis, complaining, "Man, Sepultura's sound guy keeps coming over and telling me that I gotta turn down. They're limiting my channels." He was all upset, and we're like, "Just tell Iggor and Max," and he was like, "No, no, no...." He didn't want to rock the boat. So we went and told Iggor and Max about this bullshit. Later, we were playing our show, and afterwards our sound guy comes back and says, "I was out there doing your sound, and here comes Sepultura's sound guy. He's standing behind me and starts tapping me on the shoulder. All of a sudden, Iggor walks up, grabs him, and goes, "No way, man, they can use all the sound they want, all the fucking lights they want." It's because they weren't scared and didn't come from that mentality where you have to make the opening band look smaller. They knew how good they were.

PETE: Great guys, all of them.

LOU: By the end of the tour, we had bonded so much, we figured, let's all have another riot together. It was in Seattle. We had gotten really close with Napalm Death; we were really friendly with the guys in Sacred Reich. We'd bonded with them, and the same thing with Sepultura. It wasn't just Iggor and Max, but Andreas and Paulo too. We had so much fun every night. Paulo would always come up to us and just start fucking around on the bass. Even to this day, when I go see Sepultura and he sees me or Pete, he'll start playing "Just Look Around" and laugh.

PETE: We had a great show at Rock Candy up there. It was total mayhem. When Napalm Death went on, we covered them with all the food that was backstage. It was just insanity.

LOU: And Sepultura was loving it. They said, "That's really funny, but don't do it during OUR set." After the show, we went onto Sepultura's bus. We were all on the bus hanging out, talking, and this drunk maniac is banging on the bus door. It wasn't locked, so he just opens it, comes in, and starts talking. Iggor asks, "Who are you?" and the guy goes, "You don't know me??? We're managed by Gloria too." Mitch from Napalm Death says to him, "You don't just fucking walk onto my bus!" Mitch asks Iggor, "You want me to throw him off?" and winds up in a fight with this guy. It was the lead singer or guitarist from the band Forced Entry, who were from Seattle. They're fighting, and they roll out the bus door. Then Mitch came back in and grabbed a bat. I guess the bus driver had a bat sitting near his seat, and I think that's when people were like, "Oh shit, our friend from Forced Entry is fighting, and some maniac is swinging a bat at him." They attacked Mitch, so we all ran out to help him, and it just exploded.

PETE: I remember Mitch hitting that guy; he pulled back the bat to hit him, and I was like, "Oh my God, he's gonna kill him if he hits him in the head," and Mitch probably thought of that, so he hit him in the knees.

LOU: Gloria comes running out of the bus, and she's freaking out, going, "All my bands are fighting! What's going on?!" I yell to Gloria, "Do you know this dick?!" He goes, "Damn right she knows me, motherfucker!" I don't even think, and I never do this, but I just haul off and punch him dead in the nose. He stumbles back, and the next thing I know, I'm flying through the air and thrown between two cars. There was this big bouncer and he looked down at me and goes, "Stay down!" But my favorite part was our bus driver. He called himself a "Tex-Mexican." He was a pretty tall guy, leather vest....

PETE: He was a total cowboy!

LOU: Jeans and cowboy boots.... When he saw someone hitting me or Pete, he was like, "Nobody hits MY boys." He had the bay doors of the bus open and grabbed some random guy in front of him and starts smashing his head against the bay doors. He could have killed somebody. Thank God nobody died, but it was a hell of a way to end the tour. After the fight, I remember Iggor and Max coming over to me and Pete, and we were like, "We're sorry about all that. That guy attacked Mitch," and they were just like, "Yeah, yeah, whatever. Let's take a picture together, of the brothers." That's all they wanted; they didn't care about the riot. They kind of loved it.

PETE: Overall, it went great. Most of the kids really appreciated it. This was still when hardcore people thought it should stay "underground," and doing tours like this was looked at as being too metal, too corporate. Some of the metal people were really closed-minded too. One guy up in the Pacific Northwest kept calling me "Vanilla Ice" because I had a flattop, but that's all a lot of these kids knew. A lot of them just thought, *Oh, that's MTV, I hate it, it's not metal.*

LOU: But there were so many kids who were like, "We saw your 'Injustice System' video on *Headbanger's Ball* and we had to come out and see your show." That was great. MTV helped us there. It was a pivotal time for hardcore. Some kids couldn't get hardcore records and didn't know about mail order. There were the punk and hardcore kids who knew about this stuff, but they wanted it to remain their own little scene, so some of them kind of snubbed us. But there were these other kids who were new, and searching for something, and luckily, they happened to catch us on *Headbanger's Ball*, or saw us in *Metal Maniacs* magazine, and were like, "What the fuck is this? Who are these guys?"

PETE: Some just found out about us by looking through albums at a record store and were like, "What's this? A bunch of kids stagediving all over each other on the cover."

LOU: But man, it was so much fun, sharing a bus with Napalm Death. We had the same weird sense of humor. Barney kept running around the bus in his fucking bikini briefs. He wasn't doing it to be funny; that's just what he wore.

PETE: We all made fun of him nonstop.

BARNEY GREENWAY: Not to be melodramatic or anything, but when I'm around those guys, it feels like it's us against the world in the most positive way. I feel really comfortable around Lou and Pete. When I see them, even at a gig, it's like meeting up with your mates at a pub. Those two have a firm grasp on reality. They understand that we, meaning those of us in bands, are not these great messiahs. We just know what to do. They don't expect stuff, or demand it, and then get disappointed if it doesn't work out. That's why they've lasted this long.

Reunited and It Feels So Good 2019

LOU: We did a lot of fun stuff with those guys and had a lot of good shows. The sad thing about that tour was the issues we were having with EK. At the beginning of the tour, Shane from Napalm Death came up to me and said, "You know, your drummer came up and told me that he just got off of heroin." I was like, "Well, he told us he's been off of it for a while." Shane goes, "No, he told me he was doing shit right before he came on this tour." I was like, "What?" The ride out to the first show was basically his detox.

PETE: That's why when Armand said he wanted to be back in the band, we were like, "Okay, EK is out." We'd do these weekend tours, and Lou and I would put money back into the band. EK and Eddie always wanted to get paid. One time, EK kept telling us that he needed a double kick drum pedal, so we got it for him. We spent a lot of money on that fucking thing. We had rehearsal one day and EK told us, "Yo, someone broke into my apartment. They stole the double pedal." They apparently didn't steal anything else, just the brand new, expensive double pedal still in the box. The robber must have been a drummer.

LOU: He walked us through the apartment, through the living room, through his bedroom, and I go, "None of this stuff was touched?" He goes, "No, man." It's kind of like he wanted to get caught.

PETE: I said, "So they went through your apartment, past your roommate's stereo, TV, all this stuff here, went into your room, didn't touch anything, but knew where the double pedal was?!" He's like, "Yeah." I said, "You're full of shit," but we needed a drummer for that weekend.

LOU: He went out one night with a bunch of people after one of our shows. We were playing the next day, and he goes, "Hey guys, I don't know if I can do the show today." He said, "We went out last night and shot up cocaine." I yelled, "Why'd you fucking do that?!" He said, "I don't know. Everybody was doing it so...." I said, "Calm down, calm down. We're going to go play the show." We calmed him down and we had this amazing fucking set. We walk off the stage and the crowd's chanting. Iggor tells us, "Go, go do another song," and EK's like, "No, I can't do it. I can't fucking do it." Craig and I go, "You're going to fucking go out there. I don't care if you have a fucking heart attack on the fucking stage. Get the fuck up there and play the goddamn song." EK's all mad and says, "You fucking guys are so mean to me." We played the song, and afterward, he was like, "Holy shit, I feel much better." Whatever was in his system got worked out.

PETE: Being in a band with that kind of dynamic was fucking awful, brutal. And EK's girlfriend at the time, a beautiful kid, super nice, died.

LOU: It scared him. His girl OD'd and went to the hospital. She got out, was like, "Let's go cop," and he was like, "I don't want to do this anymore. We have a chance. You're clean." She was like, "Fuck that, I want to get high." She went back and OD'd right away. It really broke his heart.

ERIK "EK" KOMST (FORMER SOIA DRUMMER): Megan overdoses and dies, and one would think that would have scared the shit out of me. But I went on another bad run for several months, until November '92, when I surrendered and got sober for several years. I moved back to Boston in 2001 after 9/11, went back to school, and became a paramedic for the city of Boston.

PETE: When we fired EK, he was like, "Dude, you're not even gonna give me a chance?" I said, "We bought you equipment, and you fucking sold it for drugs. You weren't even gonna show up to rehearsal tonight because you didn't want to." He understood, but he kept saying, "Come on, give me another chance." It was tearing at my heart, but I had to say "No," and I hung up. Thankfully, he's doing well now. He's a good guy.

EK: As far as my addiction on that tour, it was running rampant. I tried finding drugs in every city. I was twenty-one and stupid. Little did I know that when we would get back to NYC, I'd have a hunk of cash from the tour and my addiction would just get worse. Being in Sick of It All was ultimately a great experience. I'm psyched I got to record and do a lot of touring with them. I still feel kinda bad that Pete and Lou, and Eddie and Rich, had to deal with all of my bullshit, but it's just a chapter, and thankfully, we're all boys once again. I simply didn't wanna die, so I found the means to get sober again. It's really tough coming back now because of all the shame and embarrassment, but I've been good. Now I'm living in LA, doing great, playing again, and working in the treatment field. I'm a grateful human being.

5. URBAN UNDISCIPLINED
(Touring with Biohazard)

PETE: The dates we did with Biohazard were interesting.

LOU: It was us, Biohazard, and Sheer Terror, and then Fear Factory was on part of the tour. There was this kid in Florida up front...

PETE: It was in Jacksonville...

LOU: Yeah, singing all the lyrics to "Just Look Around": "the whites that hate the blacks, the blacks that hate the Jews." On his neck he had a rebel flag tattooed with flames around it. He couldn't have been more than sixteen. I remember talking to him afterwards, and I'm like, "You know, our lyrics aren't pro what you seem to be into," which was bigotry. I don't know if that changed his mind at all. I don't think it did, but it's weird to see some of these people loving those lyrics. I'm like, "You realize it's not pro-hating each other, right?"

PETE: I'm jumping back to the D.R.I. tour, but do you remember when we were playing, and there were tons of very regular, nicely dressed white dudes in the back of the show? They were there to recruit kids for the Klan.

LOU: Yeah, that was in Pennsylvania.

PETE: They weren't starting any trouble at all; they were there just like, "Hey kid, how ya' doing?" and preaching their spiel to kids.

LOU: It goes back to the Allentown riot where that tour manager said, "I don't care WHAT they said to you, this is a RACK and ROLL show." You're either that guy, or you're a stand-up person. It sucks because sometimes shit like that is there and you're like, "If I say something, are we gonna get jumped after the show? Like, at the Trocadero in Philly, it was known to happen to some bands, but it never happened to us. There was one show where that had happened, and we had to stand up for ourselves. I also remember a show where we came out afterward, and these skinhead guys were attacking two girls who were talking shit to them. We just turned the corner to see what was going on, and they thought us and our friends were coming to kick their asses and they ran. Then the next time we played the Troc, the venue was getting death threats: "Sick of It All's gonna get shot, we're going to kill them." We had Big Charlie and one of his friends come down with us, and NOBODY said a word the WHOLE show. Big Charlie was on one side of the stage, and his big friend was on the other, just watching the crowd.

PETE: That was a really weird time, not necessarily at our shows, but in general.

LOU: I'm worried about it happening at the shows again though. I remember Snapcase telling us about Russian skinheads coming to Germany or wherever they were playing, maybe Poland, to see their shows, and they were Sieg-Heiling. The band said something about it from the stage, and a full-scale riot broke out. Their drummer, our friend, got his jaw broken; he was just standing there and somebody clocked him.

PETE: Anyway, back to that Biohazard tour.... That was the biggest tour we did in the U.S. in support of *Just Look Around*. It was a full United States tour with them.

LOU: We had been trying to secure a tour for the album, and our agent, Stormy suggested to Rage Against the Machine that take us out, but they took hip-hop artists instead. I worked in the mailroom of the management company for Pantera, and the assistant manager suggested, "Hey, Pantera, Sick of It All and Biohazard should go out together. They're two hot New York bands." But their manager said no, it would be too much. That was my first taste of "No, these bands are too energetic; my boys don't need to deal with that shit," and he put them out with White Zombie.

PETE: Every single night there was a fight or a riot. Really fucking lame! California, I don't think it was like that, but everywhere else. After a while, it was just like, "Ugh." Like I said, instead of bringing a road crew, we brought all our friends. It was kind of our version of the Fresh Air Fund.

LOU: We took all the inner-city kids out to the country for a while.

PETE: We brought Ezec, Minus....

LOU: Minus was with Biohazard. We brought Toby and Big Head Jerry. Jerry was the voice of reason. Ezec and Minus would be hanging out with Evan, and they'd get dragged into "Hey, that guy looks like a Nazi, let's go fuck with him." It was our first tour with Craig, who had just come off the Agnostic Front tour. He did AF's farewell tour of Europe; he did their last show in Prague and flew home. He had two days at home, then he came on tour with us. He was in a world of shit, that guy. We started at the Graffiti Club in Pennsylvania. Sheer Terror went on and did well, then Biohazard went on and fucking killed it. I remember Craig coming backstage and saying, "Those motherfuckers are killing it! We gotta show 'em! We gotta show 'em!" So we opened with "Clobberin' Time," and the place was cheering, ready to go. Craig starts playing the riff, and then he runs and jumps OFF the drum riser into the crowd. That just set the whole thing off. The place exploded! I don't want to offend anybody, but there were nights where they purposely did shit that would fuck our show up.

PETE: It was only Evan who was straight up like, "This is a competition," and he would do stupid shit. At one of the Texas shows, there was a barricade. He tells the venue, "We don't want this fucking barricade," so they took it down for Biohazard and they had the sickest, GREATEST show, but they put the barricade back up for us.

LOU: They actually took the barricade away for the whole show. Biohazard was told, "We'll take it down, but you just gotta be careful." Then Evan starts yelling, "EVERYBODY ON THE STAGE! GET ON THE STAGE! EVERYBODY ON THE STAGE!" Now three hundred people are on the stage. Sick of It All is about to go on, so they push the crowd back, put the barricade back up, and we're going "Are you fucking kidding me?! You're gonna fuck our show up?!" The club was like, "We don't care," and that was it.

PETE: Evan said, "Well you guys wanted to go on last." Then, of course, every person in that crowd thinks Sick of It All purposely had the barricade put back up.

LOU: When we played "Violent Generation," I would talk about what the song was about. It was about CBGB, and the very next night, Evan said the same thing I said, but about one of Biohazard's songs. I went up to him said, "If you ever fucking do that again, I'll fucking kill you," and he was just like, "Oh, I was just joking around, man," He would actually steal shit I said.

PETE: He would steal everything Lou said, and then he would wear everything I would wear, and HE would wear it the next day!

LOU: He was so hurt that they had to go on before us. We didn't really care about headlining; that was the booking agent's doing, and the funny thing was that a lot of the promoters were saying, "Sick of It All should go on last because Biohazard is known, but not so much outside of New York." Anyway, it ended up being a good tour.

PETE: There was a really good fight that happened in Arizona. We were banned from playing in Arizona for years. Our friend Duck was living out there. He was either still in the Marines, or he was just living out there. Anyway, we're playing in this tiny club, the Mason Jar, and all the guys from Sepultura come down. We're playing, things are going well, and there's a bunch of Nazis there. There was this one black kid, the tiniest guy there, who loved Sick of It All. Before the show, he came up and told us, "I really love you guys, but this town is really sketchy." The show went on and you'd see him getting picked on by these GIANT dudes, throwing him around.

LOU: It started during Biohazard's set. I remember them stopping the show and saying something about it, and the Nazis were like, "Yeah, yeah..." and then they finished their set.

PETE: We were playing, and I noticed they were really hurting this kid. I thought, *If I go down there, it's gonna be fucked,* because there were HUNDREDS of these assholes. The club was super down with those guys too, and all the bouncers were with THEM. So, I went down into the crowd. I took my guitar off in the middle of a song and was like, "Hey, what the fuck?! Leave this guy alone!" Somebody said something to me, so BOOM, I punched him right in the face! Then all hell broke loose! EVERYBODY was fighting.

LOU: I said, "Hey, we didn't come here to see you guys start trouble and have fights, we came here to play." This guy walks up and he's got a Hitler haircut and this silver swastika around his neck, and he goes, "Yeah, yeah, just fucking play your music." We start playing again, and that's when the fight broke out. That guy came running at me, so I punched him in the face. All of a sudden, I get hit on the side of the head by another Nazi, and somebody's arm goes past me and cracks the guy right in the nose. It was Craig. Me and Craig are just hitting these guys and they start running. The bar area was separated by big barrels with ropes in front of them, and the Nazi guy runs past the bouncer and me, and Craig stops short. As soon as the guy hits the bar, everybody turns around, and they're all wearing SS shirts, t-shirts with the double bolts on them. They look at us and I was like, "We're gonna die!" But then, the whole fucking crowd charged them! It was insane.

PETE: I think it made the cover of the newspaper. Good times!

LOU: Billy from Biohazard broke a pool cue and stuck the jagged end in some guy's neck.

PETE: Everyone was fighting and throwing shit. It was like an actual cowboy barroom brawl, chairs flying and shit. Jerry jumps up on top of a table with one of those plastic beer pitchers, nothing in it, and all these guys are surrounding the table. This guy goes, "You better not throw that, boy," and BOOM, he lets it go. It flies, and for some reason everything is silent, and then it goes BLEEEEOOOP! It makes this weird noise, but it doesn't hurt the guy. So, everyone starts fighting again. Minus attacked this one guy with an eight-ball in a sock; this guy's fucking face was smashed to pieces. There was blood everywhere. A fucking police helicopter landed right in the middle of the street. Riot police were there.... Of course, these dicks tell the cops, "It was the singer and the guitar player who started it," so me and Lou were fucked.

LOU: Actually, they said it was YOU! The cops came in, sent everyone outside, and divided us into two groups. On one side were all these Nazi fucks, and on the other side were us and all these kids.

LOU: They were asking, "Where's the guitar player? He started it."

PETE: Iggor from Sepultura grabbed me and said, "We've got to get you out of here." I put a baseball hat on and walked right past everyone who said it was me. We're walking, and I see the kid who got hit with the eight-ball. He looked like a mummy. They had his fucking head wrapped and it was twice the size of a basketball, blood still pouring out of it. There was some kid there who said, "I'll take you guys out of here," so we drove away and met up with the band somewhere else later on. We were banned from playing in Arizona for a LONG time.

LOU: Years later we were doing a tour with Helmet and we checked with the police department. There were no warrants or anything for any of us having to do with that. We were a little worried that there might be repercussions, that some of these guys might come back. We were told, "Don't worry, the sheriffs check IDs at the doors at these concerts." And they were doing just that. They would check guys' IDs to see if they had a warrant or a felony or something. They actually got a bunch of the Nazis we had fights with, who came back to fuck with us. I remember talking to the sheriff and he was like, "Yeah, we got this guy, and this guy." He showed me a picture, and I recognized the kid's face—it was the guy with the silver swastika, a total steroid monster. Maybe he was coming to apologize, I don't know.

1. YOUR RECORD CAME OUT ON SONY HERE, AND NOW PEOPLE SAY THEY HATE YOU!

LOU: I remember Marc from M.A.D. Tour Booking calling Armand, who was working at the label at the time, and saying, "Sick of It All has to come over to Europe." Armand gave him my number and Marc was telling me, "You have to come and show the people that you are not a sell-out band." I was like, "What the hell are you talking about?" He goes, "Your record came out on SONY here, and people now say they HATE you," and I'm like, "Why would they hate us because of the label it came out on?" I wasn't of that idea that *labels are evil*. But that was his initial motivation, for us to come and prove ourselves overseas.

MARC NICKEL (M.A.D. TOUR BOOKING): I started in punk rock in 1978 as a kid in Germany. Some of the American bands that were coming over in the early eighties would bring us flyers; they brought fanzines. My friend started the first record store here that would import hardcore, and another friend started the first record label. He brought Circle Jerks, Bad Brains, and Angry

Samoans, all their records over here as licenses. I was very close with that whole thing, and with what was happening in America at the time. I think it was in '82 that we booked our first shows, but we weren't calling ourselves M.A.D. yet. A couple of years later, I went over to America to network. I was in New York in the mid-eighties when Sick of It All, the Youth Crew, everybody started to get around. I was also in Frisco, Boston, and Washington, D.C., with the Dischord people. I was hanging out with *Maximum RockNRoll* people: Tim Yohannan, everybody, and the funny thing was that they had always hated New York hardcore, but I had always loved it. When I was in New York and saw Sick of It All for the first time, I said, "Damn, that's the real deal!" They played the music we wanted to hear. And the message, all the angry things we feel... it was different from, I guess you could say, the "student music" we were getting from Washington, D.C., and San Francisco. Those bands had nothing to do with our life here in Berlin. Life over here, especially in the bigger cities like Berlin, was just like New York. Plus, that New York sound was the sound we all liked, so we basically sat down and said, "Let's do this. Let's get these guys over here." The only problem was that the New York bands weren't the richest people on the planet, so the question was: *How do we get them over here?* The guys in SOIA said, "If you can buy us four plane tickets, we'll come to Europe."

LOU: *Maximum RockNRoll* was like the punk rock bible back then. It was how so many people found out about bands and different scenes in America. Outside America too: they had all these scene reports from Europe, Asia and other places. They HATED New York! They especially seemed to hate Agnostic Front because they were skinheads. They would talk shit about all the NYHC bands as if they were all these fascist, Nazi goons.

MARC NICKEL: You know, people always say we are like the biggest lawyers for NYHC. Punk and hardcore came from the streets; we had huge riots in Germany with cops and very active anarchist circles. With *Maximum RockNRoll*, every time I spoke with them, it was a one-way exchange. I told them, "You're fighting for and preaching these ideas and you're attacking New York." I said, "You have big problems over here with fascist people, but you know, in New York, I never saw anything like that." When I first went to New York, I actually didn't know what to expect because of what I'd seen in *Maximum RockNRoll*. I went straight from the airport to Tompkins Square Park; I didn't know anybody in New York, so I just walked up there with a sleeping bag on my back. Frenchie Da Skin was sitting there, and he welcomed me with open arms because I told him why I came. I slept in some squats with rats on the floor, with some of the early Warzone women. I met Raybeez and everybody running around there, and the first thing I thought was, *Wait a minute, everybody's very together here. They don't care if you like metal, have long hair, short hair, are a skinhead or a punk. Black, white, Hispanic, it's like one huge family.* All these kids, especially the Lower East Side kids, lived in fucked-up squats and buildings most Europeans wouldn't ever squat in. When I went to the first show, I was like, "Whoa, it's like another world." Where I came from, basically everyone was white. Yet, what's crazy is that, back at the *Maximum RockNRoll* headquarters, I saw the biggest Nazi record collection ever in their hall closet. I said, "What is this?" And they said, "Oh, we collect everything." I said, "Sure, everything in hardcore and punk, but what does Skrewdriver have to do with punk?! They're not part of our scene. Why do you have their records?" Anyway, that was typical. But what I liked about New York, especially about Lou and Pete and Sick of It All, was that they presented their message without really just saying it. They were living it. They were living this tolerance. They were living this "everybody's welcome" attitude. I mean, they play huge, major festivals over here with bands like Slipknot and Slayer, yet they sit together with fans, talking to them as normal people. That's a big reason why people like them so much. That's why people respect them.

PETE: We went over to Europe for the first time sometime after *We Stand Alone* came out. We asked Armand what he wanted to do, because he had left the band by this point, and he said, "If you're going to Europe, I want to be the drummer." Without even thinking, we said, "If you're gonna drum for us in Europe, you're gonna write the second record with us too." He said, "Deal," and that was it.

Mark Nickel and Armand, sweating in Europe

LOU: Some people warned us, "The scene there is very political," but I didn't really care. The first show we played in Berlin, the first show of our first European tour, I was walking through the crowd to get to the stage, and this drunk guy corners me. In his heavy German accent, he starts going off on me about what our country has done to Native Americans, and how we've destroyed their culture. I'm all panicked and I just blurt out, "What about what the Germans did during World War II?" and he says "Oh, you Americans always bring up World War II."

PETE: As far as the tour itself, it was one of those things where when you're in it, you're having fun and all that, but you have those moments where you're like, "This fucking sucks!"

LOU: There's only one moment I remember that I hated. We played a lot of squats and a lot of youth centers, and they were all great shows. But there was one night where it was freezing-cold, and we used to change our clothes just before going onstage. They were used to punk bands rolling up and just hanging at the bar all day until it was time to play. So we went to this squat and asked, "Is there a room where we can hang out and change?" They took us across this courtyard in the freezing-cold to this other building. We walk into this room and there's one tiny space heater in the middle of the room, and a lightbulb that was turned on. So we changed our clothes, put our coats back on, and just sat there around this heater until it was time to go on. We walked back across the courtyard and go into what used to be a bomb shelter. There were about six or seven hundred people crammed into this bomb shelter.

PETE: And EVERYBODY'S smoking cigarettes!

LOU: We go through the door, and it went from being below zero to over one hundred degrees with tons of humidity because of all of the body heat that was trapped in there. And, like Pete said, you stepped onstage and the smoke would get trapped. In those bomb shelters, there were these low oval ceilings and the smoke would stay at head level on the stage. It was brutal. But those squat shows were amazing! Incredible energy.

PETE: Everybody there was very politically-minded compared to us, like we'd heard. They really liked talking politics. Anytime anyone would ask me anything involving the government, I would just be like, "Yeah, I don't know," and would walk away. I'd be like, "Hey, Richie's making a funny video over there, I'll see ya later." I left it up to Lou to be the liaison to the people.

LOU: We would have to play our set twice sometimes, and then throw an AF song in there.

PETE: Yeah, we would do "With Time."

LOU: What's weird is, considering what Marc had mentioned about people being pissed at us because of Sony, nobody really even mentioned it. They would rather talk American politics than "Why are you on Sony?" I remember doing a fanzine interview and we were like, "We didn't know the record label had been bought by Sony, or that our EP had been released on Sony here." I said, "What am I supposed to do, quit the band and lose everything?" That was the era when people were struggling with the idea of how hardcore should be. Do it yourself in the basement, blah, blah, blah. You end up going down a rabbit hole of weird discussions like, "Well, if I did a label out of my basement, I'd have to quit my job. How would I pay my rent?" And they'd respond, "But you could move into a squat." NO! No, I can't move into a squat.

PETE: Meanwhile, the people asking us all these questions were finishing their degrees, becoming doctors, and basically pretending they were punks. We were actually playing the music, living this life, and trying to make a living from it. That's the way I've always looked at it: these people aren't in bands; they're going back home tonight, and we're gonna be sleeping in a place with no windows.

LOU: I thought, *And YOU should go back to working at McDonald's, instead of trying to be a lawyer. How about that?!* I liked you better when you were flipping burgers. It's the same thing as far as I'm concerned.

PETE: Another funny thing is that some of the people who were running the squats, and I'm not talking shit because they're our friends, were very, "Fuck the government! Fuck this!" but it's pretty much the government that funded their squats. Now many of them run HUGE festivals. Big rock festivals sponsored by cigarette companies and beer companies. It is what it is.

LOU: But all that aside, when the music came on, they went crazy. They were used to hardcore and punk, but they weren't used to the New York vibe. Sure, AF and Gorilla Biscuits had gone before us, but we had our Jackson Heights groove thing going on. The name was a bit of a joke, but that was how our sound was developing at the time. "Disillusion" was part of that. The whole

Just Look Around album had a huge New York groove style to it. I remember playing a squat; it was that one where it was freezing-cold, and we would bust into "Indust." or one of the other groove songs, "The Shield." Armand would be yelling to me, and he'd nod his head, and there'd be just a row of punk girls with mohawks and dreadlocks getting down to the groove of those songs. It was so cool. You didn't see that mix of people at our American shows.

PETE: It was kinda dancy. Instead of just blasting fast stuff, dare I say there was a little soul to it.

LOU: They didn't mosh like New Yorkers; there were circle pits and a lot of pogoing and shoving.

PETE: And a lot of stage-diving!

LOU: Yeah, they were REALLY into stage-diving.

PETE: When the punk ladies were feeling the groove, the guys were like, "Wow, the girls here are so into it," and then they started feeling it, which was great.

LOU: People had started regularly filming the shows at CB's, and that's when the New York dance style started to spread out. I remember talking to the drummer of NOFX, and he goes, "I fucking love you guys, but what the hell are your fans doing, fighting the floor?" I told him, "Hey, it's either that or we run around in circles like your fans," and we laughed.

PETE: By the time we got to Germany, the wall had just come down. There was no more East and West Germany. The country was in transition, which was weird to see.

LOU: Our first show in Berlin was completely sold out, and the crowd was crazy, and we were like, "This is great! Europe's the greatest!" We were all high on our amazing first show in Europe. I remember getting in the van and Marc's going, "But that was

Berlin, it's different in the rest of Germany, don't expect this every night." Sure enough, we went into former East Germany that night and played in a bar to maybe fifty people the next day. There were guys at the bar with leather pants and mullets with Scorpions shirts on, who were just hanging out drinking beer and watching us. The greatest thing was watching them, with their mustaches and mullets, buying XXL Sick of It All shirts and tucking them into their leather pants.

PETE: They were basically into anything heavy. It wasn't like some places in the States where people are like, "Yeah, I'm into metal," but wouldn't give you a chance if it wasn't a specific type of metal. That's something really great about Europe. When we started playing festivals, you really saw that openness.

LOU: Those first two tours were basically us establishing ourselves. We played every small town that Marc could get us a show in. We played every youth center, every little club, every squat. I think it was on the second tour of Europe that he first got us on a couple of festivals. I think we played in Denmark with Henry Rollins and Iggy Pop. The crowd was going crazy, but I did a stage-dive into the crowd. I ran and dove, everybody moved out of the way, and I hit the dirt. Flat-backed right into the dirt, BOOM! And people just stared down at me, because they had never really seen hardcore. This was a whole different audience. So, I got up and Marc helped me back onstage.

PETE: Some of the people in the West were like, "Yeah, it sucks that the wall came down," but when you went to the East, you got to see what Germany there was like. We would drive through some towns and Marc would say "Oh look, they're westernizing." There'd be ONE store with a bright pink awning, and I'd be like, "Are you kidding me? That's westernizing?"

LOU: And he'd tell us about how, before the wall came down, all those towns were grey and miserable, every one of them.

PETE: Even on a sunny day, they seemed so grey and shitty.

LOU: Everything closed at six o'clock. We'd be like, "Let's go get some food," and Marc would tell us, "No, everything's closed." We'd ask, "What do you mean, 'Everything's closed?' It's Germany. Where do people eat?" Marc would reply, "In their homes." I'd say, "But what about travelers? We like to eat too!"

PETE: The club in Leipzig is called Conne Island. We played an anniversary show over there celebrating thirty years of the club. It's still the same guy who booked us back then, and the shows are still pretty great. There's basically nothing there, then the train stops right out front, and people come piling into the club.

LOU: The first time we went, we did a sound check; it was freezing outside, and we thought, *Let's go see what's around.* We took two steps out of the club, and there was NOTHING. There was the town, but it was closed down. Now we go there, and it's like a whole different world.

PETE: We learned what "squat gruel" was at that club. They set up a dinner table in the club, and if the kids were already in the club, they got to eat too. Everyone gets to eat for free. Sometimes, we didn't get shit because of the kids eating all the food.

LOU: Squat gruel was like a big pot of boiled rice and boiled vegetables, sort of like chili.

PETE: Basically, cans of Veg-All thrown inside a huge pot. And, according to Craig, to make perfect squat gruel, you have to throw an old dirty boot in it too.

LOU: We eventually started to transition from playing squats to clubs, but we still played squats in certain areas. When we went to Estonia, we always played this one squat because they were so into Sick of It All. One time we were starving, and they made the squat gruel for us. They had this whole table laid out. I was standing there with Armand, and I said, 'I can't eat this shit again! There's a pizza place right across the street," so we cut out to the pizza place. The girls who made the dinner for us were so hurt I had to apologize. I made up an excuse, "Oh, I didn't know this was for all of us, I thought it was just for the crew. I'm so sorry!" They kept asking, "You don't like the food?" I said, "Um...I really thought it was just for the crew!"

PETE: We played that HUGE squat in Milan. I think there were four thousand people there, and it was like five bucks to get in.

LOU: There were fucking Italian supermodels there just because it was five bucks to get in, and it was cool to go there. They could smoke weed in there without being harassed by the police. It was like the place to be. In 2001, we took Rise Against on tour and played that squat. Rage Against the Machine had played it, either that year or the year before. People had been calling them sell-outs, so they decided to play a squat. They did three thousand people, and we did four thousand people, and then, six months later, Wu-Tang Clan played there, and six thousand people showed up, so they won! I loved Rise Against, and they were going on first. I walk over, and they're all standing behind the stage. I say, "What's up? Is this fucking great or what? Look at that crowd!" Joe was so nervous, and he goes, "We've never played to a crowd this big before." I told them, "Just go up and do what you do." They were having a great set, and Joe almost fell through the stage. He jumped and broke a hole in the stage. Fast-forward a decade, and I get a text from Joe: "Hey, we're in Frankfurt, they're expecting ten thousand people tonight." I ask, "Is that a festival?" And he goes, "No, it's our own show." In my head I'm like, *What the fuck?! You were so scared to go on in Italy that one day.*

PETE: The first time we went to Russia was interesting.

MARC NICKEL: We snuck them over the border during the Iron Curtain period. The punk scene had been there since the eighties, but we never had the chance to go because it was quite dangerous. It would have been dangerous for us to get caught. It was even dangerous for the kids to go to the shows. We were the first to sneak bands behind the Iron Curtain to the Czech Republic, Hungary, and East Germany when the wall was still around. That's why the New York hardcore bands were so popular in Eastern Europe compared to the California bands. They went there before everybody, before the whole wave started, and they were there for the kids when they needed them most.

2. HELLO MARC, A BAND JUST CANCELLED, I HAVE ROOM FOR SICK OF IT ALL
(Festivals)

MARC NICKEL: Agnostic Front was already established in Europe. The squatters, the punks, loved them, but the big metal festivals were afraid to touch AF because of their fans. They were worried about hooligans coming to the shows. Sick of It All was a bit easier. It's funny because they had the same fans, but for the metal festivals, SOIA wasn't as scary. I'd been trying to get them on some of those festivals for a while, and one day I got a call from the guy from Dynamo Open Air in the Netherlands, a legendary festival. The guy called me and said, "Hello Marc, a band just cancelled. I have room for Sick of It All." Dynamo was basically fifty to sixty thousand people, free entry. It didn't really matter who played; it was kind of like a big metal party for everybody. They didn't really pay the bands because they had free entry, so the attitude was, "You want to play here? Just be happy." I called them, and they had this manager at that time, so we had a conference call that I'll never forget. He said. "That's stupid. A festival like that is nonexistent." It was Lou who said, "We've heard of that festival. Whatever Marc has suggested so far has been 100 percent right, so let's book the festival." They overrode their manager right on the phone with me. And they didn't do it just once; they did it a couple of times. Since that point, that manager always worked against me whenever he could, with every little thing. Anyway, we agreed to play Dynamo. It was completely crazy. We were stuck in the festival traffic with probably twenty thousand people on the highway. From Germany, there's one highway to get there, and we didn't prepare properly. The bus driver was not prepared either, so we just drove there and got stuck in traffic. The police had to come and find a sneaky way to bring us to the festival because Dynamo back in the day was completely unorganized. We made it to the backstage area, and the band was speechless. Pete, Lou, and Armand turned around and said, "Marc, we will not sell any merchandise here," and I asked, "Why?" They said "This is completely commercial; they're selling merchandising and taking a percentage. Our shirts will be too expensive for the kids."

LOU: Sick of It All has always maintained, *we can make money without robbing the shit out of our fans.* Anytime we've gone on tour with a bigger band, we've had to fight to get it in our contract that we sell our t-shirts for OUR price. Otherwise, we'd have to match the headliner's price, and our fans aren't used to buying shirts for fucking, going back to the nineties, twenty bucks. Jeez, we were selling them for fifteen and people were complaining. Then you had the festival prices.... It could get ridiculous depending on who the headlining band was.

MARC NICKEL: I had to tell them, "This is not a hardcore party here. This is a huge metal festival. Everybody knows how it is," and they still refused to sell merchandise. So, we sat down, and I eventually talked them into it. It was the first show of their tour. They had a whole truckload of merchandise for the European tour, because back in the day, you got everything at once. When the show was over, there was nothing left! First show, everything was gone. They sold all of the merchandise. They were the first hardcore band to ever make it up there at a festival that size. But during the show, the craziest shit happened to the band. The stage was so huge they didn't know where to go. They went out there, the intro started, and, BOOM, the electricity was gone! The guitar went out, with ten or fifteen thousand people who had already started dancing and slamming, and there was no sound, but the audience was not stopping. We all went into a complete panic, because we couldn't figure out what had happened to the sound. It turned out that someone unplugged an extension cord. That's why all of the guitars and everything went out, so they decided to just start again. It was one of the craziest moments I've ever seen at a festival. It was the first time Lou had to walk out in front of a football stadium-sized audience, sixty or seventy thousand people, with no music.

LOU: That was pretty crazy. We'd played some pretty big shows before Dynamo, but nothing like this. It was just heads as far as you could see. We weren't sure if any of them would know who we were, but a lot of them did, and we won over a lot of the rest.

MARC NICKEL: Dynamo was a huge win. All the merchandise was sold, and everybody talked about it. When the sound was sorted out, they killed the show. So right away, other people were starting festivals in Europe, and they all took Sick of It All. They said, "Wow, hardcore really works for our metal audience!" This was maybe 1993. They opened the door in Europe for every hardcore band basically. Part of their success was also the nice and easy way they worked. They were polite, never made issues about green and yellow M&Ms, and were always OK with what they had. Then they opened the doors to the alternative festivals. That's what made Sick of It All so huge over here. They played with everybody, and they never preached anything; they never told anyone what to do like other bands did. It was always about the music and fun.

LOU: When *Just Look Around* came out, and we didn't know this, it got licensed to Roadrunner Records in Europe, and it was doing great. We had no idea it had been doing great; we just went over there and shows were selling out. I remember talking to Zack from Rage Against the Machine when they first started going over there, and he said, "Every club we go to, they're blasting the whole *Just Look Around* album." I was like, "At YOUR shows?" and he said, "Yeah," so it was a big deal, but we didn't know that. Also, we had begun doing really great at the festivals in Europe at this point.

PETE: We were getting on all the bigger metal and just rock and alternative fests, whatever you want to call them.

LOU: And we'd be billed over some of the biggest bands. We played a lot of those huge festivals. In some cases, we played them three years in a row, like Full Force. We did the first three of those, and we were a headliner on the first one.

PETE: Resurrection, we headlined the first three of those. Now it's headlined by the fucking Scorpions.

LOU: At Full Force, it was Anthrax, Sick of It All, Ministry, and Slayer. We had an amazing set, and I remember Tom Araya standing there on the side of the stage as we were walking off after the show. He didn't realize that all of Ministry was standing behind him, but he laughs and says, "How the fuck is Ministry going to go on after YOU?!" I'm like, "Shhh, they're right behind you." It was amazing to hear him say that, and he didn't give a shit that Al Jourgensen heard him say it.

PETE: The Reading festival was a really weird one because it was The (International) Noise Conspiracy, Dashboard Confessional, Coheed and Cambria, Bouncing Souls, I think Jimmy Eat World, and then Sick of It All headlining.

LOU: We came out onstage to "We Are the Champions." It was fucking great!

PETE: That's when Reading was actually good. Now it's just total mainstream garbage.

LOU: Well, it's like most every other festival. People just buy tickets before the bill is announced because of the event. Look at Punk Rock Bowling; unless you're friends with them, you get shit money. They're like, "You can play our fest or not, we don't give a shit. We can throw on so-and-so, who's younger and will take half the money you want."

PETE: It's kind of like working a regular job. If you ask for a raise, they begin thinking, "Maybe we should have hired that other guy. He doesn't have a family to support."

LOU: We did the seventh or eighth Punk Rock Bowling. When they approached us to do it, they were like, "We really want you guys to play, but please don't ask for a lot of money because it's a little punk fest." I looked at him and said, "You know there are pictures on the internet, right?" It's not a little punk fest. They had over ten thousand people the year before we played it. Let's just say we got a small fraction of what the headliner got.

PETE: They paid for our hotel but not our flights, so there went half the money right there.

LOU: I don't understand some of these people who come from punk rock. I'm not saying, you know, just give money away, but we've played shows for hardcore kids, guys in bands that we've helped. When we'd get to the venue, there'd be nothing for us to eat. They'd give you just enough to go eat pizza with, and it's like, you came from the same background as us. This is our dinner. Sometimes, they're worse than the big scumbag rock-and-roll promoters. If you come from our scene, you should know better. We don't ask for much, but Jeez! We're not four years old. Can you do a little better than pizza money?

PETE: We just played Hell Fest, but we had to play on Slipknot's day, which they called Knotfest. We'd done Hell Fest on the main stage three years before and got really good money. We also played the first Hell Fest, which I thought would give us some pull, but because they wanted us to play on the Knotfest day, we played much earlier in the day, and were paid a lot less than we got the last time we played. It makes no sense, except to the promoters. I guess if we had just decided to break up, took a few years off, and then came back and said, "We're back. We want to play Hell Fest," we'd be getting tens of thousands of euros to play. Plus, they screwed us out of playing with Manowar!

LOU: I saw the original schedule, and instead of us being higher up on the bill, or headlining the hardcore stage, they made us one of the openers on Knotfest. It was in either 2010 or 2011 that we headlined the hardcore stage. It was called the Warzone Stage. When we went on, it was packed from the stage all the way through and around the bend, so that nobody could get in or out the whole time we were on. That's why they put us on the main stage a few years later. Why hardcore is treated like this I'll never know. Generally, in Europe, hardcore is treated like "real music," not like it is in the States, where promoters look at it as some shitty little thing. Anyway, if we had been a metal band, we would have been second or third from the headliner this year. Story of our lives!

3. ALWAYS WITH US
(Embracing the Culture)

MARC NICKEL: Sick of It All was the first band I'd met that was interested in the culture of where they were playing. Most bands would just hang out in their dressing rooms until showtime or walk around close to the venue. But these guys, I showed them every fucking place in the world. I always told them, "We're on tour here now, but who knows what will happen tomorrow?" Every show looks the same, I know. After sightseeing, sometimes they were like, "Marc, another castle???" but they went to everything wherever we were. And because of this, the people in each city respected them more. They saw that they cared about where they were. Plus, they'd talk to everyone.

PETE: By now I've seen all these places, the Louvre, the Colosseum. But now, I get to take my daughter to these places when she comes on the road with me during summertime, and I know a little bit about them so I can teach her. Lou does the same thing. I mean, who knows if we'll get to do this again?

MARC NICKEL: We'd visit the Schloss Neuschwanstein, which the Disney castle was modeled after, the Alps.... We did all these things. We went to football matches. I know all the guys in all the firms all over Europe, so it was easy for me to get us in without any trouble. We had been in Cologne and it was Cologne versus Leverkusen. We went to the gate, and the hooligan police saw us and went, "They don't belong to Cologne, they don't belong to Leverkusen, who are they?" They heard my Berlin dialect and must have thought, *this is dangerous. Tattooed guys, the way they are dressed.... Let's put them in a special place.* So, the police brought us to an empty block, an empty section of the stadium. The empty block is there so that opposing fans can't get too close to each other. So, me and the boys are sitting between the Cologne and Leverkusen hooligans in an empty block in the middle of the stadium. Just us in this big block, and both sides decide to fuck with us. It was a little crazy, but nothing really happened. When we were leaving the stadium, one guy went up to Pete and said, "Fuck your mother," trying to set him off. I immediately tried to get us going in the direction the cops wanted us to go. They're NEW YORKERS, if you know what I mean. It was hard to pull Pete away. I said, "Stay together. I don't know those guys. There's like fifty of their supporters behind those trees waiting to fight. Let's just go to the bus." It was difficult for me to explain to Pete, Lou, Armand, and everybody what the hell was going on there, and it was probably one of the most bizarre things they'd ever seen. I have to say, they always stood behind me. I never had the feeling I was by myself. I knew they were there for me. For instance, we used to have problems with bootleggers. They would basically set up a shop outside the venue and sell lots of t-shirt designs. At one gig, Sick of It All went after them, and it got ugly. The bootleggers were very organized at that time, but we beat them up, took the merch, and brought it in for the kids for free. That was the game for three or four cities. The bootleggers didn't know who I was, but they picked Berlin for their revenge attack. We had the whole firm there. Definitely the wrong place to try to attack the band. The bootleggers got beat up very badly. We had it in Holland too. Then we went to England—that's their hometown—and they were ready. They came with black masks and Molotov cocktails and attacked us. We had a street riot with them, the band against them. Scary, you know. The police came because it was out in the middle of the street. Nobody helped us. It was just us and them. The police came and said, "You should leave the country; this is organized crime. You should go. They will come to your next show again. We can't protect you all over." I said, "Let me make a couple of phone calls to certain people I know, and I think we'll get rid of the problem." I spoke with the people from the

London firms, and SOIA never saw the bootleggers again. Other bands had these issues and tried to fight the bootleggers the way SOIA did, but they all failed because they never had the backup those guys had. I've heard stories of other bands making that kind of call, but the people who helped us said, "We won't do it for THEM." There's a reason Lou, Pete, and those guys got that kind of support. They'll have that for life over here.

PART IX
ALONE

1. JUST SMACK THOSE KIDS ALREADY!

LOU: Our *We Stand Alone* EP was released in Europe by Sony with a bunch of live tracks added to it. We came home from our European tour and were like, "We need to do a New York show, and CBGB is gone, but everybody is playing ABC No Rio." We approached them but were told, "We don't like the kind of crowd you draw." We thought, "What does that mean?" That was the answer: they didn't like the crowd we drew. I mean, I sort of understood what they were saying, but they knew us. Many were fans of our band.

PETE: By that time, the scene had started getting pretty dumb.

BILL FLORIO (*SMASHIN' THROUGH* FANZINE): I'm assuming they had spoken with Mike Bullshit, who booked the shows at ABC. He had been put in the hospital after getting beaten up by some of the people who used to hang around Sick of It All. He was probably terrified. While they personally had zero to do with that, some of their hangers-on were the worst of the worst.

LOU: We were totally against that shit that had gone on at CB's. That was at the time when we started writing for *Just Look Around*, more social and political stuff. It wasn't about fighting. We wrote a lot about the violence in the scene and also the violence in the city. The song "Just Look Around" was written about what happened in Brooklyn, in Crown Heights, what happened between the African-American community and the Hasidic community. People lived together there for decades and it started exploding into race riots. That's when the AIDS crisis was really bad, and we wrote songs about that. But somehow, all these kids down there made us the poster children for everything they thought was wrong with New York hardcore. I don't remember all of the specific zines, but I remember on the back of *Smashin' Through*, they had taken Mötley Crüe's promo shot and glued our faces onto Mötley Crüe's bodies and wrote "Alleyway Crüe" in the Mötley Crüe logo. I wish we had a good image of that because if we made a shirt of it, we'd probably sell a ton of them!

BILL FLORIO: Before ABC No Rio started up, around '88 or '89, I started the zine. I interviewed Sick of It All for issue number two, and I think it was the same week Adam from Born Against was passing out these "Sick of It All Built Missiles" flyers. Born Against only had a demo out and had played maybe three shows by that point. They seemed to be trying to make a name for themselves. Anyway, Pete and Lou and those guys were fired up about that and talked about it the entire interview. I really didn't know what they were talking about, so for the next issue, I interviewed Born Against to find out what that was all about. I had all these questions about what Sick of It All had talked about in their interview. I was printing the issue with the Born Against interview and had the stupid idea to put the Sick of It All/Mötley Crüe thing on the back-cover. I was folding them, and I got a call from Pete. He was really angry and said, "I need this guy's address; you know where they live," all while I'm looking at the Mötley Crüe thing. I told him I'd only been to their house once and didn't really know where it was. It was basically a case of the Born Against guys opening up their big mouths and me opening up my troublemaker senses.

Back of Smachin'Through Fanzine #4 (1990)

PETE: None of those kids ever came directly to us. We were just being lumped in with the tough-guy aspect of hardcore, which sucked.

LOU: When someone says "tough guy" to me, I think, *It's just a guy who carries himself with strength and goes about his business, but if you cross him, you're probably gonna get what you deserve.* That's the way we carried ourselves. We never went out to start trouble. We'd always give people chances. As soon as somebody says something negative to you, you don't just beat them up. We never did anything like that. But nobody would come and talk to us. I remember Pete and I went to see our friend Trevor's band. They came up from Florida, and I loved their 7-inch, so we went to ABC No Rio to see them. We went there and people were shitting themselves. Sam McPheeters actually left that day; he left the building and ran away. We walk in and some guy from the band Our Gang says, "We just want to make sure you guys aren't going to make any trouble." "Do you ask everyone that?!" I said, "We're not here to make trouble." Even though Trevor put us on the list, I paid the five bucks to get in.

PETE: We MADE SURE we paid to get in.

BILL FLORIO: What's funny is I used to edit these wedding and bar mitzvah videos, and at one point, I made a reel of wedding and bar mitzvah bloopers. I gave a copy to my friend Artie who roadied for Sick of It All, and he shared it with the band. Apparently, they loved it. Fast-forward to around 2006, and I ran into Pete at a show and told him I was the guy who made the blooper video. He said, "Oh man, that's the funniest thing ever," and we talked about it for a minute. I then decided to tell him I was the guy from *Smashin' Through* who put their heads on Mötley Crüe's bodies, and he actually had no recollection of it. I was surprised.

LOU: Those guys also LOVED making fun of our In-Effect jackets.

PETE: Those were cool jackets!

LOU: When that stupid debate happened on WNYU, one of those kids commented, "You could have done your own thing with Sick of It All, but what do you have now? Just some fancy jackets." We thought, *your reason for hating us is because we got JACKETS from our record label??? That's your problem, that we got jackets?!* That fucking debate.... It was the singer of Born Against and two kids from some fanzine; I can't remember their names, but they were generally nice kids. I never really knew the guy from Born Against, but I knew the kids from that fanzine and the kid who ended up drumming for Born Against; he does sound all over New York now and works for the Bouncing Souls a lot. The thing that got me really mad was not that they hated us for "selling out"; it's that they had been our friends and somehow couldn't just come up and talk to us about this and have a normal discussion. They had to attack us with the "Alleyway Crüe" photo and all this stupid shit. The debate was just idiotic. I remember all the phone calls that were coming into the station while it was going on. People were saying, "Just shut up and play music! Who cares what label they're on?!"

BILL FLORIO: When that debate was happening, I was at band practice and was basically told not to walk down University Place, where the radio station was. They told me that Lou and Pete were trying to find out who the *Smashin' Through* guy was.

PETE: Nobody cared about it. Anthony Comunale called up and said, "Just smack those kids already," and he was friends with them too. He almost formed a band with some of them. For us, it wasn't super serious. I think we all just let it explode. I just wanted it to leave. We're not tough guys, but if you keep messing with us, and we get pushed too much, you can't be a sucker.

LOU: It kept going on and on and on. Towards the end, I remember someone going, "All right, it's over," and we all started screaming. As we were leaving, I turned to that kid John and said, "This is fucked up! You were my friend, man, what the fuck?" He just sat there with this weird smile on his face. I got mad and shoved him, and he fell over a chair. Everybody was like, "Oh man, Sick of It All just attacked the guy." No, we didn't, and I even apologized to him. It's funny because he and I laugh about it now. Like with everything in life, later on you feel differently. When we left and got downstairs, the two kids from the fanzine were there, and I asked, "Hey, where's that guy from Born Against?" They told us, "Oh, he ran away. He and his girl jumped in a cab because they thought you were gonna kick his ass." I was like, "We're not gonna beat anybody up," and he said, "We know that." That's when they actually gave us their whole reasoning behind their bullshit: "You guys could have been the Minor Threat of New York hardcore. You could have started your own label. Just think what you could have done." I replied to them, "Maybe we could have, but we WORK jobs to earn a living. We do this band, and then we come home after a weekend of shows early on a Monday morning, put our equipment away, and return the rental van at 4 a.m. Then we go home, most of the time not even going to sleep, and then at 6 a.m. we go right to fucking work!" That's what we did for YEARS, and they're gonna tell me I'm gonna run a record label in the middle of all that?! Then they had problems with how we handled the lyric sheet inside our first album because we wanted the album to be distributed everywhere.

PETE: We did what we did so we could reach as many people as possible. That was a big deal. Most places in the country didn't have a store like Some Records, dedicated just to hardcore or anything like that.

LOU: Most kids didn't know about magazines like *Maximum RockNRoll*, or where to get hardcore records, so they would go to their local mall or some chain store. Most of those places had policies against carrying records with curse words on a lyric sheet or lyrics they thought were "questionable." Well, WE were "questionable!" So, WE decided not to put our full lyric sheet in the album. We only had "Injustice System" on there, but you could write away for the lyrics for FREE. Most of the time when people got the lyrics, they got a fuckin' sticker too, so I still don't see what the big deal is. There was still cursing, if that's so important to everyone, all over the record. We snuck it past everyone.

PETE: This kid told us a story about going to a Sam Goody store. There was no "hardcore" section, so he's looking through the "S" section and comes across *Blood, Sweat and No Tears*. He looks at THAT cover compared to all the rest, and he sees Jorge, total skinhead, flipping over the crowd, and Fern dancing to our band, and there's Walter with his alternative haircut on top of the pile, and he's like, "Wow, this is fucking cool," and it made him buy the record. There were black skinheads on the cover of the record. Most hardcore people had never seen that on an album cover.

LOU: As curious as I am sometimes, I CAN'T listen to that debate. Somebody sent me a link once. I played it, and within five seconds of it, I thought, "This is so dumb." I do remember thinking, "I understand their position to some degree, but they're not presenting it correctly at all." All they did was make fun of our In-Effect jackets, and we were like, "Fuck this!"

BILL FLORIO: Bottom line: Sam and those guys lost that debate. And what's crazy is that everything Sam was complaining about, he did later with his own label. He mismanaged it into the ground. He did a distro deal with Dutch East on the suggestion of this guy Charles who was also in on the debate. They ran out of money and did a deal with the most expensive, shitty distributor. They had a falling-out over it, and I don't think they ever spoke to one another again.

PETE: I wish I still had my In-Effect jacket.

LOU: I think I still have mine in storage. Or maybe I did something dumb like give it to a girl. I remember walking in Flushing, Queens, wearing that jacket, and some people were like, "Yo, that's a baaaaad jacket!" Once, I was sitting in a Wendy's, which turned out not to be a good place to wear that jacket, and these two guys go, "Harder than you?! Yeah, let's see how hard you are!" I started eating my food as fast as I could, like, *I think I'm gonna go now.* To this day, our friends in the California scene don't understand that New York was more of a street scene. Yeah, they had their gutter punks and all that, and punk was a brutal scene growing up in California with all the gangs and shit, but the way it is now, it's bordering on pop-punk 90 percent of the time. Our friends out there would always ask, "What's with all the fucking hip-hop?" and we'd be like, "That's New York." When we were on tour with Agnostic Front, the first time we went out with them in '91, we went up to Quebec. The place went absolutely crazy, and I remember going backstage and sitting there with these two French-speaking skinheads. They say, "We like your music very much, but why do you speak BLACK in between the songs?" I said, "Speak BLACK?" And they go, "Yes, you speak like a black man." I remember me and Pete look at each other and Pete says, "We're from New York, everybody talks like this," and they walked away. They couldn't understand why we were like, "Yo, what's up?" like everybody in our neighborhood. Our freaking mailman talks like that.

I think many people will like... hear some reserve final judgement when I hear some vinyl. Let's face it, SFA are the gods of NY hardcore, unfortunately I'm an atheist.
— Nick

SICK OF IT ALL

PART X
JUST LOOK AROUND

1. WE'VE GOT MORE THAN THREE DAYS THIS TIME. THAT'S GOOD.

PETE: We were ready to record our second album. Of course, we went back to Normandy because it was so much fun the first time, and Tom fit in with us right away.

LOU: I remember Tom saying, "Whoa, we've got more than three days this time. That's good." We did a whole week and didn't go in there with twenty-one songs either.

PETE: I gained about ten pounds recording that album because all I ate were Hot Pockets. I was like, "Wow these things are tasty," and couldn't stop eating them.

LOU: We got more into a rhythm with *Just Look Around*. Instead of "OK, everybody play together," which is what we had done before, Tom would concentrate on just Armand to start. He'd be the main focus, then we'd do the bass tracks, and then we'd do the guitars and vocals.

PETE: It was more separated, so you could get your stuff down a little bit better. On the first record, if I fucked up, I'd have to do the whole song again, which was absolutely nerve-wracking. I'd finally make it through, and then Armand would tell me, "You messed it up. You've got to do it again!"

LOU: Tom was hard on us, but not as hard as he would have been if he was being paid more.

PETE: I remember him saying, "If I was actually producing this thing, NONE of these songs would be good enough yet."

LOU: Yeah, but he did enjoy a lot of the stuff that we bought. Richie and Armand and all of us were making stupid videos again; that was another big part of that recording. We would come up with dumb scenarios all the time. We were in a little town in Rhode Island; what the hell else are you gonna do when there's that much downtime? Now the failure of *Just Look Around* was the album cover. We wanted an eye, but we wanted inside the iris to show either a decaying city or a skull. But no, they just took a picture of my eye and threw it on the cover. And then, in typical Sick of It All fashion, not due to us, we told the label this isn't the cover we wanted; we wanted this and this. The response was, "But we've got to print it now or else you'll lose your window to have your record released when we have it scheduled for."

PETE: Shit like that's been happening for thirty-plus years! Anything we say is met with "That's way too much money, or we have to be done by tomorrow." How the fuck does that happen?!

LOU: We had a few songs written already, which we had been playing towards the end of our tour in Europe. There was one we were calling "Midget Head," and all the lyrics were just "midget head." That song became "Never Measure Up."

PETE: There was this one part, when it was ending, where Richie would just yell "MIDGEEETTT HEAAADDD!"

LOU: He was actually making fun of our merch guy. He had a normal-sized body but the head of a dwarf.

PETE: We had that song and a couple others, but they didn't have lyrics yet. When I was writing for the album, I wasn't trying to do anything specific, but like we were saying about the last songs written for the first album like "Alone" and "Disillusion," those had more of our feel. That's what would just come out. It's not really metal—it's hardcore—but it was Sick of It All hardcore. Like "Midget Head," there's a lot of chugga-chugga-chugga in there, but it was really fast. I was trying to write things that seemed powerful to me. When I write music, I listen to my favorite bands and artists a lot. I get influenced by them. I listen to Eric B. & Rakim, and I listen to Bad Brains. I'll listen to AF, Cro-Mags, all that stuff when I'm trying to get my juices flowing. Usually a riff will pop into my head and I'll just take it from there.

LOU: Richie wrote "Just Look Around." He began playing the bass riff, built it up to "da da da da daaaaa," and we kicked in. A lot of the songs actually came about from us making jokes. In one case we were joking around about how one of the guys from Biohazard would move when he played. Richie goes, "He moves like this," and would play what he thought that movement sounded like. Pete was like, "Wait a minute, listen to this," then Armand would join in, and that's how that song formed. It was us basically making jokes.

PETE: But later on, when we'd play these so-called jokes live, seeing people actually grooving and dancing to it instead of running in circles, we realized that groove had a really positive effect on people. And we had used jokes and humor to create a lot of that stuff. We were just fucking around, and cracking up, and somehow, these jokes became songs.

LOU: But I was still THAT guy, angry about everything when it came to lyrics. As soon as I heard the music for "We Want the Truth," for whatever reason, the words just came out. I wasn't thinking ahead of time, I'm going to write a song about being lied to by everyone. If you're a kid growing up, and you're disillusioned by what your parents tell you, or what your school tells you, or the government.... When I heard that music, it just came to me and worked. "Locomotive": when Pete started working on the music to that, I wanted to write a song about how I fucking hated going to work every day. But there are other songs like "Violent Generation," which was just about the stupidity going on in the hardcore scene at the time, the gang shit.

PETE: Of course, the people in the scene it was written about took it like, "Yeah! WE'RE the Violent Generation," as if it was their anthem.

LOU: Armand came up with the lyrics for two songs, and he came up with the music for "Indust.," which was just a joke title at first. He thought it sounded like a bad version of industrial music. Then it became "Indust.," as in "ashes to ashes, dust to dust," but we squeezed it into one word. Same thing with "The Pain Strikes." He wrote it about the AIDS crisis and nobody, at least from our side of hardcore punk, was talking about that. A lot of people came up to us, people who were in the closet and out, and told us they really appreciated it. I did an interview with *Anti-Matter* fanzine, and I remember Norm saying he wanted to interview us. I thought, *Norm hasn't been to a show in like two years, is he still doing a fanzine?* We sat down and he told me, "I think it was really important that YOU guys, with YOUR following, did this. I'm not saying you guys aren't smart, but you have a very tough-guy following," and I was like, "Holy shit, (thankfully) there are people who still pay attention to the lyrics." We wrote about AIDS because it was so important. Then there's the song "Just Look Around...." I remember sitting at home watching the news, and there were all these riots in Crown Heights. There was a car accident where a Hasidic man hit a young black boy. There was chaos for days...weeks. I couldn't understand it; different groups of people turned it into "I hate this religion" and "I hate those people."

PETE: To this day, when Mei and I watch the news, I think, "Why would people spend so much energy on hating other people, wasting their lives and their time on this?!" And it's NEVER gonna go away.

LOU: By the time we were done recording the album, we found out that the record company, Relativity, was getting rid of In-Effect. I was never given a full answer as to why. In my head, I was just like, "Why would they get rid of it? Did they just want to absorb it into Relativity? Was it just a business thing?" In-Effect seemed to be doing well. They dumped Combat Records too. Then I found out that Sony bought the company, so basically, they decided to get rid of all the labels other than Relativity.

PETE: Just more bullshit we had to deal with.

PART XI
REAL ROCK CONCERTS
(TOURING)

1. TIME DOESN'T MATTER, AGE DOESN'T MATTER

PETE: If I'm sitting home for too long, and I don't mean this like, *Oh I hate being stuck at home with my family*, it gets to me that I'm not playing a show. I get antsy if I'm sitting still. Generally, touring is fucking boring, except when I'm warming up and getting ready to go onstage to play. It's like any other job; there's a routine and it can bore you to tears, but it is the greatest job anyone could have. In the end, I just look forward to playing shows, and I'm totally sincere when I say that. When the intro comes on over the PA, I'm ready to lose it.

LOU: We all are! Going onstage and having people sing back the words you wrote or go wild when you go into a song or a riff, and watching people's faces light up and scream like at REAL rock concerts.... Even now, I get excited when we go into a song like "Death or Jail," where it starts with the guitars, and all of a sudden, the crowd just cheers, and you're like, *Holy shit, they love our song!* I feel so alive. Time doesn't matter; age doesn't matter. All the time, people say things like, "You guys look so young, how do you stay so young?" It's because we're doing this! But prepping for tour.... Sometimes, getting my voice ready for tour is kinda funny. I try to book studios to practice in because I pace back and forth when I sing. I need room, so if the ones I usually book aren't available, I'll just drive around in my car, screaming, That's always fun. Someone once suggested that I take some band money and build a vocal booth down in my basement. I was like, "That's a great idea, but I don't stand still, so I'll wind up feeling trapped in a box."

PETE: That's how I practice backup vocals. I just sing along to CDs while walking around. People on the street think I'm some kind of lunatic.

LOU: I was hanging out with Milo from the Descendents, and we were talking about bands that never want to rehearse and end up driving around town, screaming in their cars. Everybody just thinks you're crazy. Milo was like, "Oh, you do that too?" I used to make a playlist of the live set. I don't do that anymore because the older songs are tuned differently. We tune down now, so when we play them live, I'm like, "Oh shit, I'm singing this too high." Luckily, I've been pretty active, but singing and moving is rough. The first few shows of a tour, I've got to pace myself. Once we're into the fourth and fifth show I'm fine. But, for whatever reason, if I move too much, I don't really lose my breath, but my vocal cords get tenser. I don't know the exact science of it, but sometimes, you don't have enough blood for the muscles in your throat; some weird thing like that.

PETE: I go to the gym super early in the morning, and I'm the only one there, so I practice the sing-alongs there.

LOU: I could do it the local woods, just run in there and start screaming, but people would be like, "My God, there's a madman in the woods!" I usually get up and do this routine that's supposed to help you burn a lot of fat. You do forty jumping jacks, forty squats, forty leg lifts, forty crunches, and then forty more jumping jacks. But the other day, I decided I'm going to be cool, and I am going to do eighty squats! I haven't been able to move until today. Why did I do that?!

PETE: In Europe, I have kettlebells, weights, resistance bands, and all sorts of crap like that. And it's easy nowadays. You can ask Google where there's a gym and it finds one for you. There's even an app called "Find Me a Gym," or some shit like that. The promoters used to hook us up with a gym, but of course, that's been cut out now because we need more money for fancy beer for Armand. My protein and the gym being paid for by the promoter is gone, but there's always a lot of extra beer at the end of the tour. We actually pay for that. Sometimes Armand actually takes extra baggage home filled with beer.

LOU: He should really open up that beer store he's talked about with the supply we get from Europe.

PETE: Beer, schmear. Anyway, lately I've been going back to basics. All you really need is pull-ups and push-ups, but you've got to switch it around every once in a while.

LOU: When we toured with the Misfits, we asked Doyle what his routine was. His abs are insane, and he said, "I've never done a crunch in my life, I've never done a sit-up in my life." I was like, "Really?" and he said, "Yeah, it's all weights." He was working out with those block weights the way people work out with kettlebells. He knows all those movements that make his core super strong without doing any crunches.

PETE: That's why I don't go to the gym on the road as much anymore. I have those gymnast's rings that come with the straps so you can hang them anywhere. You can do an entire body workout with them.

LOU: I do this whole Diamond Dallas Page thing. When he was leaving wrestling, he could barely move, and his doctor told him he'd be lucky if he could walk within the next year. He was freaking out, so he got really into yoga, and it loosened him up. I do it to strengthen my back. Craig liked to tell us that we were doing yoga wrong: "No, no, no. You've got to straighten this out. What are you doing?"

PETE: We'd go to our friend Franco's boxing gym in Berlin. He's like an absolute killer. He brings us to the gym, and I'm doing my thing. Craig hasn't worked out in weeks and he does squats, which is something you don't do on tour because then you can't walk. So Craig tries to work with the weight he was able to do five months earlier. I don't know if he was just trying to impress Franco, but he goes down once and throws out his back. So, of course the guys from Sick of It All are in this tough-guy gym and everybody's watching us, and all they hear is "Aggghhh," and Craig's lying on the floor in the middle of the gym. Franco runs over like, "What the fuck happened?!" He's like, "I used to do be able to do this and that," and now his back was completely fucked up. When I do stuff on tour, it's just to maintain. When I'm home from tour, I'm rebuilding and getting bigger. I take the first two days off, then I start going back to the gym in the morning for an hour or two. Now, I work out twice a day, and then I ride my sand bike.

LOU: I'll tell you one thing about our shows—I think us not taking everything so seriously rubs off on the crowd. It's always been this way. You know how everyone's all angry at hardcore and metal shows? Well, they are at our shows too, but we try to keep it fun, even though there's definitely a release of anger going on. We did our first show at the Limelight when *Scratch the Surface* was out, and the president of the label, Sylvia Rhone, was there. Her specialty was definitely more R&B than rock.

PETE: It was a fucking great show. Packed, crazy....

LOU: She brought the head of R&B. I can't remember his name, but he was a nice guy. We finished the show, and she came down to see us: she said, "My babies, my babies," and hugged us, which I thought was really weird, but she was always nice to us.

PETE: VERY weird!

LOU: I remember her hugging me and I'm thinking, *this is the woman who signed TLC and tells them what to do.* Then the guy from the R&B department comes over and he tells us, "You know, I go to all the label's shows no matter what the music is, whether I understand it or not. I've been to a bunch of Pantera shows. You have a similar vibe, but yet your crowd...when you guys play, everybody is smiling. It's not like that at the Pantera shows." He loved that we played super aggressive, angry music but that everybody had a smile on their face. I thought that was really cool. It's something we strive for, but it's probably why we were never as popular as Pantera; most people would rather hate than be happy.

2: JUST GOOFING AROUND IN THE VAN

LOU: At the beginning, we'd ride in the van with Rest in Pieces or the Token Entry guys or whoever. We did a few weekends with AF or Youth of Today, just goofing around in the van. The first time we ever did more than two or three days was that run with

Exodus. Then we went out with D.R.I., AF, Bad Brains, Biohazard, Sepultura.... I can't even remember what order they were in, but the one with D.R.I. was our first really long tour. We never even tried to do a budget, and we were getting paid fifty to seventy-five dollars a show, but the label did help us rent a van. Thankfully, our brother Steven was road-managing because we had no clue. There were some nights where he was able to talk the clubs out of taking a percentage of our merch. He'd say, "C'mon, look at these poor guys. They had to open the show...they're just a bunch of kids."

PETE: But that was ruined one night in Texas. My brother was in the office with the club manager, talking him out of taking a merch percentage. The guy was saying to Steve, "Man, your boys were so cool. They're a great band, really nice kids. I'm not going to take a percentage of your merch tonight." Now while this is going on, we were in the dressing room, and Richie, who loves to egg people on, (jokingly) asks Armand, "Hey, what are you going to do if the Nazis show up, man?" He finds a pipe somewhere and starts hitting this thing that turned out to be the water heater with it. He's smashing it and denting it. Thank God it didn't burst and burn us all to death. Steve comes in with the manager and asks, "What's that noise?" and there's us, laughing our fucking heads off as Richie's smashing this water heater. The guy's like, "What the fuck are you doing?!" It was a typical Sick of It All skit, which we ended up calling "The Nazis Are Coming." Back then, people would always be like, "Yo, Nazis are going to show up tonight." It was a problem then and we were just making fun of it.

LOU: They did show up a couple of times. It was in Kansas. They were quiet when we were playing, but when D.R.I. was on, they were throwing pennies at D.R.I. I remember a girl coming up and telling me, "Those guys are going to jump you when you go to your van." So, we were all backstage; I think it was six of us.

PETE: We were like, "Well, what the fuck are we going to do?" I remember Squirm looking at us and saying, "You know what we're going to do," and he flips a table over and breaks off the table leg. We're all like, "Yes!" So, we all break off table legs and kick open the door. We're yelling, "LET'S FUCKING GO!" We head back to where the van is, and we see all of them standing there. There's like ten of these Nazi jerkoffs, and they see that we're not scared. They all jump in one of their fucking moms' station wagons, and we were like, "Well, I guess that's what happens when the Nazis come."

Squirm Handling Nazis

LOU: Richie's antics, which quickly became OUR antics, got us through so much boredom. There are so many of these "concepts" that still live on today. We'd get to a hotel after driving all night, and everybody would just get to the room and get into bed. We had this one roadie who would go right in and just pass out. We would sneak into the room, get two guys on one side of his mattress and two on the other, and start lifting the mattress. Just before he'd start to realize what was going on, somebody would yell, "Trapped in a world!" and we'd flip the mattress over with him on it. Then you'd pile all the furniture in the room on top of the person: chairs, desks, the TV, everything. That's "Trapped in a World." Somewhere there's video of all of this.

PETE: Are you getting the picture of how fucking boring touring can be?

LOU: Even though we were treating it that way, the road isn't always the fun and games you hear about. I suppose it can be if you're making money.

PETE: When shit sucks, it sucks! You play in fucking Gainesville or someplace like that, and, you know, forty-two people show up. You still have to play. You can't be angry at those forty-two people because they actually came and you owe it to them. I mean, someone who goes to their day job knows they have a paycheck coming. I don't, and that's a really hard way to live. But I would never, ever change this for a job. Bring on the forty-two people and the hurting knees.

3. *JACKASS* BEFORE *JACKASS*

LOU: We were *Jackass* before there was *Jackass*.

PETE: Yeah, we definitely act like jackasses!

LOU: We just didn't have anybody to fucking bankroll us.

PETE: We had this VHS tape of those guys before they were famous. Someone gave it to us while we were on tour. I guess you could call it a "dare" demo tape they made. It made me think, *we do stupid shit like this all the time*. One time, Craig bought some mace, you know, pepper spray.

CRAIG SETARI: We had a day off at the Jersey Shore, and I had just finished doing laundry. I was headed back to our bus, which was parked by the beach. I had this mace which I had bought down south a week earlier. I was outside by the beach and decided that this would be a perfect place to shoot some mace into the wind and see how it works. I put my bag down and sprayed some in the air. Right at that second, the wind changes direction, and the mace blows right back into my face, right in my eyes. I can't see anything, and I stumble over to the boardwalk, where all of these homeless guys are. I was convinced they were going to rob me. Anyway, I make my way to the bus, and the guys are all cracking up about something. I'm like, "You're not going to believe what happened," and they're like, "Wait, wait..." They were watching a VHS tape of Jackass, and they say, "This idiot just maced himself!" I'm like, "No, you don't understand." Then they saw me struggling to keep my eyes open, tearing up, and realized that I'd just maced myself too. It was ridiculous. They were dying laughing at me.

PETE: It was me, Lou, I think Mei was there, and Armand, obviously. We're watching this tape and we're like, "Wow, these guys are fucking idiots. Who the fuck would mace themselves?" The second someone said that, Craig opened the door of the bus, "I just maced myself!" He was testing his mace. I was dying.

LOU: He's like a little kid. He got some mace and couldn't wait to use it. When he first got it, we were like, "What are you going to use it for? In case of emergency?"

PETE: What kind of an asshole would do that?

CRAIG SETARI: I took a week's worth of roasting over that, a week's worth of abuse.

PETE: So stupid. Then there was the time EK bleached his hair with some crap that made his head blow up like a balloon....

LOU: Oh my God, we had the day off in Texas on the New Titans tour, and EK went and bleached his hair. It was summer, and the hotel had a swimming pool.

PETE: He didn't just bleach it—he bleached it and relaxed it in one shot. All kinds of crazy chemicals at once.

LOU: He does all this shit and then goes night-swimming with this girl he'd met. Let's just say, we don't stay in the fucking Ritz-Carlton. It wasn't a really shitty hotel, but it had the kind of pool where you could smell the chlorine from twenty yards away. We're all going about our business, and he decided to stay on the bus because he wanted to be alone with the girl.

PETE: Out of nowhere, the girl frantically knocked on one of our doors and said, "You have to come. Something is wrong with your friend."

LOU: We were like, "What do you mean?" We go to the bus, and EK's sitting there. He looks up, and he had his shirt over his head, covering half his face. He pulls it off and his head was three times its normal size, all swollen up, so much that his ears were facing forward.

PETE: Yeah, his ears were bent. His eyes were completely closed. His lips were fucking huge.

LOU: It was really fucked up, and we were all freaking out. We go, "We've got to get you to a hospital. Let's go to the tour manager." Us and Napalm Death were sharing a sound guy, who was also the tour manager. We go knock on this guy's door, and he's sitting on his bed. We tell him, "We've got to take EK to the hospital." Pete says, "Show him EK." He takes off the towel. The tour manager yells, "Oh my God!" and jumps up off the bed. He picks up the phone, looks at EK, and puts it down again. He goes, "Oh my God," again, and picks up the phone again. He didn't know what to do and was panicking. EK looks at me, and goes, "Man, that looks fucked up," and we all began cracking up. After a minute or so, we're like, "All right, call an ambulance." They ended up taking him to the emergency room. They looked at him and told him what we already figured. He put too many damn chemicals on his head and then went swimming in a ton of chlorine. It all seeped into his pores, and his body was fighting it, trying to push it back out. So, it was creating pus. We were all sitting there, going, "Poor EK, poor EK," and Richie blurts out, "Poor EK??? Imagine the fucking girl he was with waking up and seeing that!"

PETE: Yeah, their date started out with her thinking, *Wow, this guy's really cute....*

LOU: And woke up next to someone who's got a fucking Mardi Gras head!

PETE: Like a cartoon.

EK: They gave me prednisone, and three or four days later, I was fine. But Sepultura was now dedicating songs to "Elvis the pumpkin head."

LOU: What sucks is we took two Polaroids, one of the front and another of the back of his head. They were so amazing, but we don't have them anymore. We had a roadie who was a klepto-collector. If he saw something he thought would be special in years to come, he would steal it. He stole Agnostic Front's banner at the end of one of their tours. I wish we had them for this book, because you cannot properly explain how crazy that guy's head looked.

PETE: In true Sick of It All fashion, it only took us a few minutes to start laughing about it. At first, we were like, "Oh my God," and then I couldn't breathe from laughing so hard. EK was like, "Yo, that's fucked up, man. That's really fucked up."

LOU: But then he looked at his own head and was like, "Man, I looked FUCKED UP!"

PETE: After all of this, the girl he'd been with kind of slipped out of the bus door unnoticed.

LOU: She probably ran to a clinic thinking, *is there some sort of venereal disease where your head explodes?!*

4. THEY'D POKE AT YOU AND POKE AT YOU UNTIL YOU'D SNAP

TOBY MORSE (H2O, SOIA ROAD CREW): Those guys were into this heavy New York style of ball-busting, which I'd never experienced before. They'd call me things like "The Girly-Man from Mary-Land." They'd just find your weakest point and try to break you to see if you could hang with them. They'd poke at you and poke at you until you'd snap. But the minute someone would fuck with you, they had your back big time. They broke me down and gave me a thick skin which I didn't have, and I thank them for that.

JOHN "DEVIL" TURNER (ALLEYWAY CREW): If you were watching the shit they would do to people, you'd think it was going to turn physical at any second, but it never did. As much as

I liked EK and Eddie when they were in the band, they were fragile and weren't a good fit at all. Sometimes it was just brutal.

(SICK OF IT) AL ALVAREZ (SOIA ROAD CREW): Oh man, it was nonstop! They would throw my cigarettes out of the van, my beer.... If you were being a prick, they'd just lock you out of your room at night. Getting into a van with them for nine hours at a time was torture. And while I caught plenty of it, I didn't get it nearly as bad as Toby or Tim Shaw or Max Capshaw. Max took THE most abuse of anyone. It was just dumb shit. It was harassment. Then throw Squirm or Anthony Comunale in the mix.... Forget it, you were done.

SQUIRM (SOIA ROAD CREW): They'd find someone's scab and just pick at it until it was a full-on explosion. I guess it came from growing up among brothers. It started straight out of the womb.

LOU: It's like this tough love, big brother thing.

PETE: It was hazing.

LOU: We got it from our older brothers and stuff, but I think it grew because of us being together as friends and as bandmates. I mean, back when Ritchie was in the band, we would always make stupid jokes about each other. Even if you were just speaking to someone and simply stumbled over a word, Armand would lose it hysterically laughing. It could be just the stupidest thing in the world, and I'd be like, "Really? That made you laugh that hard?" But then it just became the norm—anytime anybody stumbled over a word or slipped getting out of the van, it seemed like the funniest thing in the world to us. I kept asking myself, "Why do I think this is so funny?" I guess we were THAT bored.

PETE: I still laugh at that stuff. Even a little stumble by someone walking by and I crack up. Somebody will yell out, "Oh, first day with the new feet?" Stupid shit that you'd hear from your dad when you were a kid—that's what we do to each other.

LOU: As far as actual ball-busting goes, the direct attacks usually involve Craig and Armand.

PETE: They're very mean-spirited people.

CRAIG SETARI: Armand and I are like mortal enemies who sometimes wind up on the same side. It depends on the day. But as far as busting balls, dealing with Roger when I was in Agnostic Front, I became a samurai. He was a master manipulator. That was the highest level of nut-cracking you could ever experience. I mean, I could get you, but sometimes I'd have to take the shots for the room, if you know what I mean. Diffuse everything. I've got a good chin—I can take a beating—but a lot of times it provides entertainment for everybody.

LOU: I'm not saying me and Pete are innocent, but we are more so just devil's advocates. We are pretty good instigators though. Sometimes Armand will say something to attack Craig, and either Pete or I will quietly throw some ammo to Craig, like, "Oh yeah, well what about his fucking bald spot?" Then Craig will use our ammo like, "Yeah, you've got a fucking nest with an egg on the top of your head!"

PETE: Nowadays with cell phones, I'll be in the back of the van texting stuff to Craig to use against Armand or vice versa.

LOU: But when those two unite and attack the roadies or anybody else, it's pretty rough. That is the axis of evil!

PETE: That's big, big bully shit with those two.

LOU: They've almost sent some of our road crew packing because of their bullying. One of the roadies once got so upset he wanted to bolt from the tour. He was yelling in Craig's face, and Craig got angry back, and we had to step in and calm it down like, "You're both wrong here. Craig, you went too far, and you, our roadie, took it too personally." We try not to let it get that far. I mean, every few years there's a huge blowout because we've been together for so long. Whether it's within the band or with the crew or whoever, it's always resolved within twenty-four hours at the longest.

PETE: It's been happening again with Armand and Craig lately.

LOU: There was an incident on a recent tour, where I think alcohol had a little bit to play in it. There was a misunderstanding involving somebody eating Armand's personal food. Craig egged on one of the crew guys to eat it. I was in my bunk trying to sleep, and Armand starts foaming at the mouth, going crazy. Then Craig starts getting angry back, and they're cursing at each other: "Fuck you." "No, Fuck you!" Our road manager's like, "Let's just separate you two." I'm in my bunk going, "Man, I really should step in and tell Armand that he's wrong, but this is so much fun to listen to." The next day when Armand was not inebriated, he sat down and rationally talked to the roadie about what had happened and admitted, "I don't actually think Craig's in the wrong on this one as much as I hate to say that."

PETE: Then there was "Cheesegate." On the last Warped Tour, everyone would go to Walmart at night and buy food. Craig bought a packet of cheese, but the bus fridge was almost too packed. You couldn't open the fucking thing without everything falling out. We don't know if his cheese was lost in the back, or if someone mistakenly threw it away, but Craig pretty much attacked one of the road crew because he couldn't find it. He was screaming at this guy in his face to the point of spitting and pushing him. It was beyond a level we've ever seen. Armand looked at me like *I'm not going out there because he's going to attack me*. He wasn't thinking clearly, and this guy who worked for us was our friend. I don't give a fuck if it was over a million dollars, you shouldn't do that to somebody. You talk it out. I had to go out there, get in between them, and push Craig away from this guy.

LOU: This was all over CHEESE!

PETE: Craig kept saying that he was being disrespected, but it was about a packet of fucking cheese.

LOU: That stunk up the whole refrigerator!

PETE: Everyone on that bus had cheese he could have eaten. This fight happened with the entire Warped Tour watching. Very unprofessional. There were bands who wouldn't leave their vehicles because it sounded like there was an actual fight going on.

LOU: With all the ball-breaking, the minute you show even the littlest bit of weakness, you're done. We have a thing when you break somebody's balls to an extreme degree—we'll say "I cracked you," kinda like "I got you." Then you make an egg-cracking noise like "CCCKKK". You cracked. Whether you react or not, you're cracked. There are times when you don't want to hear it or really don't want it, but you're still getting attacked. You're still being harassed.

PETE: I'm always egging Craig on against Armand. At that moment when it's silent and Armand's fucking blitzed out of his mind, I'll be elbowing Craig, doing the "CCCKKK" really low, and then he'll go, "CCCKKK." Then Armand will be even more pissed, and while he won't show it, you can see that we've completely gotten to him. It spread all throughout hardcore. Everybody uses it now. Hoya uses it all the time. Over the years I've kind of gotten out of all the attacks and stuff. I stay quiet a lot because I don't want anyone attacking me. But if I have a great one-liner, I'll shoot it out there, and if it's about Craig, he'll laugh, and I'll be like, "All right, I had to do it." He'll tell me, "That was a good one. It was a good one." But it's not attacking him the way Armand does.

LOU: True, but those two are thick as thieves.

PETE: The guys in Rancid have always said, when they're looking to hire road crew, "If they've already worked for Sick of It All, they can definitely work for us. They've already passed the test." A lot of our roadies have gone on to work for them because, obviously, they pay a lot more than we do and are much friendlier. Those guys are like, "Hey, how are you doing today?" We're consumed with trying to get somebody to "CCCKKK" the second they wake up.

5. HEAD IN A BAG

LOU: Easily, the weirdest, most fucked-up thing that ever happened to us on tour happened outside some Masonic Temple in Pennsylvania. Naturally, Richie kept doing the pose from The Cult's *Sonic Temple* album all weekend because we were playing a MaSONIC Temple.

PETE: We've experienced some weird shit, but this incident takes the cake. It was after our set, and it was a shitty neighborhood. Most of the kids who came to the show had been dropped off by their parents, who were going to pick them up after the show.

LOU: The crowd was really young, actual kids that came to the show. We loaded everything out and were talking to some kid whose mom hadn't come to get him yet. He was stuck in this shitty neighborhood, so we told him to hang out with us. He said, "There's this weird guy over there standing on the corner." He was next to the venue holding a paper bag. The bottom of the bag was soaking wet, and he was talking to himself, standing pretty close to us. Being total idiots, we're like, "Hey, look at that guy, look at that guy!" pretty loudly. He started looking over at us and saying, "I'm going to fuck you up! I'm going to kill you like this guy!" Then he reaches into the paper bag and pulls out a human head! He was holding it by the hair. I was laughing because, as always, Richie was doing something stupid, but you know when you're a little kid and you think you've seen a ghost? You get that chill up your back. That's what I felt. We were like, "Oh shit!!!" We jumped into the van, but I was still laughing. Now the guy's coming towards the van. We're telling our road manager, who was behind the wheel, "Get the fuck out of here. GO, GO!" The guy's getting even closer to the van, and I was just laughing harder because I was so nervous. We took off up the block, and there was an empty parking lot there, with a ton of police cars at the corner. They were looking for a guy who had just killed somebody.

LOU: Before we met that kid, some guy and girl came around and said, "There's a guy over there, watch out. He said he's got a human head in that bag." We were like, "Whatever," and blew it off. Then he came around the corner and had something in his waist. You could see there was something in there that could have been a gun, but it might not have been. That's when he began talking. I don't remember him pulling the head out, but I remember him opening the bag and seeing a bunch of hair in his hand. That's when I was like, "Fuck this," and jumped in the van. We took off, and I remember all these cops pulling into the parking lot where the guy was and chasing him with their guns out. We were laughing and carrying on in the van; Richie was yelling stupid shit out the window. It was pure insanity. We wound up driving somewhere so that the kid we had with us could call his mom.

PETE: A year or so later, we ran into some kids who were at that show, and they told us that the guy was on the cover of the newspaper the next day and a body was found without a head.

LOU: I never found anything online about it, so who knows, but yeah...a head in a bag.

Head in a Bag by Lucy Koller

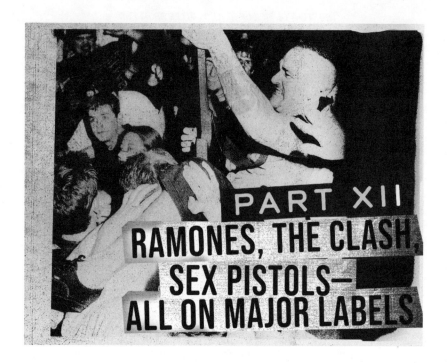

PART XII
RAMONES, THE CLASH,
SEX PISTOLS—
ALL ON MAJOR LABELS

1. SCRATCH THE SURFACE

LOU: After *Just Look Around* came out, we kept saying, "Hey, the album's out, why is there no advertising or promotion, even in New York?" It was super frustrating. There was this big show in New York at the Palladium that year with AF, Murphy's Law, Nuclear Assault, the Lunahchicks and a whole bunch of other bands. Pete and I actually made our own flyers and went out and glued them all over the city and handed them out near the Palladium. Not that it was beneath us to hand out flyers, but we didn't expect to HAVE to. In-Effect was gone, and the people left at Relativity were doing nothing. We thought, *we have to get OFF this label, they haven't done shit for us!* Then it got really confusing because we wanted to look for another label. Roadrunner was interested, and I remember Relativity being willing to sell them our contract for a reasonable amount. But then, as soon as East West raised their head up, Barry Kobrin, the president of the company, raised the price to something like $200,000, that son of a bitch!

PETE: There was this older rocker dude with poodle hair at East West named Derek Oliver. He had worked for Roadrunner years earlier.

LOU: Apparently, he had been coming to see us when we did the Amnesty International benefits and some other bigger shows. Plus, he saw that the scene was growing, and he liked us.

PETE: I remember talking to Steve Martin, who was our manager at the time, and he goes, "Wow, overnight the price for your contract jumped to $200,000 because East West is interested in you." We were like, "Can they actually do that?" Steve was like, "Yeah, Barry can do whatever he wants."

LOU: We hadn't been paid royalties yet for Just Look Around, so we went to get paid, and they told us, "Oh, no, no, no. We licensed the album rights to Roadrunner for Europe, you need to get paid directly by them." Just Look Around had done really well in Europe. It was everywhere We never saw a dime from it. What Relativity was telling us was total bullshit. THEY were supposed to pay us. We hired a lawyer, and he told us, "I don't know how much this is going to be worth, but I don't think it's going to be worth spending your money to fight."

PETE: The first tour we did in Europe on Just Look Around was good, and the second was amazing. There's footage of us playing the festivals that summer, and the whole place was bouncing, thousands of people bouncing up and down.

LOU: I knew hardcore kids were gonna talk shit if we decided to go to a major label. One of the reasons we went to Europe in the first place was because Marc said, "I want to bring you over here to prove to everyone that you're not sellouts." We hadn't even known that the We Stand Alone EP was being sold by Sony over there. So, we knew there might be a little backlash, but, growing up loving rock and metal, it seemed like a natural progression: going from doing it yourself to indie to major. Look at every classic punk band: Ramones, the Clash, Sex Pistols, all on major labels.

PETE: We wound up having an opportunity with East West, and we went for it. We just wanted the best chance to reach as many people as possible. We thought we deserved it.

LOU: When all was said and done, they let us write whatever we wanted. They never tried to turn us into Green Day or anything like that. We wrote our darkest album up to that point, *Scratch the Surface*. It was the first time we wrote all together: Craig, Armand, Pete, and me. And I don't care what Armand says, that was my favorite time writing an album. We spent all summer in Chinatown. We had a rehearsal space and had the whole spring and summer to just jam and make noise and laugh. The songs came from that process

PETE: What came out was just what we were writing. There was no pressure to be anything but Sick of It All. I remember doing a zillion interviews, and every interviewer kept asking, "Is that label trying to change you?" and I kept telling them, "They signed us to be who we are, why would they want to change what they just paid for?"

LOU: We had almost the whole record written, and Toby came to watch us rehearse and hear the songs. He looked at us and was like, "You guys are still playing fast stuff? Nobody likes that fast stuff anymore. They like that groove shit like Biohazard." We were like, "Fuck that! THIS is what WE play. We're not Biohazard!"

PETE: We decided to go back to Tom Soares because we trusted him. Tom was our guy. But the first day we got there, he said, "Everything has to change on this. This is a MAJOR label; this is the big time." The first mix of the record was way too slick and didn't sound like us. It wasn't mean, and the sounds weren't dirty.

LOU: If you listened to the old Twister Sister live stuff they'd broadcast on the radio, it was so aggressive and dirty. Then you bought *Under the Blade*, and it was good, but it was tame as fuck. That's what Tom had us sounding like. We were like, "We gotta dirty this up!"

PETE: Even Derek Oliver—he didn't say he didn't like it, but we knew he didn't like it. It just sounded safe.

LOU: So, we brought in Billy Anderson to dirty it up. He'd worked with the Melvins and L7. We needed someone to make it sound mean.

PETE: Billy and Tom worked on one song together, which I thought was the best track, "Consume." Unfortunately, I think Tom was kinda hurt that we brought Billy in.

LOU: We were trying to explain to him, "This is us, we gotta sound like us," and he thought he was gonna push us into the realm of Metallica. I mean, c'mon, we're not going to be played on the radio; that's just a fact.

PETE: When Billy came in, we were doing "Maladjusted" and were looking for an effect for Lou's voice. Tom was like, "We have this computer here, and there's thousands of different distortions. Let's start with number one." Billy goes, "How about we do this?" and just grabs this knob on the giant fucking board and turns it to ten, and we're like, "YEAH, it sounds great!"

LOU: He came in and gave it the grit it needed. I really think if Billy and Tom could have worked together from the beginning, it would have been an even better record. Lyrically, there's some introspective stuff on there. Armand really stepped up. That was the first time he had written some songs and we worked together. If I brought in lyrics, he'd go, "OK, let's try this or that." He had great melodies to put in there. Take the song "Scratch the Surface": I was sitting there thinking, *How am I going to approach this?* Armand said, "I'm gonna try it, all right?" I was totally fine with it, and the way he wrote the lyrics to that was amazing. Then with a song like "Step Down," I wrote the original lyrics, and Craig HATED them. So, Armand changed them, but not too much. One of the lines Craig was making fun of was actually left in there, and all of a sudden, Craig loved the song.

PETE: Craig was always self-conscious about how we were going to appear to his old band or his friends. It wasn't about our fans—it was about what Stigma was going to think or what Matt Henderson was going to think. But Craig has THAT sound!

LOU: I remember the guys in Anthrax and Rise Against saying that with every record they do they start with Craig's sound and build from there. I've heard this from them and their producers. Craig, like Armand, is just naturally musical. Together, they seemed to lock in from the get-go, but it's funny because they fight all the time. Craig's like, "You're going too fast here, or you're going too slow," and Armand's like, "No, YOU are!"

PETE: Instead of listening to each other, they'd rather make fun of each other. Even live, to this day, we play a song called "Uprising Nation." I start it and set the tempo. Armand keeps the timing with me, but then when he kicks in, he jumps up the tempo so fast like a blast beat. Craig starts yelling at Armand while we're playing, and Armand just looks the other way like, "Nope, that's the timing." It's so fast that I have a hard time playing the riff. He's a big fan of having his way.

LOU: Truthfully, they're a perfect fit, and it was a perfect time to have Craig in the band. Agnostic Front was miserable at that point. They hated each other. As soon as they broke up, Craig had two days at home, then left on tour with us.

PETE: When people heard the finished album, they were just like, "Holy shit!" There was no backlash, nothing.

LOU: When it came out in Europe, they had six-foot-high by six-foot-wide posters of the cover, which said, "The legends from New York City, Sick of It All's new album Scratch the Surface." They were all over Germany and elsewhere.

PETE: I remember Marc calling me, and he was ecstatic, all laughing and happy like a giddy little kid. He said, "You should see the fucking train stations when you pull in. The entire platform is filled with these giant Sick of It All dragon posters. It's the craziest thing I've ever seen!"

LOU: We gained so many new fans, and I think the influx of new blood really helped to quash all the bullshit from the naysayers. Not to discredit our older fans—they loved the fucking album—but people just didn't care about what label the album came out on. There'd be people who would be loyal to labels. How the fuck can you be loyal to a label?! Anyway, we decided to try something a little different with the videos we made for the album. "Scratch the Surface" was the first video, and it was gonna be a live thing, but we stressed to the director, "We don't want this to be everybody all pissed off and angry," so, at the beginning, he filmed all of our friends just hanging out and laughing, having a good time, talking. Then we go into the song, and the place goes crazy. That was perfect. With "Step Down," we took it further. I give credit for the whole concept to Pete because he brought up the idea of the line dance from *Soul Train*. We wanted to do a hardcore version of that. We added elements to try and make it more fun, like getting what looked like an old lady to crowd-surf, and Toby dressed up as the leather man from the Village People. He understood that we wanted to show humor.

PETE: I loved the idea of showing all the different dance styles and keeping the humor in it. It was a weird time for us and hardcore in New York. As we started getting bigger, more people started attaching themselves to us, and we had to shy away from a lot of them. We were playing the Limelight, and this guy we knew wanted to get in for free, and all this guy ever did was beat up our fans. Then, we would have to protect HIM from the security trying to toss him out. At that show, we said to him, "We're not letting you in tonight," and he said, "Yo, you're gonna play me like this?" and we said, "YES, that's the end."

LOU: He stood outside and talked shit about us the whole time.

PETE: After a while, we realized this was becoming our lives, so we weren't going to surround ourselves with people that might take it away from us. Fuck that!

LOU: When it stops being fun, why do it? I remember when Fat Mike's wife Erin saw us on MTV for the first time. All of NOFX was watching it, and she turned to Mike and said, "I thought NOFX was supposed to be funny. THESE guys are funny!"

PETE: Obviously we're funny; we were on *Beavis and Butt-Head*.

LOU: I was just glad they didn't tear us apart. They actually made their own dances up. Sometimes you'd see a band on there, and they'd be like, "Look at these losers," and they'd make fun of them.

PETE: That would have been pretty good too.

LOU: I loved when they'd show some metal band and say that one of the guys looks like an office worker. Beavis would be like,

"What's THAT guy doing in the band?" Butt-Head would say, "It's his cousin; he had to stand in for the real band guy 'cause he's with some chick."

PETE: That's when I knew Sick of It All was on its way to "making it"!

2. BUILT TO LAST

LOU: *Scratch the Surface* was so successful for us. We were touring the world, going everywhere: South America, Europe, Japan. We were just living on the road, and the label finally hit us up and said, "Hey guys, it's been two years. You're ready for another record." We were like, "Sure, we've got some ideas." They were really on us to get a producer for this one too. We wound up going with GGGarth Richardson, who had worked with bands like Rage Against the Machine, Red Hot Chili Peppers, L7, Alice Cooper.... Pretty sure his name is spelled with a triple "G" because he stutters a little.

PETE: We recorded at Sound City in California because that's where he recorded the first Rage Against the Machine album. He wanted to record us pretty much as a live band, which is the way he said Rage did it. His idea was to set Armand up in a big room with PA monitors so you could really feel the drums. I'm not trying to talk crazy shit, but GGGarth did 1 percent of the production work on that record. The engineer, Greg Fidelman, did 99 percent of it. He did all the recording, and he made sure everything was on time. He had great ideas. GGGarth would be sleeping in the other fucking room, then come in and be like, "That's out of tune," and leave again.

LOU: GGGarth was kind of phoning it in. He loved to talk. He would talk about when he recorded Rage or this band or that band. He'd barely be there most of the day. Then at night he'd go, "All right, I'm going to edit drum tracks." I'd be like, "Edit?" He'd say, "Yeah. I'm going to cut the best takes into the songs." I had to sit around a lot. I'm the singer, so I'm the last guy to do anything. He would do the drums, then the bass and guitar tracks. I finally start tracking a verse, and we get to where the second one should go, and I stop him: "Wait, stop, stop." He says, "Why? What's the matter?" I had to tell him that the whole second verse was missing. He's like, "What?" He had edited out the whole second verse of the song. He wasn't there when we were recording, so he didn't know how the song went.

PETE: This is back when you had to cut tape with the razor. It wasn't Pro Tools. We're like, "Fuck!" We had to rerecord the whole fucking thing.

LOU: Most of our recordings were fun, and for the most part, so was this one, but there was an unnecessary amount of stress with the rhythm section because there was a friggin' video game in the lobby. *Arkanoid*!

PETE: Armand and Craig are so fucking competitive. That's why whenever we're on tour and one of them wants to play foosball or a game of pool, I shut it down. Those two cannot just play for fun—they HAVE to win!

LOU: They're sick freaks. They're like, "My high scores are better than yours!" Then, when Armand would do drum tracks, Craig would unplug the machine so that the high scores would disappear, plug it back in, and go, "Look, I got the high score." Armand would be so concerned about beating Craig, he'd stop giving a shit about tracking drums. He would rush through a take just to play *Arkanoid*.

PETE: You know how when a band's recording they have a big piece of paper on the wall where you check off what's been recorded, song by song? Well, instead of Armand putting a check in the box to show what he'd finished, he would draw a rude picture of Craig's mother in the box. Then Craig started writing shit. Instead of recording the music, these fucking idiots couldn't stop attacking each other.

LOU: It did make for an amusing time though. We were in California. We lived in an apartment together for a month. We got rock as fuck! Toward the end, we reached out to the label to see if we could get a little more time with the record. Naturally, they said, "We don't have money for that. We MUST keep this on budget!" Then we get this call from them, just after we asked for more recording money, to tell us that the original KISS was getting back together, and they're doing three nights at Madison Square Garden. They told the promoter that they wanted all the hot, young New York City bands to open, and they asked for Sick of It All for one of the shows. The label people said, "Yeah, we'll fly you guys to New York, and then back to California to finish recording. We'll pay for the flights and everything." We looked at each other like, "You won't give us more money to finish this record the way we need to, but you're willing to fly us to New York to play for an audience that's going to boo us because we're not ROCK enough. We were like, "No, fuck that," so they took CIV instead. I know D Generation played one of the other nights.

PETE: We stayed out in California and finished the album. We did the mixing at Chick Corea's place, the jazz guy. Great studio.

LOU: Here's a typical Sick of It All moment: I'm not saying we are great musicians, but we have some really good songs. I know people who don't listen to hardcore who like us because we've got a little bit of melody. It's not just fast part into mosh part. You can sing along. But, of course, every time somebody who's an actual musician comes into our recording session, all they hear is the dumbest joke track we have. There's a joke song that Armand and Craig did as a hidden track at the end of the album. Of course, Chick Corea, a world-renowned fucking jazz musician, walks into the studio and hears this nonsense called "I Take Shits" blasting over the speakers. He says, "Sounds good, fellas," and walks out. We all just sat there with our heads in our hands like, that was *fucking Chick Corea*! He did get one of his conga players to play on the song "Jungle," so he couldn't have hated it too much.

PETE: When we came back to New York to master at the Hit Factory, Redman was sitting outside the studio when they were fucking playing "I Take Shits." This is the fucking song Redman gets to hear from us.

LOU: At the same session, Missy Elliott walks in and hears that fucking song. She's like, "Damn that's some crazy white boy shit." I'll tell you what though, that recording, that's when Craig and I stopped being friends. Before that, Craig would come to my apartment, we'd go to the gym together, we'd cook rice and beans together. We'd laugh our asses off and then we'd go our separate ways. We lived together while recording and I got stuck with Craig. The first day, there's fucking six big towels for us to use. He thinks it's like a hotel, so on the first day, he used all six towels. I was like, "What the fuck are you doing?" He's like, "Ah, housekeeping will give us more." I'm like, "It's not a hotel. These are supposed to last us until the end of the fucking week." It was like *The Odd Couple* times one hundred.

1. TOO PC FOR THEIR OWN GOOD
(924 Gilman Street)

PETE: Remember when we played Gilman in Berkeley?

LOU: Oh God! We were on tour with Bad Brains and had our own show at Gilman on a day off. I never do this, but for some reason, I said, "I'll go inside and see what's going on," to find out where we should load in. I never do that because I hate talking to people, but I'm like, "This place has a great reputation and is supposed to be super open-minded. It's gonna be great. I walk in and say, "Hey, I'm from Sick of It All, and we're wondering where we should load our gear in." The guy goes, "Listen: first of all, we know about you New York bands," and I ask, "What do you mean?" He says, "We've had guys like you here before. We don't want no trouble. We don't want no shit. You can load in over there." THAT was the greeting I got from this supposedly ultra-open-minded scene guy. We're getting ready to play, and I see they have this sign: STRICTLY NO STAGE DIVING. *I'm like, how is this a punk show?* But, whatever. I had to laugh because the club was already coming down hard as hell on us. They had all of these bouncers, and outside there were fucking NAZIS all over the place. Not guys you think might be Nazis, but full-on NAZIS! Skinheads with swastikas on their arms, standing outside their club. So we're playing our show, getting a great reaction, and there's this drunk woman standing in the crowd who keeps yelling at us and spitting on us. She's screaming, "Go home, you faggot straight edge! Go home!" I go, "First of all, we're not straight edge. I don't know why you keep saying that," and she's like, "Fuck you," and keeps spitting at us. Then, in the middle of a song, I hear this horrible noise, and I see her grabbing Pete's guitar strings. She's trying to disrupt our show because we're "faggot straight edge." She's not just drunk but high as a fucking kite!

PETE: Turns out, she was the head bouncer's girlfriend. Gilman's got a reputation for being super PC, but the bouncer's girlfriend keeps yelling "faggot" at us.

LOU: So, she's grabbing Pete's strings, and he pushes her off with his foot. He didn't kick her, just shoved her with his foot while trying to play. The bouncers are standing in front of the stage to stop stage diving because, you know, us "New York bands," but it took this guy a good five minutes to notice that his girlfriend was lying on the floor, pretending to be hurt. He finally turns around and starts screaming until the other bouncers come, THEN he tries to attack us. I'm yelling at him over the microphone, "You should have fucking stopped her from spitting at us." Now there's chaos going on. The other bouncers are trying to pull him away, people are screaming, and then, out of nowhere, the side door kicks open, and the NAZIS start running around, Sieg-Heiling. We're just like, "What the fuck is going on?!" You know who got the Nazis out? Us and our fans! Not the people at the club. Fast-forward a few years later, and we were playing this festival in Sweden, when Green Day had just broken big. We walk up to do our set, and all of the Green Day guys are there. Billie Joe comes up to me and says, "Man, I haven't seen you guys since you played Gilman." I go, "Holy shit, you saw that? You saw when that girl got knocked on her ass?" And he says, "Yeah, she was a good friend of mine, but she was a junkie." When we first started going to Europe, there was a fanzine that was the equivalent of *Maximum RockNRoll* called *ZAP*, and they did an exposé on Gilman. This guy went and lived in the Bay Area for a month and went to all these shows. He wound up writing, "For such a supposedly PC place, it's absolutely not." He wrote this whole article about how un-PC and closed-minded many of the people there were.

PETE: And New York has a bad rep.

LOU: It's like when *Maximum RockNRoll* kept attacking Agnostic Front, accusing them of being Nazis. They reviewed our first album, and they just panned it: "It's a bunch of guys playing metal disguised as punk and hardcore." If you listen to that album now compared to what people call hardcore these days, it's a fucking punk album! It kind of hurt because, growing up in the punk scene, you're like, "I can't wait for *Maximum RockNRoll* to hear our stuff," and they just ripped us like that. Fucking horrible.

2. DROWNING IN GERMANY

PETE: We were playing a festival somewhere in Germany. It was us, NOFX, CIV, H2O, and a bunch of others. Sick of It All, H2O, and CIV were all touring together. It was in a big field, and behind the stage there was a huge lake. It was normally a vacation spot with a little beach and all that shit, and in the middle of the lake was one of those floating docks. We all said, "Hey, let's go swim out there," but Craig and Armand weren't awake yet, so it was just me, Lou, and the guys from CIV and H2O. Everyone took off swimming, and I looked over at Lou, who was kind of behind me, and I saw that he wasn't fairing very well.

LOU: I was struggling big time.

PETE: I don't know if you remember, but I said, "Lou, you okay? Fuck this, let's go back." You said, "I can't make it." I had no idea what was wrong.

LOU: It had been like a thousand degrees in the bus the night before, so Armand, Craig, the roadies, and I stayed up most of the night, got maybe two hours of sleep. Somehow Pete slept. My arms and legs were just dying and giving out.

PETE: So I said, "Come over here and grab onto me, and we'll go back to where our feet can touch the bottom." Lou came towards me, kind of panicked. We were facing each other, and I was floating. You put both of your hands on my shoulders and almost went down, so you pushed off of me to get back up and get air, and you pushed me all the way down under the water.

LOU: Yeah, now I'm drowning my brother too.

PETE: I sucked in an entire mouthful of water. I made it back to the top, but I was choking. There's water in my lungs, and I'm trying to breathe. I'm trying to keep myself up and keep Lou up, so I'm using one hand and both legs, and there's no oxygen. So, we see Craig coming down to the lake. The buses were parked right at the edge. We start yelling to Craig, "Come here. Come here." Of course, he thought we were fucking with him, so he just waved to us like, "Fuck you, forget it." It took him a second, but he realized we were really in trouble, so he started running, jumped into the water, and swam toward us. We were pretty far out. Craig was almost to us, so I said, "Lou, I'm going to push you that way. I have to get out," because my legs were cramping. There was no oxygen anywhere in my body, so I shoved Lou towards Craig, and I went underwater. I swam as hard as I could, with no oxygen, underwater. I remember straightening myself out, just so I could touch the ground. Only the tips of my toes were touching the ground, and my head was just above the water. I started to breathe, and I walked my way to the shore. I didn't even see Lou or Craig get out of the water.

LOU: Normally, I'm not a bad swimmer, but as soon as we got to that point, my legs were killing me, and my arms felt like they weighed a ton. I couldn't move. But Craig swam out and dragged me back to the beach. I was so weak and shaking, I could barely walk. I climbed onto the bus and just collapsed in my bunk, passed out. I woke up hours later. Fat Mike loves bringing it up every time I see him: "Remember when Craig saved your life?"

PETE: Every time I think of this, it still scares me. That could have been the end of Lou.

LOU: Hey, it was at the height of Sick of It All, so it would have been great. We could have just ended the story there.

3. FUCKIN' BUS DRIVERS

PETE: Fuckin' bus drivers.... We were playing Resurrection in Spain. The show was way out on the coast, so you had to fly into a major city and then vans would take you out to the festival site.

LOU: It was probably a three-hour drive.

PETE: It was fucking long. Anyway, it was three in the morning, and we had to get to the airport by six. We get in the van, and we're saying to the promoter, "This guy better not have been driving all day long," because we knew he must have been. He had been picking bands up since six a.m. the day before and driving them to the festival. Mei was with us and speaks Spanish, so we went up to the guy, and she asked, "Hey, have you been working all day?" and he's like, "Yeah." She goes, "Oh, maybe you should take a rest before driving." He started in with this whole machismo bullshit: "I don't need any rest. I don't need any coffee." He was a total dick. So, we all get in the van, and we're driving along, and everyone starts dozing off. I was half asleep with Mei sleeping on me. Suddenly, I hear Craig screaming. We all open our eyes, and we're headed towards the side of a bridge. It's over a ravine, so Craig screams, and the guy wakes up and throws the van to the left. Thank God there was nothing next to us. We were skidding all over the road, and finally, the guy pulls us straight. We started fucking screaming at the guy and made him pull over at the next truck stop. I went in and bought him a Red Bull. Someone went in and bought him a shot of espresso. He was going to get his ass kicked, but then Mei kind of calmed everyone down. This dick was too macho to say that he was wrong. Couldn't admit his mistake of almost killing everybody in the van. Craig saved us. He was about to fall asleep, but just before, he looked out the window and thought, *we're getting really close to those guardrails*.

LOU: The crazy thing is that we found out Madball had the same guy. He did the same fucking thing to them. We told our friend who set up the whole thing, "If one of your guys is in that position, he has to tell you, 'I can't do it, I'm way too tired.'" You've got to get another driver.

PETE: Not kidding, I think everyone who comes to our shows in Spain is on coke or speed or something.

LOU: We had this German bus driver who was great. He was a total eighties rock guy. Had a mullet, wore sleeveless shirts, and had a huge gut. He would introduce himself to women as if he was James Bond. His name was friggin' "Hammerhead." He'd say, "My name is Head...Hammerhead...Licensed to fuck!" I swear, "Licensed to fuck," and we're like, "You're the grossest man we've ever seen." But he was that old-school bus driver who would say things like "I got a long haul tonight" and go do a bunch of coke and speed. We were headed to a show in Germany and had to get on the ferry with the bus. So, we're all off the bus, on the ferry hanging out. Hammerhead's walking around, and Marc tells him, "You should probably be sleeping. You should be resting." Hammerhead says, "No, I'm good, don't worry." We all get back on the bus, and we're dead-tired. Marc goes, "Okay, it's four hours to the festival. We'll make it there and wake up in time to play." The bus gets off the ferry, and we all pass out. Then, for what seemed like a few minutes, the bus wasn't moving anymore. Marc sticks his head out of his bunk out and asks, "Are we at the festival already?" He looks at his watch and goes, "There's no way we could be at the festival yet," so he gets up, and I get up with him. It was a double-decker bus, and we were upstairs. We walk forward and see that we're stopped on the side of the highway. Marc's like, "Shit, did we break down?" We go downstairs where Hammerhead is passed out over the steering wheel, drooling, because his body crashed from all this speed that he did. He couldn't sleep on the ferry because he was so high, and when he got off, he didn't have any more speed and just passed out. Marc just grabbed him and yelled at him. Shook him. We ran and got

Red Bulls, and then we had to call the festival and tell them we were going to be late.

PETE: Luckily, when we showed up, the way the stages were set up, there was a two-hour gap between bands, so we had two hours until we went on. We were on the second-biggest stage with Prodigy, and the main stage had The Cure and I think Aerosmith. They set the stages up so that you could see the bands playing on both.

LOU: We made it there an hour late, and all I remember is the stage manager walking up to us and saying, "I had to go onstage and tell seven thousand people that you were going to be late. It was not fun. You have to hurry." Our roadies looked at us and went, "Don't worry." All of us grabbed equipment, and we helped the loaders and the roadies get our gear onto the stage. We ran and got ready, and within ten minutes, we squeezed in a line check, and the stage manager was like, "I have never seen a band and crew move that fast. Thank you so much." He was so happy.

PETE: That was a great show too.

LOU: Yeah, it was fantastic.

4. BRUSHES WITH GREATNESS

PETE: We were backstage at one of the first festivals we ever played. It was in Denmark. We didn't have much room back there, and suddenly, one of Henry Rollins's guys comes through and says, "You guys need to get out of the walkway. Henry is going to walk by." Marc was with us and was like, "Fuck you." We had nowhere to go, so we just sat there, and when Henry walked by, he was like, "Hey, guys. What's up?" It was no big deal.

LOU: It wasn't him, it was his people, but there are so many cool artists who hire people to be assholes on their behalf, so they don't look like assholes themselves.

PETE: Later that same day, we're hanging out, and Iggy Pop walks by. We're all like, "Holy shit, that's Iggy Pop." He comes over to me and says, "Hey man, how are you doing? You live in my neighborhood." And I'm like, "Yeah, I live down the block." He says, "Great to see you, man," and then walks away.

LOU: His wife came out first and said to you, "I know you." Then Iggy came out.

PETE: I was like, "Yeah, Iggy Pop just said hi to me. I'm so cool!" I remember being at catering, somewhere in Austria. The bill was Judas Priest, Slipknot, us, and a bunch of other bands. I saw K.K. Downing from Judas Priest sitting there eating, so I got my food and was like, "Oh, there's a seat right over here," and I sat down next to him. He's one of my heroes, and he was super cool.

LOU: Remember when we hung out, talking to him, Glenn Tipton, and Ian Hill? Ian Hill was the coolest of all of them. He was shooting the shit with us, and then later that night, Clown from Slipknot came into our dressing room and then one of the guys from Leftover Crack. He was plastered. It's so weird at those festivals, you get this mix of people hanging out. You know, Priest, Slipknot, Sick of It All, and fucking Leftover Crack! If you had told me any of this in advance, I would have told you it's a joke. There are people I wish we could sit down and hang out with at catering. Lemmy would have been number one.

PETE: I'd have Jerry Seinfeld there.

LOU: Joan Jett. I guess we're talking dead OR alive, so Rodney Dangerfield. Eddie Murphy. Dave Chappelle. Those are guys who come off the top of my head.

PETE: Redd Foxx!

LOU: Oh my God, when Fred and Esther are going at it on Sanford and Son, their insults are fucking brutal!

PETE: Fred goes, "All these people running around saying, 'Black is beautiful,' then they see you, and they're like, 'Well, wait a minute. I don't know.'"

LOU: That album *You Gotta Wash Your Ass*.... On the cover he's standing there grossed out by the smell of a donkey....

PETE: Fucking hilarious!

LOU: Richard Pryor, George Carlin. We'd have to have Vinnie Stigma and Jimmy from Murphy's Law too. If Seinfeld is there, he'd be like, "Why don't these guys have a show?"

PETE: If there was anyone I'd see at catering who'd make me get up right away and switch tables, it would be Craig Setari. Just kidding.

LOU: Oh, I'd definitely want Dee Snider there because he's fucking hilarious!

PETE: We had that whole experience with Twisted Sister at Graspop a few years ago.

LOU: So many people don't really understand Twisted Sister because most grew up seeing them on MTV. They were an incredible, balls-out rock-and-roll band. Those records are NOTHING compared to the way they are live.

PETE: Sometimes we talk about our love for Twisted Sister, and people just look at us all weird. They'll ask, "You like "We're Not Gonna Take It?" We're like, "Yeah, but you know, their other stuff is way better." They were the biggest unsigned band in New York for years. They worked harder than anybody and everybody.

LOU: I got to see that famous Palladium show they did. They sold the place out, like three thousand tickets, without a record deal. My best friend's older brother was a Twisted Sister freak and knew about the show. It was like ten bucks, so I asked my mom for ten dollars. I told her that we were going with my best friend's older brother, so she said, "Okay." Decades later, they're doing their farewell tour, and we wound up on the same festival bill as them. They were playing on what was supposed to be our day off, but someone pulled out and the festival asked us to play as "special guests." We had been all psyched about our day off because we were going to get to watch Black Sabbath at another festival, but about two weeks before, we got a message from our booking agent saying they want us to play Graspop. We were like, "Shit. Okay, who's playing that day?" Our agent tells us it's Iron Maiden and Twisted Sister. We said, "We're fucking doing it!" Instead of seeing Black Sabbath, we went and played.

PETE: I don't really remember how I met him, but I connected with Twisted Sister's risk-management guy, a financial guy. He was hanging out with them on the road. They were about to go on, and I texted him asking where he was. He said, "I'm on the side of the stage, just come up." So, they let me and Lou stand on the side of the stage.

LOU: We had all been on the bus. Pete and I were like, "Shit, Twisted Sister's going on." Everybody wanted to see them, but everybody else was drinking, and we were like, "Yeah, yeah—we'll be up there in a minute," but Pete and I ran over there right away.

PETE: So, we get up there, and the guy introduces us to their stage manager, and she says, "Come stand over here." She takes us to the left side of the stage, Mark "the Animal" Mendoza's side.

LOU: We were next to Jay Jay French's wife and daughter.

PETE: They're about to go on; the AC/DC "Long Way to the Top" intro is playing, and Lou and I are like little kids, super psyched.

They came out and just started tearing it up. We knew every single song and sang every song. We were literally screaming along on the side of the stage. They had to be thinking, w*ho the fuck are those guys over there?* But, at some point, Dee Snider noticed us. He actually seemed to know who we were.

LOU: It was during one of the guitar solos, when he runs behind the amps to grab a drink of water. He ran right to Pete and said, "You're in Sick of It All, right?" Pete went, "Yeah," and Dee went, "All right!" Then he ran and did one of his crazy Dee Snider kicks. During the next solo, same thing. He came over to Pete again, and Pete said, "This is my brother Lou, the singer."

PETE: I didn't just say "Yeah" when he asked me if I was in Sick of It All; I grabbed him by the collar and screamed, "FUCK YEAH," in his face! I was so excited. It was this guy who was an idol of mine, and now he knows me and Lou.

LOU: Dee goes back out, and all of a sudden, Armand and Craig show up. I'm like, "Where were you guys?" I'd been texting them, letting them know we got a great spot. They had been on the other side of the stage behind the monitor guy. Armand, all jealous, says, "I thought we had a good spot too, but Dee Snider's not coming over there to say hello to US." It was funny because, between songs, you could see Mark Mendoza walk over to Dee and ask him who we were, and then he nodded his head towards us. Mark came over, and out of everybody, he went right to Craig. He somehow sensed Craig was the bass player and said to him, "That's how you do it, motherfucker," and Craig yelled back, "Bass mafia!" It was just hilarious. It was so much fun because, like Pete said, we were there screaming and singing all the words. Jay Jay French's wife was filming the show and turned and filmed all of us going crazy on the side. Then Dee said to the crowd, "This is for the hardcore," and he dedicated "Under the Blade" to us. Then, during "S.M.F.," they have the lyrics "If sick is what they call us, then sick is what we'll be." Dee turned and pointed at all of us when he said, "Then sick is what we'll be." It was just a really cool moment. It was like a childhood dream come true. Another great one was with Joe Strummer.

PETE: It was in Italy in 1999.

LOU: The festival doesn't exist anymore—it was just something a promoter was trying out—but it was us, tThe Offspring, NOFX, the Bouncing Souls, and Joe Strummer and the Mescaleros.

LOU: There was a guy who roadied for The Offspring, and he told Joe Strummer, "You've got to see Sick of It All." We played our set and had a really good show. We're coming off the stage, and there's Joe Strummer standing there, and he's clapping. He says, "You guys are fucking brilliant. Fucking amazing." I'm like, "Holy shit, Joe Strummer just said we were amazing." Luckily Pete had the sense to ask if we could take a picture with him. Armand and Craig, of course, had already run off the stage and disappeared, otherwise they would have been in this incredible photo too.

PETE: The roadie guy told us that Joe Strummer never hangs around during or after the shows. He wanted to go straight to the hotel, but they told him he should stay to watch us, and he did.

LOU: This didn't happen at one of our own shows, but we went to see Rocket from the Crypt and The Get Up Kids at Irving Plaza. I'm in the balcony watching The Get Up Kids, and they had just come off the stage. Right before they came over to talk, the bouncers came and pushed everybody aside. They made a wall around a table, and in walks fucking Jimmy Page and Robert Plant. I said to the guys in The Get Up Kids, "Do you see who's over there? Fucking Robert Plant and Jimmy Page," and the guy goes, "Who cares? I'm talking to Lou from Sick of It All." I started laughing and said, "You've got some weird fucking perspective, kid."

5. SEPTEMBER 11, 2001

PETE: We were touring in Japan when it happened.

LOU: We had a great show in Tokyo, our first of two nights there, and we went to the hotel. We were in the lobby and said, "We'll all meet in the lobby in twenty minutes and go out to eat." It was us and all of AFI. We went up to our rooms, turned on the TV, and saw that image of the top of the twin towers burning. I was like, "What the fuck?!" I changed the channel and saw it again. I was like, "What the hell is going on?" I remember all of us running into the hotel hallway trying to figure out what the fuck was going on.

PETE: When we were leaving the show, the lady who was in charge of taking us around had a cell phone. She said, "There was some sort of accident in Manhattan. A plane hit the twin towers." She made it seem as if a little Cessna went off course and had an accident. I was like, "Oh, that's fucked up." Then, when we got into the rooms, I think the second plane had just hit, and you heard everyone in the hallway. We all tried to call our parents. It took twenty-four hours to get through. My dad was working right in that area. He had to walk from the twin towers all the way to the 59th Street Bridge. My dad doesn't walk anywhere. He had to walk to and across the bridge and get back home from there.

LOU: Our dad and Armand's dad both worked right across the street from the towers.

PETE: I wasn't able to get back until two days after the tour ended because planes weren't allowed to fly into the United States yet. When I got off the plane, a soldier said, "Welcome home." I was just like, "Holy fucking shit!" Until I got back to the U.S., I couldn't truly realize what was going on here. I had been six thousand miles away.

LOU: I actually stayed in Japan another five days, and when we landed, there were still military people all over the airport. The guys from AFI weren't allowed to come back to the U.S. as early as us because they weren't booked on a U.S.-owned airline. We were on American Airlines, and the only people on the plane were American citizens. The plane was actually pretty fucking empty.

PETE: They kept telling us, "No, you can't fly, you can't fly to New York. We can fly you to Michigan, and you can get a car, or we can try to get you home from there." By the time we got to the airport, we were told, "You're going to be one of the first flights back into New York from Japan. You're going straight to JFK." Coming in to land, you saw everything still smoldering. I was living on the Lower East Side, so Mei was there when it happened. She said she woke up, tried to listen to the radio, and all there was was static. She said she looked out the window and it looked like a zombie movie: thousands of people walking uptown covered in white powdery shit. As soon as I got home, we went down there to see if there was anything we could do. The police were like, "There are so many volunteers already, there's really nothing you guys can do, but thank you very much." People may remember that there was a lady who pretty much started the whole "Thank you" sign thing along the route to the towers. She had a giant sign that said "Thank you." After a few days, there were thousands of people there with signs, and Mei was there too. The lady turned to Mei and said, "I have to get home," and gave Mei her sign. A photo of Mei holding the sign wound up in Life magazine. She happens to be wearing a Sick of It All shirt.

LOU: A couple of years later, we were all hanging out in front of your apartment, and there was that big power outage. Hundreds of people were walking down the street asking, "Do you think it's the terrorists again?" It was still fresh in everybody's minds.

PETE: Then a couple of months later, maybe a year later, there was a plane that crashed taking off from JFK. Anytime something unrelated happened, everyone assumed it was a terrorist attack. On the news, for months, they kept saying that the fires were out, but every evening, the winds would change, and you could see the smoke coming from Battery Park all the way up to the Lower East Side. It was fucking gross, and it was just super sad walking around and seeing all the flyers with missing people on them. That was absolutely heartbreaking.

LOU: After the 11th, we still had shows in Japan over the next few days. All of the handlers and Japanese crew kept asking, "Is there anything we can do to make it better for you guys?" They were very concerned about us. We were all freaking out, trying to call our families. We thought, do we just sit here in the hotel and be depressed, or do we play the shows? We decided to play the shows. It was a good distraction from all the news back home. When they asked, "What can we do to make it better?" we said, "Take all the barricades away." That was the only thing we could think of. It did help because people went wild, and it got us in a better mood. But, as soon as we were done, we were back in the hotel talking to our families and calling everybody we knew.

PETE: I remember finally getting through to my mom. There was fear in her voice. I asked, "Is everything okay?" My dad was in the background talking, and you could hear fighter jets flying over Queens. I was like, "Fuck, I can't wait to get home," to be able to see them and just try to help or whatever.

LOU: And to think she had been a child in France when the Nazis invaded. It's always fresh in her mind, having lived through wartime. What's crazy is that, if you go back to the *Yours Truly* album, we did an animated video for the song "District." This is a year before 9/11 happened, before the towers fell. The artist came up with this concept of demons as real people, and the screen would flash, showing who was and wasn't a demon. At the end of the video, when the music starts to climax and really kick in, it shows the twin towers collapsing, and the dragon rises from under the towers. About two months after getting home, I got a call from the director and he was like, "So, the towers, man, how fucked up is that? You know, in the video." I was like, "Holy shit!" That freaked me out. I had completely forgotten about that part of the video. Now, people ask, "How come you don't play 'District?' " and it's because I think of the video and get all nervous. I don't want ANYONE to think we're condoning or making light of the attacks. We made the video a year before it happened, but people are crazy.

PETE: Well, we could have been Slayer and released an album called *God Hates Us All* on the day it happened.

LOU: Yeah, that was fucking crazy! There was that rap group The Coup, who had an album cover with a photo of themselves and the towers blowing up behind them, but they created the cover before it happened. They decided to hold back the album so they could change the cover. Not too long after all of this, Dropkick Murphys asked us to go on tour with them, and it was intended to try to bring some normalcy back. We had to think about it, but we went up there every night and did "Injustice System." We never hid our lyrics from the crowd, and we didn't feel anyone got angry because of what we were saying. It really wasn't until social media became prominent years later that we'd post something and hear things like, "Oh, come on with your leftist, fucking bleeding-heart bullshit." Most bands just promote themselves on there, and I'm not saying that we don't. We do, but we do shit for other people too, like a podcast or an important show. Recently, I posted something about a benefit for immigrants, and it was mostly immigrant bands playing. It was about kids who grew up here but had come from different countries, American citizens with backgrounds from elsewhere. I couldn't believe some of the fucking comments on there: "So, you're supporting illegal alien bands now?" I'm like, "Um, I don't think if they were illegal aliens they would be advertising their show." How fucking crazy is that? People can be assholes.

PETE: Everybody LOVES to hide behind that keyboard. They would never say anything like that to any person standing in front of them.

LOU: I understand if you have an opinion, and you really, really believe there's a big fucking immigration problem here, but why attack a band for supporting another person's rights?

PETE: The person who posted that comment was probably eating a sandwich, saw our post, put his or her sandwich down, wrote the dumb comment, and went out to walk the dog. It doesn't truly mean anything to them. It's just bullshit thrown out there in a split second. They just love that the guy from Sick of It All is writing back all mad.

LOU: There was an article recently about how they want to start teaching the history of the gay rights movement along with the civil rights movement in schools. I couldn't believe the number of people from the hardcore scene, and even just people I've known my whole life, who said shit like, "Great, they're going to start teaching gay history. What about straight history?" I'm like, "Jeez, they teach that all the time." They don't understand the struggle that community has had to go through. I always like the argument "It's against the Bible." I'm like, "Do you follow everything in the Bible? If you did, you'd be wearing a bonnet like they did on *Little House on the Prairie*." Then there's "And man shall not lie with man." Yeah, but it also says, "And women shall cover their heads when in public." It also says, "On Sunday, you cannot touch the skin of a pig," which is weird because when is American football played? Mostly on Sundays with a pigskin! How did they predict that? I don't know.

PETE: I guess God is against football!

LOU: And women's hair for whatever reason. People are ridiculous. On our next tour of Europe, after 9/11, we were somewhere in Germany, and this guy from the club came in with a shirt that had a plane made out of the Nike symbol flying towards the twin towers. Of course, it said, "Just Do It." We're not rah-rah America guys, but all of us looked up and went, "Take that fucking shirt off. Get the fuck out of here with that shirt!" He was like, "It's just a shirt," and we were like, "It's not funny." I get the whole big corporation Nike thing but still, people died; it was horrible.

PETE: No matter who was behind it, innocent people died. Moms and dads with kids died.

LOU: When we were on that Dropkicks tour, we were in Lawrence, Kansas, getting breakfast at a diner. The waitress asks, "Where are you from?" We go, "New York," and she says, "It's a shame what happened to the people in New York." I had to remind her, "What happened in New York happened to all of us.

1. IF YOU HAD BEEN WITH FAT,
YOU'D ALL OWN YOUR OWN HOMES BY NOW

LOU: One thing about being on a major label is, every month, the person in charge of your band disappears. We weren't happy because the people who were behind us for Scratch the Surface, who had pushed it and made us successful in Europe, were gone. There was always someone new, and after a while, they didn't even know we were on the label because we would be touring so much. In Europe, the guy who took over for us used to be the EDM guy. He tells us, "I don't know what to do with a rock band. We just put out 12-inch singles for the music I work with." In America, we were asked to do Warped Tour, so we sat down with Steve who was managing us at the time. He's like, "If you guys really want to get off the label, we need to make you look undesirable." So, we came up with the idea to take as much tour support as we could, so it looked like we were in debt with the label. We got a really nice tour bus, plenty of per diem; it was great. The funny thing is, even after all that, they wanted to sit down with us and talk about doing another record. We only had a two-record deal. Who knows what would've happened? I mean, I don't think we would've written *Call to Arms* the way we did. We just got lost in that major label shuffle. For instance, we toured Australia, and the stores would have all of our indie-label records. They had the Revelation stuff, the In-Effect and Relativity stuff, but they didn't have *Scratch the Surface or Built to Last*.

PETE: They even had *Live in a World Full of Hate* on Lost and Found Records.

LOU: We were like, "Why the fuck are we in Australia, and all they have are our older records?" People told us, "Well, you're on EMI here, and EMI only ships to chains. They don't ship to independent stores here." That's when we became really disenchanted with being on a major label because we knew that if they could have found a balance between the chains and the mom and pop stores, it could have kept Sick of It All alive.

PETE: We'd been hanging out in Steve Martin's office, and Dexter from The Offspring was there. They were HUGE at that time. He wanted to sign us to his label, Nitro. When we would play with The Offspring at the festivals in Europe, he would come watch us, him and Noodles.

LOU: He is a very nice guy and said, "We have AFI, and it'd be great to have you guys." He was really into the band. So, he sends an offer, and it was really good, especially for an indie. Then Fat Mike sent in an offer for us to be on Fat Wreck Chords. Steve was like, "Holy shit! Mike, what are you doing?" because the offer was way better than we expected. Mike says, "I love these guys. I love the band, and they're my friends, so I want to help my friends." Steve told him, "Okay, I'm going to talk to the guys. Let's see what happens." A few hours later, Mike sent in another bunch of numbers, which were insane. Basically, Dexter sent an offer for X amount, and Fat

Mike sent the biggest X's we'd ever seen. Mike said, "I want to help the bands I believe in," and he saw that we'll tour no matter what, whether it's to play to two people or twenty thousand.

PETE: He did his research and told us, "These are the numbers you did on *Scratch the Surface* and *Built to Last*. If you had been with Fat, you'd all own your own homes by now with the royalty rate I'm giving you." Then, Epitaph wanted to make us an offer. They had a guy who, I guess, used to work at some major label, and he took us out to lunch. It was right out of a movie. He was sitting there, stuffing his face and telling us, "Epitaph is the biggest punk label around, so how can we be the biggest punk label without the biggest hardcore punk band in the world?"

LOU: There was food flying out of his face, and of course, Armand and Steve were just looking at each other, not listening to a fucking word the guy said. They were ready to burst out in laughter. We thought we were meeting with a super cool indie, not some Hollywood nonsense.

PETE: Of course, all of our hardcore friends kept telling us, "You should sign to Victory." Tony Victory was like, "I really want you guys," so when we got the offer from Mike, Tony looked at the royalty rate Mike offered and said, "Good fucking luck to Mike trying to make any money off of you guys." That's what he said. In the end, we got more shit for signing to Fat than we did signing to a major because we didn't sign with some East Coast hardcore label. There was no East Coast hardcore label at the time. They all wanted us to sign to Victory. Thank God we didn't because look at all those bands now. They all have lawsuits against Tony.

LOU: I don't even really know how Mike knew we were free and looking for a new label. We definitely didn't call him, but, forever, when we'd see him, jokingly we'd say, "Hey, want to sign Sick of It All?"

PETE: The whole thing happened through friendship, running into each other on the road and at festivals. The first time we ever met him was at Some Records. It was the day of the Cro-Mags' record release show at CBGB, and NOFX was playing somewhere else in the city that day. Mike says, "Hey, we're playing down at..." wherever it was. I go, "Yeah, but the Cro-Mags record release show is today." He says, "But you can see the Cro-Mags anytime. Come see us." I say, "Sorry man, it's the Cro-Mags." To this day he remembers that story and tells us, "You know, Vinnie and Roger showed up. They were the only guys who came to our show. All you other guys were at your Cro-Mag, Krishna lunch, or whatever, show."

2. CALL TO ARMS

LOU: We recorded *Call to Arms* near Times Square at a studio called the Big House with John Seymour. Turns out, he lives five blocks from me. I'm not 100 percent sure how we decided to work with him, but he was a good guy. I liked him. Pretty sure he worked with Alice in Chains and later did something with the Bouncing Souls.

PETE: Craig and Armand decided that they were back into getting a really raw sound.

LOU: Everything else around that time was getting heavier and more produced. All the bands were using triggers for the drums, and we were like, "Fuck triggers! We want a natural sound." Honestly, I didn't love that recording for several reasons, one of the biggest being that I was sick the whole time. I sang that whole album with a fucking terrible cold. It was one of those situations where you get this much money, you have your window, and if you want the album to come out when it's scheduled, you have to record it right then. It was what it was. It was also another one of those cases where we had some great songs but they were played too fast.

PETE: Like "Sanctuary." It's so fucking fast; it's ridiculous. I heard it on Pandora the other day. It's faster than we play it live.

LOU: When I was bored, I'd just look out the window, and there was fucking Times Square below me. I'd go hang out in the Virgin Megastore for hours, reading books and looking at shit but never buying anything.

PETE: Metalcore was the thing when we went in to do the album. Earth Crisis had done their metal record; VOD and Converge and all these bands started to happen.

LOU: Yeah, it was '98; All Out War was around, Hatebreed had started.... Armand always wanted to make sure we stood out. My job was to go in and scream. I didn't know anything about tuning down or anything like that. "Oh, they're tuning down. What the hell does that mean?" I just scream until they tell me it sounds right.

PETE: In any case, Armand and Craig insisted that the album be raw. It's weird because we were going to be on Fat.... Maybe that subconsciously influenced them to want to be more punk. They were definitely into having raw sounds, but overall, I think they just wanted it to be more Bad Brains. If not Bad Brains, definitely older punk style.

LOU: "Let Go," the opening track, is such a blatant fucking hardcore song. It's fast and crazy and has a cool dance part.

PETE: We definitely went in the opposite direction of what everyone else started to do. Those all sounded like metal albums, and we didn't want to get caught up in that.

LOU: It was all just becoming metal. This was the time when hardcore really just dumped all of the punk out of itself. It was the generation of Snapcase, Strife, and Earth Crisis, and when they talked about their influences, they'd mention bands like Pantera. Knowing them as people, especially the guys in Snapcase, we would talk with them about Murphy's Law and Minor Threat, but when they wrote music, they were influenced by Pantera and other metal bands of that moment. I was like, "Where's The Exploited? Where's Motörhead?"

PETE: You can't have hardcore unless there's punk in there. If someone says you can, that's wrong, and they don't know hardcore. They know nothing about the roots. Discharge.... There would be no Sick of It All without Discharge. There would be no Sick of It All without Motörhead.

LOU: That generation of kids and bands were about something else musically, so we purposely did the opposite.

3. YOURS TRULY

LOU: Oh God, my favorite album cover. We were trying to be all Manhattan-artsy or something.

PETE: This was the era of Boy Sets Fire, and Snapcase was really popular. Quicksand...their album covers had that weird, nontypical style. Didn't necessarily look "hardcore."

LOU: Our manager at the time, Trevor, met the artist, Phil Frost, through some DJ. Phil was a graffiti guy, but he did these weird faces you see on the cover all over the place. He told Trevor that he loved Sick of It All, so Trevor got the idea to have him do the cover. I was like "Okay, cool. He's gonna create a cool cover," but when I saw the final result, I was like, "I don't get this, I don't like it at all." Trevor tried to sell it to me like, "This is something new," because the music, while still Sick of It All, was definitely us branching out. He was trying to appeal to that next generation of hardcore and take us to another level. Alternative rock was big, I guess. I remember telling Armand that I hated the cover, and he asked, "What do you want, a skull with flaming dice for eyes?" I went, "As opposed to this, yes I do!"

PETE: The funny thing is that every other album that came out that year had, like, a deck of cards with a spade behind it, or a skull with a switchblade. A photo of the band around either a pool table or a poker table with beer on it, smoking cigars.

LOU: Everybody wanted to be Social Distortion.

PETE: Fat Mike told us he thought it looked like "Nairobi hardcore." He asked, "You sure you want to do this?" and we said, "Well, we already paid for it."

LOU: Yeah, what a fucking scam that was. Phil sold it for millions to some Italian guy. Somehow, Craig made out like a bandit. He got like three paintings from the guy because he became his friend.

PETE: Phil's a really nice guy. I'm not putting down his art at all, but for us, it wasn't right. Unless it was being released in Nairobi, then it would've been fucking great.

LOU: It is one of my favorite Sick of It All records.

PETE: We got into this serious band discussion about whether or not to tune down in order to make the album heavier and more powerful. I think we should have, but I don't think the album lost anything because we didn't. I do think it would've made the songs even more powerful though.

LOU: The look and sound of hardcore had completely changed by 2000. The new generation was establishing itself, and the scene seemed to be more splintered. You had the Snapcase and Quicksand side, and then in the other direction was the Hatebreed and All Out War dirty metal side. Sure, Snapcase is heavy, but in a different way than straight-up metal.

PETE: But we should always do what we want and what feels right to us. What we did kept the album sounding like us.

LOU: Around then, I remember reading an interview with Jamey from Hatebreed. They asked him what he'd been listening to, and he said, "*Yours Truly*, it's my favorite album of the year." When we went on tour after the album came out with Boy Sets Fire and The Hope Conspiracy, I was thinking, *Oh my God, people are going to murder each other to these songs*. At that point, we hadn't learned about what we call "the two-year curse." We make a record, and nobody moves to the new songs when we play them live for the first two years. Then, when we make the record after that, all they want to hear is the shit from the last record. It's like clockwork. It always works out that way.

PETE: I love that album because it's so diverse. A little bit after the record came out, I walked into a bar and this drummer friend of ours, completely drunk, goes, "I'm really loving your new record, except for that one song..." I asked, "What song?" He didn't know any of the names, but I knew he was talking about "Turn My Back." It's a rocker song, kind of an AC/DC rip, but played Sick of It All style. He goes, "What the fuck is that Buckcherry faggot shit?" He was so drunk, but that record is us playing whatever we fucking wanted.

4. *LIFE ON THE ROPES*

LOU: Interesting recording that was. That was just us and Dean Baltulonis.

PETE: Yeah, it was more of a band production thing. We did it in Brooklyn at a place called Atomic. It doesn't exist anymore, like most studios. It was a great place in DUMBO, really nice.

LOU: I don't mean to out him or anything, but Craig was involved in a lot of extracurricular activities at that time. He was really into getting high then.

PETE: All day, he was drinking and getting high, and everything was going pretty well, but sometimes, he was just absent. Armand had to play some of the bass tracks because Craig just didn't show up.

LOU: Even when he was there, he kinda wasn't. I remember everybody would be showing each other songs, and we'd be like, "What have you got, Craig?" And he'd be like, "Um, I got this thing." It would be like half a riff. We'd be reminding him, "Hey, we're going to the studio. You know your shit, right?" He was like, "Yeah, yeah. I fucking know. I know." Then, when we went in, he was like, "I don't know what to do on this one, guys." Armand would go in and show the part to him, but then Armand would just wind up playing it. I'm not trying to put him down; he was having real problems.

PETE: His extracurricular stuff really did get in the way. You could see it; he looked terrible. We got John Joseph to sing on one of the songs. It was Craig who contacted him. So, John shows up at the studio. Craig had been there, but as soon as John showed up, Craig slipped out the door. He came walking back in with a beer. It was fucking noon. Even John was like, "What the fuck?" This is the guy who asked me to come?" It wasn't like Craig.

LOU: John finished his part, and we wanted to take a photo with him, but Craig was nowhere to be found. So, we took photos without Craig, and then, leaping ahead a little bit, when we went to tour Europe for that album, and the photos of the three of us and John Joseph were put on a bunch of flyers as Sick of It All. Craig was so pissed. He goes, "What the fuck is this?" We're like, "We didn't plan this. You left when the photo was taken." The photos made it look like John Joseph was our bass player.

PETE: Armand refers to that time period as "Brian Pasty." That was Craig's nickname because he looked like his name should have been Brian, and he was very pasty, all fucked-up looking. Whenever we talk about Life on the Ropes, those guys are like, "Yeah, total Brian Pasty."

LOU: There are a lot of good songs on that album. Armand wrote this really heavy song called "The Land Increases." People tell me they love that song, but, naturally, when we played that live, nobody cared. It was that two-year curse. "Fakin' the Punk" was a good one too, and the opener, "Relentless." I love that one. And again, trying something different, we recorded analog and then moved it to digital. But what happened because of our lack of knowledge and the engineer's lack of knowledge was that when we transferred from analog to digital, we lost so much of the brightness and heaviness of the recording.

PETE: It just became weird and dull. It was all flat. We played it for our friend Artie from Indecision before it was transferred to digital. He was like, "Holy shit, it's so brutal." Afterward, even the engineer was like, "What the fuck happened?!" Something went wrong.

LOU: On top of all this, we were having problems with the label, especially overseas. We were drawing anywhere from five or six hundred to over a thousand people every night headlining in Europe, but when we looked at our record sales, they'd tell us that we'd sold TWO albums. Literally two albums sold in Munich where we sold out a fifteen-hundred capacity room. We were like, "What the hell is going on? How's that possible???" Fat Europe just dropped the ball. It was so disheartening, because when we first joined up with Fat, they flew me and Craig over to Europe and we did a press tour, which we had never done with any other label. When *Call to Arms* was about to come out, we had press all over the place, and it was great. But then it just started to fade. I mean, we were killing it at these festivals, blowing bigger bands off the stage, and there was no press anywhere, and nobody from the label would come to the shows. We played Full Force and had an amazing show. Afterward, we called the girl from Fat. I said, "We just played Full Force. We blew the place away. Why is there no press? Why aren't you here?" She goes, "Oh, you know I don't like the heavy stuff." That was her answer. That made me so angry, and I was so hurt. Every other band had twenty different magazines taking pictures and talking to them.

PETE: Our record sales were fucked, and it was because of Fat overseas. In our heads, we were like, is it the album covers? Is it because of the whole streaming thing starting to take off? I remember people telling us, "We got your new album for free on this Russian site." But even Mike admitted to us later when we said we were leaving the label, "Yeah, I understand. The European operation has been really slipping." That's all I remember him saying.

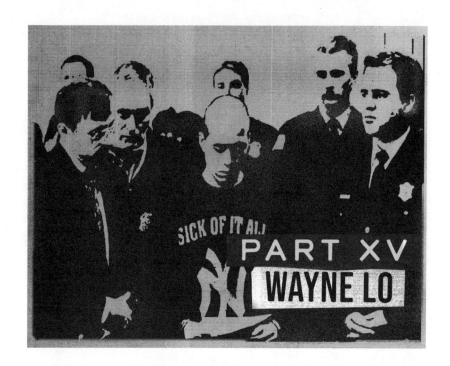

SICK OF IT ALL PART XV
WAYNE LO

1. MY GOD. IT'S ON THE COVER
OF THE *DAILY NEWS*!

LOU: We were in Rome when we found out about the Wayne Lo shooting. It was either our first or second time there.

PETE: We heard about it from someone who had just seen the story on CNN, which you were able to get over in Europe. There was a guy in Massachusetts who'd shot people while wearing one of our shirts.

LOU: I actually remember the show where he must have gotten the shirt. It was a new design, and the first place in New England we sold it at was in New Hampshire, right on the border of Massachusetts. There were tons of college kids. There was a big hardcore crowd, but there were also a bunch of random people who came to check it out because it was a college town. He had to have gotten the shirt at that show. It was close to his school too.

PETE: What's crazy is that we used to joke around, saying things like, "Man, we need some nut in a tower with a Sick of It All shirt on to do something messed up to put us on the map." Not too many years later, this fucking maniac pretty much did it. Makes you rethink some of the things you joke about.

LOU: We called our parents to see if they'd heard about it, and they said, "My God. It's on the cover of the *Daily News!*"

PETE: I remember thinking, this sucks! It's on the news. *This guy killed people wearing our shirt, and it's plastered everywhere.*

LOU: Then there was the fucking *New York Times!* They said we were part of the skinhead culture and were racist. Just like everybody else, when they heard "skinheads," they automatically thought Nazis. You'd think the *New York Times* would know better. We reached out to them, but they wouldn't give us any space to offer our side of things. We wrote a letter to them. We gave everything we had to say to Armand, and he wrote it with his brother.

PETE: The *Times* wouldn't print it, but the *Village Voice* did. People appreciated it and immediately took our side. They realized how irresponsible the *Times* had been saying shit like that without doing any real research.

LOU: All they had to do was ask us about it. I guess because we weren't of the stature of AC/DC or Judas Priest, who got to offer their comments after people did fucked-up things with their shirts on, or with their tape in their pocket, they felt it was okay to jump to conclusions like, "These guys are Nazis." Afterward, we'd have fans who would want to talk about what Wayne Lo did, and I was always like, "What about him?" Dead-serious. What was I going to say? The guy killed two people and injured a bunch more. So fucked-up.

PETE: That shirt he wore was one of our biggest-selling shirts ever, the dragon with the N.Y. under it.

LOU: THE best-selling shirt we ever had! He said he wore it as more of a statement. It's not like he was a big fan of the band; he was wearing that shirt as a statement.

PETE: I remember wearing one of our first tour shirts in the city, near a Crunch gym, and these business guys were like, "Sick of It All, me too! Where do I get one of those shirts?" The name "Sick of It All" can be taken a lot of ways.

LOU: Every interview for the next two decades, we had to answer Wayne Lo questions, and we weren't really allowed to play in Massachusetts for a while. I remember our agent, Stormy, saying that the promoters wanted the story to die down. We were being shown on the news as if we inspired the shooting. Remember, after

September 11th, all the shit that Anthrax had to deal with because people were sending fucking anthrax around? Then there was that band, ISIS. For a while, we were "that Wayne Lo band."

PETE: He's in jail for the rest of his life. He got two life sentences. He was actually on some show not too long ago, talking about the shooting. He was saying that he was a little crazy and confused, and that it was all for a girl to notice him. And the thing is, he's super intelligent, but he's socially fucked up. He didn't know how to talk to this girl. He wanted to impress this girl, so he killed people's children. The dad of the student that was killed wrote a book called Gone Boy, and the first chapter is called "Sick of It All." He doesn't mention the band or anything, but it took me by surprise. I read it and was just like, "This is so fucking horrible."

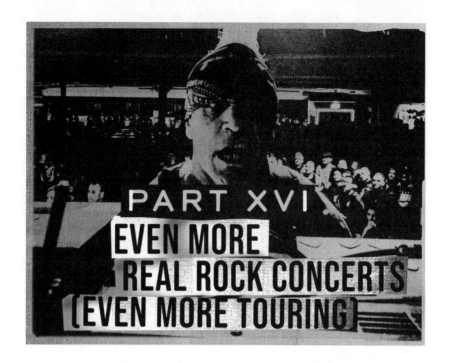

PART XVI
EVEN MORE
REAL ROCK CONCERTS
(EVEN MORE TOURING)

1. FUCKIN' SLAYYYEEERRR!

PETE: It may have taken us thirteen years, but we finally got to tour with Slayer!

LOU: In 1999, we did the Slayer tour. The year before, we were in Argentina playing a show, and the day after our show, there was a huge metal festival. It was Kreator, Soulfly, Slayer, Iron Maiden, and I forget who else. Most of those bands flew in a few days early, so the promoter invited a bunch of them to come see Sick of It All. It was sold out, twenty-five hundred people, the night before this huge metal festival.

PETE: Let me tell you a couple of things about that show.... A week before we'd gone to Argentina, we were playing at Toad's Place in Connecticut, and it was a dismal, piece-of-shit show. We were giving it 110 percent, and the people at the show had a good time, but it was shitty overall. It was the state of hardcore at that moment in that town. It seemed like people couldn't be bothered. Fast-forward to the show in Argentina: we're onstage, and nobody speaks English, but every motherfucker there was singing our lyrics in English. I'll remember this to the day I die; the place was going fucking berserk, and you turned to me and said, "This is why I'm in a fucking band!" The place was going absolutely sick! If I was in Slayer watching this, I would have been like, "God damn," and that's what happened. They came backstage, and Kerry King was like, "Dude, that shit was fucking amazing!"

LOU: Then Kerry and Tom put us up for their Slayer U.S. tour. They were like, "You guys are fucking great! The way you played, and that crowd reaction...." A few months later, we got a call: "Hey, do you guys want to do the Slayer tour? You'd be main support over Meshuggah." We were like, "Holy fucking shit!" But we made a lot of mistakes on that tour. Kerry King was cool as shit when we met him in Argentina, but on the tour, he was very standoffish.

PETE: Yeah, really weird.

LOU: For that tour, I really didn't want to play the more melodic stuff we had. I only wanted to play our heavier and harder stuff. Armand insisted we play "Sanctuary" because it would make us stand out. Anyway, we used EPMD's "I Shot the Sheriff" as an intro tape. So, the lights go down, and the place just starts cheering. Then, our hip-hop intro comes on, and there's dead-silence. But then we come out, and to get people into it from the start, Pete and I jump straight onto the barricade, and the place starts going crazy. But we go into "Sanctuary" and just lose them again.

PETE: So, Lou, exactly how many fans did we gain from doing that tour?

LOU: One. We got exactly one new fan, but he's still a fan to this day and still buys all the records. So, in another sixty years, he'll have helped us pay off the tour support. But we had a good time on that tour. We were playing in Georgia, and after our set, we were sitting at the merch booth. We would hang out the merch booth most of the night and then go find the highest spot in the venue to watch the Slayer crowd from. It was amazing, just watching from above. This guy comes walking up to the merch area, with no shirt on, a totally diesel, bald-headed, crazy-looking guy. He says, "You guys are pretty badass." He turns to walk away, and on his giant back he has a giant pentagram, and around the pentagram in giant letters it says, "I killed Christ." This was tattooed on his body.

PETE: Remember New Mexico?

LOU: Oh yeah. We're at the merch booth, and the Swingin' Utters are in town and come to see us play. We're talking, and Slayer is about to go on. They're like, "All right, we're going to go." I say, "What do you mean you're going to go? You're not going to watch Slayer?" They're like, "Nah, we don't do metal." I tell them, "You have to watch Slayer," and they're like "Okay, okay." So, another funny thing: we were standing there with them and counted—now they weren't all together—SEVEN Mexican dwarfs walking around the show. SEVEN!

PETE: Then Slayer went on, and the place was going absolutely apeshit! The Swingin' Utters guys' faces were white as ghosts. They were like, "We've been to shows in L.A. back in the day when it was scary, but I've never seen a crowd like this." People were ripping their t-shirts off and setting them on fire. I was like, "Yup, that's the Slayer crowd."

PETE: We had fun with Slayer; they were cool. I remember our interactions with Jeff Hanneman. At the first show, he walks into our dressing room completely drunk and goes, "Oh shit, this isn't my dressing room. Hey guys."

LOU: We were playing at a casino in Vegas and sitting at some video poker table is Jeff Hanneman with six Jack and Cokes in front of him. I go, "Hey Jeff, you know you're going on now." He just sat there, and we bullshitted for a while. Those were my interactions with Jeff Hanneman on that tour.

PETE: My memory of that Las Vegas show is that, when Meshuggah was on, the fire alarm wouldn't stop going off throughout their entire set. It was ridiculous that they couldn't stop this fucking thing before the show started.

LOU: Meshuggah was great as fuck to us. They were super cool. And we had a good time, especially with Tom Araya. We were in Reno in a fucking giant rodeo ring. It had the sawdust floor and bleacher seats. It was like five thousand people. We started playing, and a small pit opened up. There were a bunch of hardcore people there from Reno. By the end of the set, we had five different pits going, and Tom was on the side of the stage watching. We're walking off, and he goes, "That's why we asked you guys to be on this tour." It made me so happy that he said that. Tom always watched us, and he would always come hang out with us before the shows. It was cool. He's a really good guy.

PETE: Because of Tom Araya, we got to meet some actual zombies. We would pull up to the venue parking lot, and sometimes Tom would come out to talk to us and say hi. As soon as Tom stepped off the bus, there'd be fifty people coming out of what seemed like a fucking swamp. Where the hell were these people coming from? They weren't here a second ago.

LOU: He would hang with the zombies for a little while and sign everything, but as soon as they would walk away, Tom would turn to us and say, "Nothing scares me more than our own fans!"

PETE: The coolest thing is when you get a text message from Tom Araya wishing you a Merry Christmas. I actually took a screenshot of that one.

2. WARPED TOUR

LOU: We did the first Warped Tour, but the way we got onto the next one, in '97, was basically because Helmet was too snobby to do it. Helmet was supposed to be on the tour that year, and somebody got in Page's ear, I think someone from the Jesus Lizard, who asked him, "What are you going to do, that Warped Tour where you play to little kids on their little skateboards?" They pulled out. Steve Martin happened to be doing press for the tour, so he told Kevin Lyman to try to put Sick of It All on, so he put us on the tour. That was one of the best lineups ever.

PETE: That was a pivotal moment for the Warped Tour. They still had Pennywise, Social D., the Mighty Mighty Bosstones, us, and Suicide Machines, but a lot more of the Blink 182-type bands were getting on it, and that stuff started to outdraw the harder bands.

LOU: That's when Sugar Ray was on it. At the beginning of the tour, nobody knew who they were, and by the middle of the tour, they had sold millions of records.

PETE: Right. And they still played on some little tiny stage.

LOU: They insisted on staying on the little stage, and there'd be like ten thousand girls waiting to see them play.

PETE: It was fun because some of the bands just gravitated towards each other. It was us, Pennywise, the Bosstones, and the Social D. guys hanging out every night. The Descendents reunited for that tour too. Mike Ness came up to us at the end of the tour and said, "If it wasn't for you guys, Pennywise, and the Bosstones, I would have gone crazy on this tour." It was really nice that we all bonded like that. Everybody was jocking the shit out of The Descendents, but every single night, Milo came onstage to watch us. It was really cool to us that the band everybody else was jocking was checking out Sick of It All every day because he loved the way we played.

LOU: You know how that tour doesn't announce set times until the day of each show? As we got closer to New York, we said to the production people, "We're not asking to be on the main stage, but we'd like to go on at a good time, maybe in the middle of the day, because New York's our hometown." They were like, "Sure, sure. Don't worry about it." We get to New York, the times get posted, and we're going on at two o'clock on the truck stage, which is a flatbed truck. We went to them to complain: "Hey, you said you were going to look out for us in New York with the set time," and they were like, "Oh, we're sorry. It's just the way it happened." I said, "How could you do that? We specifically said we'd even open the rest of the tour, but please just don't screw us in New York, and you just did." They actually said, "We didn't know you were from here." Are you fucking kidding me? I don't want to badmouth them because that tour did a lot of good for us, and Kevin Lyman put up with a lot of shit from us that he didn't put up with from other bands.

PETE: Yeah, Kevin was really good to us.

LOU: That being said, we go to our stage at two o'clock, and I don't know who was on the main stage at that time, maybe Less Than Jake or Limp Bizkit, but easily more than five thousand people started marching over to the truck to see Sick of It All. We start, and you have to picture it: on the side of the stage is Mike Ness, Kevin Lyman, Fletcher from Pennywise, Steve Martin, and Stormy. The place is going absolutely ape-shit.

PETE: Craig was doing his Craig shit, jumping around, running....

LOU: I found out about this a little later, but Craig stepped back into a hole in the stage and twisted his ankle. So, when we stopped and I was addressing the crowd—"Hey, what's up, New York?"—I said something about us being on at such an early time, and Craig goes, "YO, FUCK THIS FUCKING STAGE, I ALMOST BROKE MY ANKLE, MOTHERFUCKERS. FUCK THEM!" He's going off like that, and we'd agreed not to complain about the stage or our set time from the stage, but still I said, "Yeah, fuck them. We're home. They can kick us off the tour if they want," and the place went crazy. We really had an amazing set.

PETE: But Craig also yelled, "Fuck Kevin Lyman," and he was right there.

LOU: Steve said that Mike Ness was in shock, but smiling, and that Fletcher was elbowing Kevin Lyman, laughing. So, Kevin Lyman grabbed Steve and said, "Come with me." He started yelling at Steve about what had happened, and Steve goes, "Well you did kind of fuck them. You fucked them in their hometown. What did you expect them to do?" So, after the show, we had to go onto Kevin's bus, and I don't remember apologizing, but I think maybe we did because he was very mad. We were just like, "Look, your people promised us we'd get a good spot in New York, and we got screwed." It got settled.

PETE: But Kevin Lyman is very cool. He really supported an entire culture in the United States.

LOU: Fast-forward to 2017, and he asked us to be on it again. It was twenty years since we'd done the tour. He said to Stormy, "I'll tell you what; your boys, every night, no matter when they go on or and how many people are there, whether it's fifty people or five hundred, they're giving 110 percent every night."

PETE: He'd actually be standing in the crowd, watching at most of the shows.

LOU: He liked us because we NEVER give a half-assed show. I mean, we played in St. Louis to thirty fucking people in 2017, but it didn't change how hard we played. I think fifteen of the thirty were from the other bands. But there were some bands, like, 2000s bands you wouldn't expect, drawing HUGE crowds that year. People love nostalgia. They miss their "Back when I was a carefree teenager" years. That tour really is its own world, but we had so many good times.

PETE: The Bouncing Souls making fun of Limp Bizkit all the time onstage.

LOU: Then Limp Bizkit coming up to us towards the end of the tour saying, "Thanks for being cool, not like those jerks from the Bouncing Souls." They're the happiest and mellowest punk band from New Jersey, and every show, they were just like, "Fuck those assholes in Limp Bizkit."

PETE: Those damn Bouncing Souls bullies.

3. ROTTEN IN THE STATE OF DENMARK

PETE: On one of our first European tours, we were going to Denmark. We had a city bus that they'd added bunks to. Everyone was completely exhausted, and we all went to sleep on the bus while it was on the ferry from Germany to Denmark. I got up at some point and got out of the bus. I went upstairs and ordered some food. There was no one around. I thought, *Wow, we're not moving.* I went downstairs to get back onto the bus, and it was gone. I was completely confused. I was like, *Where the fuck is everybody?* The ferry had just been packed with people and vehicles. I was like, *Okay, maybe I'm on the wrong floor.* So, I went to the next floor, and by then, the boat was moving again. This was before everyone had cell phones. I went to the captain's door and asked, "Can you tell me which way we're going?" He said, "To Germany."

LOU: We were in the bus, and some voice came over the driver's radio. We were leaving the parking area, and they flagged us down. They asked, "Is one of your crew missing?" We said, "What do you mean?" Then we all looked around and realized, "Oh shit, Pete's missing." Our driver said, "We just got a message from the captain saying we should wait because Pete was on his way back to Germany, and he'll just ride back again." If they didn't stop our bus, we would have gotten to wherever the hell we were going without Pete.

PETE: Thankfully, it wasn't a crazy ferry ride. It was maybe two hours. It was like a magic trick: I go upstairs, I run back down, and every vehicle in the world is gone. Everything and everyone was gone. And I was running around like a nut: *Where are the cars? Did I go in the wrong door? I've got to talk to somebody.* I didn't even have my passport with me. It was in the bus, and I didn't have any other form of ID at all. So stupid!

4. FUCKING HAMMERHEAD

LOU: A lot of English and European cities weren't built with modern traveling in mind, so there's no place to park your tour bus. We were playing the London Astoria 2, and had to unload the bus, and then the bus would go park somewhere. You'd do your show, and then the driver, in this case Hammerhead, would come back, and we'd load up again. Well, Hammerhead decided he was going to come back early. We start loading the bus, and the police came over and said, "Hey, you can't park here." All they wanted him to do was drive around the block and come back, just to allow traffic to get through more easily. It's their job. It was one in the morning, and there was no traffic, but they wanted him to move. There were five cops, and instead of trying to explain what we were doing, and that we didn't need long, Hammerhead looked at the cops, pointed his finger at them, and said, "Excuse me, I am German. You talk to me with respect!" This is right into the cop's face. The cop was like, "Oh, really? Okay, we're taking your bus," and they arrested him.

PETE: Took him right to jail.

LOU: He was being belligerent to the cops, and now we were all freaking out. We didn't know if they were really going to take the bus, and if they did, where it was going to go. The cop got onto the bus, and he was trying to start it and get it in gear, but he left the door open. I ran onto the bus, and he was telling me to get off. I go, "This is my fucking house. I've got to get my money and my stuff off of here," and he just looked at me. I grabbed my wallet, or whatever was in my bunk, jumped off the bus, and he drove away. We're like, "Fuck!" The club is closed, and we're all sitting in the street with our equipment. Steve, from The Business, works security all over London. He went down to the police station and spoke to them on our behalf: "Yeah, I know the driver's a dick, but the band, these are good guys. They're just a band trying to get to the next city." He got our driver out of jail. He got the bus out of lockdown, and all of us off scot-free. Steve saved Sick of It All's ass that night.

PETE: Once again, Hammerhead fucked everything up.

LOU: Fucking Hammerhead.

PETE: I actually think Hammerhead OD'd. I remember someone saying that.

LOU: That's sad. He was a dick, but he gave us good stories.

PETE: Remember that time he was coming down from speed, standing in front of the bus with his pants unbuttoned and wide open? He was halfway bent, doing the junkie lean with all the kids from the show passing by. There was spit coming from his mouth, touching all the way down to the floor, and we were like, "This is the motherfucker driving us. That's our bus driver." But somehow, if any lady walked by, he'd still find the energy to hit on her.

LOU: Now, there are so many rules to make sure it's safer, and the drivers can't drive for a crazy number of hours. It's like this digital tracker that the driver has to use, almost like a punch clock in a warehouse.

PETE: There's even a point when the driver has to take forty-eight hours off. In the middle of a tour, your driver might have to leave. Well, he could just sit on the bus, but you have to hire another driver. So, you're paying for both drivers, and one guy just gets to hang out. You're still paying him his per diem. It's smart but expensive.

LOU: And there are ways drivers can cheat it, but if they're caught cheating, they take away their license forever.

PETE: Sometimes we have to get a driver from another tour bus—because they all know each other—to move our bus because our driver doesn't want to get a fine. They don't do anything like this in the States, but they probably should.

LOU: With truckers too. Only pilots have these kinds of rules...and Hammerhead.

5. NEW YORK UNITED

PETE: We did a tour with Madball in Europe called "New York United." We were all excited because the Barcelona show was sold out in advance, and we had a day off the day after and were staying in Barcelona. The show was amazing. Madball tore it up, and then we came out, same thing. Great club, great people working there, total fun. After the show, everybody was psyched. The bands and crew had the day off, so everybody who drank had already been drinking while the show was on. The party had already started.

Somebody involved with the show owned a bar down the block from the venue and said they would keep it open all night for us. My wife, Mei-Ling, was working that tour and was pretty tipsy even before we got onstage, and Armand was drunk before he got into the shower. Both bands headed over to the bar. Even though I don't drink, I went to check it out, but I only stayed maybe thirty minutes. It wasn't my scene, but everyone else stayed while I went back to the bus and went to bed. Strange thing was, I woke up maybe four hours later, dreaming that Mei-Ling was calling my name. It sounded like it was coming from the downstairs of the bus, but it was just a dream. Regardless, it woke me up, and I noticed she was not in her bunk. I called our stage manager Noodles, and he told me Mei was wrecked, but that things were okay. I was worried, so I went down to the bar to check it out.

When I got there, both bands and all the crew were standing in the street, absolutely blasted out of their minds! Everybody was crazy drunk, and they were talking about how they lost Freddy. No one had any idea where he was. They weren't really making any sense because they were so fucking drunk, but Mei-Ling told me that Freddy was really drunk and wandered off while talking to his wife on the phone. They tried calling him, but he wasn't answering his phone, and nobody knew where he was. They were all getting worried, so they decided to make a very loud and drunken search party. I was standing there with Mei-Ling and said, "You know what, I'm going to go this way," pointing to the left because the entire crowd of drunks went to the right. Mei-Ling said, "Okay, you go, you go find Freddy." It was fun, like she was sending a dog to go out to go fetch something.

So, I set off jogging down the street. Mind you, I had just woken up and was kind of in a daze. I ran down the street, made the first right, and kept on jogging for three blocks, then made another right. The reason I remember all these turns and twists is because I wanted to remember how to get back to the club, so it's stuck in my mind. I kept running two more blocks straight, and I saw a police car on the corner. I was at a red light, but I kept jogging in place because a tattooed man in his pajamas with a blonde mohawk looked a little out of place, and I didn't want them to be suspicious of me running around the streets at four a.m. So, I kept jogging when the light turned green and went one more block straight, two more blocks to the left, made another right, and then saw a whole bunch of police cars. I thought I was running towards a police station, so I slowed down a little.

Then I saw a circle of policemen looking down at the ground as if they were holding someone there. I slowed down and jogged around them and found one space open in the circle of police. It was Freddy on the ground, and the policemen were holding him there. I walked right into the circle, pointed, and yelled, "Freddy!" and he looked at me and yelled, "Pete!" All the policemen turned and looked at me all super startled because I had walked right up on them. Three policemen pulled me to the side real rough and tough, and the rest were just smiling and talking to Freddy. Now these policemen were yelling at me in Spanish. I just kept speaking to them in English. Then, out of nowhere, every police officer suddenly was able to speak English. They started asking me who I was, and how I knew Freddy. To make things simple, I just told him that Freddy was the singer of the band I was in, and we had just played a show nearby. Then the policeman told me that Freddy fit the description of somebody who had just assaulted some old man in the street. While they were talking to me, they still had Freddy on the ground, and one guy had his foot on the side of Freddy's head, holding him down. Freddy was talking to them in Spanish, but they didn't believe that he was the singer of a band from America. I told the officers the story about us playing the show, so they let Freddy up, and they stood us next to each other. Then the man who was assaulted came up to look at us, and he told the police that it wasn't Freddy.

They told us we could go, so Freddy and I walked back to the bar. Everyone was right in front, all drunk and cheering, acting like absolute idiots, which was hysterical. They decided that me finding Freddy was another reason to celebrate, so they went back into the bar for one last round. Then, the sun was coming up, so we all walked back to the bus. Armand walked straight into a tree and then apologized to the tree for walking into it. When we got back to the bus, I got into my bunk and Freddy came over and thanked me for looking out for him. Then they all did Jägermeister shots until nine or ten in the morning. I woke up a few hours later, and there was vomit all over the bus because Armand had thrown up all over the place. For the rest of the tour, Hoya gave Armand the nickname "Vomitface." That's the story of me somehow knowing which way to run to find Freddy in the middle of Barcelona.

PART XVII

THE CENTURY MEDIA YEARS

1. DEATH TO TYRANTS

LOU: We decided to leave Fat. We were just like, "All right, let's just step back and see what's going on." We were speaking to different labels, and someone at one of the labels gave us this advice: "Find a label where the people in charge love your band." From the first day we met them back in '92 or '93, Century Media had always championed Sick of It All. They loved us. They asked us when we left East West to go to them, but we went the route we did. We were thinking, *We don't actually fit in with most of the Century Media bands, but....*

PETE: They started this sublabel called Abacus, which focused more on hardcore and metalcore bands, as opposed to Lacuna Coil and Moonspell.

LOU: When the guys started bringing songs in, we were excited. They were raw and heavy and definitely sounded like us, but with a new energy. I was just like, "Holy shit, this stuff is fire!" It was what *Life on the Ropes* should have been. "Take the Night Off" was definitely us, but in a new style.

PETE: I wrote "Take the Night Off." I wrote "Uprising Nation," and stuff like that. I had no specific plan, but that's what came out.

LOU: He didn't sit down and say, "Here, I'm going to write some Buckcherry faggot shit!"

PETE: No, actually I'm going straight AC/DC!

LOU: We were rehearsing in Park Slope, right next to the sanitation department. I was living in Jersey by this time, but I'm not taking the train; I'm driving to rehearsal. Armand lived in Westchester, so every night after rehearsal, he and I would be there with these shitty little handheld recorders we used to record rehearsal, and then we would go, "All right, let's go home and write lyrics." I would drop Armand off at Grand Central, and I would drive home. It would take me maybe an hour to get home after dropping him off. He would text me from the train like, "Hey, I wrote lyrics to this." He wound up writing the lyrics to every song on that album, except one. It blew me away! People would ask me, "Does that piss you off?" I'm like, "No, he wrote great lyrics." I was used to taking my lyrics to him anyway because he'd be honest. He'd tell me, "These are great," or, "No, we should change this. I pictured you coming in on this offbeat, not on the beat." It worked.

PETE: Our record sales went back up, and I think the attendance at our headlining shows picked up again. We never equated it to being on Century Media. We just thought it was the ebb and flow of hardcore's popularity. With Century Media, we were back to putting Sick of It All out there and showing people we're still here and making great records.

LOU: I remember when we played them the rough mixes for Death to Tyrants, during "Take the Night Off," the president stopped the tape and said, "We have to put this record out." He loved it that much. He was really excited.

PETE: A little bit after the record came out, Dropkick Murphys asked us to do some shows in Europe with them.

LOU: It was funny because they were saying things like, "You're big in Europe, and we're big in Europe, let's do the tour together." I was thinking, Y*eah, you draw six THOUSAND people there, and we draw seven HUNDRED people.* We always had an Oi! influence, but we were still hardcore. We loved those Oi! gang choruses, which was basically what Dropkick Murphys did, so when it came to playing to a Dropkick Murphys crowd, we thought, *Oh, shit, we don't even have to say we're Irish or anything.*

PETE: *Death to Tyrants* was the first album we worked on with Tue Madsen. He flew in and lived in Staten Island with us, recorded and mixed it all there.

LOU: When we were originally writing for the album, we were still touring. Everybody was like, "Who should we get to produce?" We loved what Steve Evetts did on *Yours Truly,* especially with me on the vocals. He and I worked really hard on those, but we needed someone else. We came up with Zeuss, who had done Hatebreed and Madball. Armand was all into it. I liked his stuff too, but I didn't want to be lumped in there with the guy who does all the hardcore bands. I met Tue when I sang on The Haunted's Revolver record. He told me, "I love Sick of It All. I'd really like to work with you. I really want to do your next record." We said, "Well, we're kind of waiting to see if Zeuss can do it."

PETE: But Tue would fly out to every one of our shows within a reasonable range of his home. He'd show up in Germany and hang out with us and watch us play. He was a fan.

LOU: It was just good timing because, when Zeuss finally got back to us, the label said, "Well, you can do it with Zeuss, but we've got to push your record back at least six months because he's all booked." Then they said, "Well, what about Tue?" And we were like, "Yeah!" Armand and I had listened to that *Revolver* record, and some others he'd worked on, and we were like, "All right, let's give him a shot." Tue kept telling us, "You never capture what you guys are like live on your records. You have to strive for that."

PETE: That's the main reason he showed up at the shows but kind of hung back. He kept a low profile, just hanging in the background like a weirdo. Later he told me, "I was trying to see how I can best capture your live sound, the energy and everything, on a recording."

LOU: I loved the whole sound he got! That record really was like a rebirth for Sick of It All. I remember people in the States saying things like, "Oh man, your new record's fucking great!" They never said that about the Fat stuff, but they loved *Death to Tyrants*. All of a sudden it was cool to like Sick of It All again.

2. BASED ON A TRUE STORY

PETE: *Based on a True Story* was our second album working with Tue.

LOU: It came out at a time when hardcore seemed to be having a little resurgence, especially in the States.

PETE: The sound of it was heavy and thick. It was a mean-sounding record, unlike *Call to Arms* or *Yours Truly*. They weren't mean-sounding records. Everything is tuned to D.

LOU: We got to work with Tue again, and we were all excited. We actually went to Denmark to record.

PETE: We lived in Denmark for around three weeks, maybe a month. I think the sun came out for one hour the whole time we were there.
LOU: We just worked, no bullshit. We just did the record. We got the best performances. I remember Pete playing the opening track, "Death or Jail." It was so Sick of It All, but with this fresh take on it, a fresh spin. We had friends fly over to do backing vocals, people from Europe. We even met Flemming Rasmussen.

PETE: He was one of Tue's mentors.

LOU: One of our friends who had flown in to do backing vocals was like, "Oh, Flemming's coming." I've never been starstruck by a producer because I don't know any better, but he was like, "He did *Master of Puppets* and *Ride the Lightning*." He came in and listened to the tracks, and he was like, "Yeah, this is good stuff. I really like it." He's a little old man, and that was really fun. But I love the sound we got on that record. Tue told me, "I'm doing something different. I hope you guys will like it because I think the record calls for this." He pushed it so that the frequencies and the volume of the record were....

PETE: So close to breaking up at the top.

LOU: It was almost too much, but I love it. I know Armand, for sure, didn't like it at first. I think Tue found a good balance of keeping it musical and making it sound like it's gonna fall off a cliff.

PETE: That's what hardcore should be. It should sound like you're trying to get to the end of the song. I think it was A.J. from Leeway, or his uncle, or somebody, said, "You gotta play punk rock and hardcore as if someone has a gun to your head." You're just trying to get it all in there before it ends. It takes away from the angst and anger if you're spending time during the song trying to show off. I'm not fucking Slash, or someone like that. I'm trying to murder somebody!

LOU: Armand hated that it was almost breaking up. But I've had people, musicians and engineers, tell me, "Dude, your new record is so fucking great. It feels like it's about to explode and be too loud for your speakers." You have to hear it in a club. Somebody put on "Death or Jail" at some bar in Brooklyn. I was there, so they were like, "Let's play that new Sick of It All." It fucking sounded like the whole system was blowing out. People were like, "Holy shit."

PETE: We had close to final mixes done while we were in Denmark. Armand calls us over and says, "Guys, come here." He goes, "This sounds fucking awful. Do you hear that? I think we have to remix everything. It's fucking terrible." Tue says, "Wait, just listen to it on this." We had these shitty little bullshit speakers, and it sounded fucking great. Armand was finally like, "Ohhh, it sounds really good."

LOU: We told him, "You shouldn't listen to the new Sick of It All album on the same headphones you use to listen to your electronic French cowboy music."

PETE: Exactly, which is one of Armand's favorite styles of music.

LOU: It's the most pretentious fucking shit you could ever think of, and of course, you need the world's best headphones to hear it. That's what he was listening to the mixes on. You've got to get into a fucking van where one of the back speakers has a screwdriver shoved in it, then play our song! But the thing is, we pushed everything so far to the limit, we realized that we were in danger of having to do every album from then on just like Based on a True Story.

PETE: We have our diehard fans who, pretty much, like whatever we do, but we appreciate the praise we get from people saying that each of our albums sounds really different, but they're still Sick of It All.

LOU: We went to Europe with Madball after that record came out, and I remember in Spain, the bartenders were holding up a sign that said, "Play 'Good Cop,' play 'As Long as She's Standing," which were kind of different for us. I thought, *Holy crap, people actually like this new shit.*

3. XXV NONSTOP

PETE: Our twenty-fifth anniversary was coming up, and we didn't really have tons of material for a new album yet. We wanted to put something out to celebrate the anniversary and also have something new we could tour behind.

LOU: I know people love the *Blood, Sweat and No Tears* album, but I can't listen to it. The songs are good, but I think the performances are weird because it was only the third time we were in a studio, and we really didn't know what we were doing. But now, because we've been playing them for twenty-five years, we wanted to record them the way they sound now. Plus, so many kids come up to us and ask, "Hey, what album is that song 'Injustice System' on?" "What album is 'Scratch the Surface' on?" Young kids who only know our Century Media albums. There's more energy and more power to those songs now. When Refused got back together, they played in Brooklyn and asked me to come down and do "Injustice System" with them. I went to the sound check to practice it with them, and they played it at the original album speed. It was so uncomfortable for me to sing it at that tempo. I had to tell their drummer, who's the ringleader, "We play it A LOT faster than that." I know rerecording that material was risky because some people consider that first album a classic, so to speak.

PETE: I remember talking with the guys about the whole idea, and we just came to the conclusion "Who cares?!" We wanted to do this, and we did it.

LOU: I really love the way we rerecorded the songs. We played them at way better tempos, and everything just sounded better. We executed them much better. It wasn't like we were going to throw a curveball at everyone and redo "World Full of Hate" acoustic.

PETE: We didn't make a super big deal out of it. We had a tour booked and had five days off, so instead of filling the days with shows, we went to Tue Madsen's house in Denmark and recorded.

LOU: The band recorded live, and I sang my parts afterward. Tue had a pool built inside his house. It was completely drained, and he would do drum tracks in there. It sounded so great. It was great watching Armand climb down a ladder and get into this pool to play drums. Pete and Craig played in the control room, which was the living room. That was it. We did the songs three or four times each and used the best take of each.

PETE: Some songs we nailed on the first take, but we would do another just in case.

LOU: I'd go in and sing at night, and then the band would record the next day, and then I'd sing again at night, and then, on the last day, we did all the backups.

PETE: There were twenty songs, so that was brutal.

LOU: We also figured, if we're doing this, let's get an updated intro from KRS-One. I just wanted him to say, "Sick of It All, blast-master KRS-One" and "You suckers" again. I didn't want him to say the year, but he said it anyway. Also, for the record, I'm not a big fan of the term "bitches." But he was cool as shit. We called him up and asked him to do this for us. When we finally got in touch with him, we explained what we were doing for the anniversary, and he was like, "Sure, I'll do it." We asked, "What do you need from us?" and he told us, "Send me three XXXL t-shirts." That's all he asked for. Oh, and a copy of the finished album. He's a cool guy, man. He just loves music. He's such an icon, not just in hip-hop, but in all music. A few years after we did the first album, I was at a friend's house, and the kids were watching one of those teen PBS shows. They had KRS-One on it, and they asked him, "Do you listen to any other music besides rap?" and he was like, "Oh, the stuff I listen to you wouldn't know." They said, "Like what?" and he went, "Sick of It All." Everybody in the room turned and looked at me, and I was like, "Ohhh, yeahhhh!" Shit, I don't even know if we ever sent him the shirts!

PETE: If we left it up to someone else to do, then it definitely wasn't done.

4. THE LAST ACT OF DEFIANCE

LOU: Going into *The Last Act of Defiance*, I remember saying to Pete, "I hope we can write more songs like "Take the Night Off" and "Death or Jail." He immediately brought in "Road Less Traveled." He had 90 percent of the lyrics written. That's not normally how things worked. Before that, Pete might play me some music and ask me for a title, but he went all-in this time. He started writing lyrics. Craig also started to come in with more lyrics and ideas for lyrics. He and Armand would work together and hammer it out, or I would add a line here and there.

PETE: With "Road Less Traveled," my daughter had just been born, and she had this little keyboard with drumbeats on it. Some generic Casio keyboard. I made the beat go as fast as it could, and I started playing guitar to it. That's how I wrote the song.

LOU: We wanted "Get Bronx" to catch on as a saying. It was just a weird thing that Craig would say: "Yo, we gotta be hard. We've got to get Bronx." Nobody knew why, but I was like, "Well, then let's run with it." We wanted to get people to start saying it, but it just never happened. They actually wrote about it in the *New York Daily News*: "Queens band wants you to get Bronx," or something like that. Craig was trying to come up with a good explanation for it, and he talked about it in several interviews. In one interview, the interviewer was like, "I get it. It's, like, New York, in your face." I chimed in: "That's not what you said two days ago." He was trying to be real PC and for the community. I remember him saying, "It's like a call to arms for the people in the community to come together and help one another." We were like, "No, it's not." I remember Armand looking at him at the interview, like, *What the fuck are you talking about?!*

PETE: Yeah, he was trying to be all super nice and thoughtful. We were like, "Why?"

LOU: But I really love that song; I love the music. Craig would come in with a couple of riffs, and we'd all hammer it out and work on it. Armand came up with the "DNC" lyrics.

PETE: I think Craig started to go up to Armand's house, and they would work on the songs together. I'm pretty sure that's how they came up with "Machete." Ernie Parada from Token Entry told Craig that "Machete" was the perfect hardcore song because it's fast and crazy, and then gets super heavy at the end.

LOU: When *Last Act of Defiance* comes up, I remember a lot of people thinking the title represented the end of the band. We had to say, "No, no. We're not going to break up or anything." It was just a cool name. I came up with this idea in my head for the cover. We talked to Ernie about it because he had done some great show posters for us. The first few things he gave us were very literal. There was a guy in front of a firing squad giving them the finger or spitting at them. I said to him, "The vision I have for this is: when I was a kid in the seventies, there was a t-shirt that said, 'Last Act of Defiance.' It had a cartoon mouse giving the finger and these giant eagle claws that were coming to kill it." He was like, "Okay, I get it now." He didn't come back with a cartoon, but he came back with this beautiful illustration of a rattlesnake eating a rat, with the rat biting the rattlesnake as he's going down. I said, "That is fucking perfect!" I remember Craig freaking out and hating the cover. All three of us were like, "This is amazing." Craig complained, "But it doesn't have the dragon on it. We've got to have the dragon on every album cover." Now he loves it. Some guy in Europe actually went online and wrote, "How dare you promote violence towards animals!" I was like, "What?! It's fucking nature—snakes eat rats and mice."

PETE: Aren't there only vegan snakes over there? Fucking people…. Anyway, here's a little side story about the opening song, "Sound the Alarm." John Joseph told a bunch of people, "I want to do a new Cro-Mags record. If you guys have any ideas, send them to me." I took one of Craig's riffs—it was more of a mid-tempo riff—and I had this alarm-sounding sort of riff, and I wrote that song. I sent it to John: "Hey, John, I've got this song. What do you think?" He never got back to me, so it became the opening track for that record.

5. *WAKE THE SLEEPING DRAGON!*

PETE: We went back to Staten Island for this one, but this time we would do rehearsals at the studio, so Jerry Farley could hear the songs, and we actually let him have some say. We never really let anyone say anything before, but this time, it helped. Jerry did a great job producing the thirtieth-anniversary EP we did under Tue's guidance, so we thought it was time to give him a shot doing an album.

LOU: Jerry really did a fucking great job on the EP, but we still wanted Tue to mix. The way he mixes us is just amazing. He gets hired by Judas Priest and Ozzy to mix their shit.

PETE: Jerry put together a mix for the EP, and it was okay, but it didn't have what it needed. Then Tue sent us his rough mix, and it was absolutely perfect.

LOU: Even Jerry said, "Yeah, Tue's got it." Jerry's been a fan for years. He worked with that whole metalcore scene as it was just growing into being platinum-selling bands. He loves melodic punk. He loves emo, but he loves hardcore. So, he has all this experience, and he loves Sick of It All. He was surprised that Armand and Craig didn't mind him saying things like "No, do this.

Try this instead." If Armand wrote the lyrics, he wanted to know what Armand was hearing melody-wise. If Pete wrote the lyrics, then he asked what Pete thought we should do here, or how I should sing it. We worked on all of that for a few weeks.

PETE: I think that really helped the album too. Usually we would do our pre-production. We'd go into the rehearsal room, put a digital recorder in the middle, cover it with a t-shirt to try to drown out the cymbals, and listen to the recordings afterwards. It was just noise, you know. It was hard to come up with melodies to something that sounded like white noise. I live in Florida, and I would have things come to me when I was doing some work, so I would record it and email it to the guys and to Jerry. At least they knew what I was coming up with. Armand would do the same. Sometimes I would record a video of me playing the parts, so they could see how they went. Everyone would mess with the stuff for a week, and then I'd fly up for a few days, and we'd all learn each other's songs. We'd do that until we had the album written.

LOU: Craig really came into his own with this album, where he could take all his weird concepts and be able to explain them to us. Before, it was hard for us to understand where he was coming from. He brought two great songs, and he had lyrics too. We were like, "Holy shit, he even wrote lyrics."

PETE: Jerry really pushed him. Craig would be bugging Jerry like, "Jerry, Jerry, are you going to come get pizza with me tonight?" Jerry would say, "Um, we've eaten pizza seven nights in a row. I'll tell you what, I'll go eat pizza with you tonight as long as you get this much work done."

LOU: Yeah, like putting a carrot in front of a horse, but, you know, pizza. We needed that because with vocals there were things that I never wanted to try; I thought I couldn't do it. And he would tell me, "Who's going to hear it if you fuck it up?! You're in the room with just me." So, we would try shit. It would have been great if we had done things like that on earlier albums.

PETE: It worked. Like with Craig, he would tell him, "Write your lyrics, put something here," and he would tell him what was wrong, and it just worked out great.

LOU: It was also great because now Pete has a voice; Craig has a voice. It's not just me and Armand writing. It's a great mix of all of us, and I liked the way everybody approached it from a different angle, with their own stamp. Armand wanted to write a song about racism. He didn't write something simple and obvious like, "Everybody, you've got to stop hating all the brown people." He looked into Robert Moses's life and thought, *that guy was a fucking racist*, and he wrote the song "Robert Moses Was a Racist."

PETE: Then there's "That Crazy White Boy Shit." People who interviewed us were DYING to know where that came from.

LOU: I would just tell them the story: "Our black and Hispanic friends that weren't into rock music would call our music 'crazy white boy shit.' We would laugh our asses off and say, 'I guess we need to have a band that's all Rastafarians.' At the end of the day, it's a tribute to Bad Brains, the greatest hardcore band ever. But they wouldn't understand that. These writers were like, "You called them 'black' and 'Hispanic.' " I'm sorry, that's how I speak! So, does everyone I know. Even now when I repost the video, somebody will pop up and go, "Whoa, that's a little...." They won't necessarily say "racist," but that's what they mean. Then somebody will write back, "Um, yeah, why don't you pay attention to the lyrics?" They're pretty damn clear.

PETE: People just fucking live for that "gotcha" moment, so everything you say or do is analyzed to death. "Hey, we're Nazis, and they play that crazy white boy shit, let's go see Sick of It All!" I pretty much never read reviews, even if they're great, and I hate message boards. Obviously, you only remember the shitty reviews, and the stupidest comments.

LOU: I think there should be an actual law where you cannot review a record until you spend at least three sittings with it. Even with our new album, one guy thought "Bull's Anthem" was about the Chicago Bulls, and this other guy wrote, "'Crazy White Boy Shit' is addressing the Proud Boys and the New Right movement." No, it's not!

PETE: Totally made it up!

LOU: I remember Armand and I talking about a lyric once. He was like, "We probably should reword that because, if you don't know us, and maybe even if you do know us, you might think, 'Whoa, what are they saying there?'" It's a fine line. Look at how people analyze comedians now—but, at least with comedians, you know what you're paying for. Their goal is to shock you a little bit, but with us, even if I say something blatantly nice, it's probably going to get misconstrued.

PETE: I wish we'd had Tue and Jerry for Yours Truly. Not putting down Steve—he was a great producer—but I don't remember him making the suggestions these guys have. When we had GGGarth Richardson on Built to Last, we would respond to his suggestions like, "No, we tried that in rehearsal and it sounded like shit." And he would just be like, "Okay."

LOU: He didn't have another plan. He didn't ever say, "Well, let me hear it and let me understand it." He was just there to get a paycheck. Not meaning to put him down, but I don't think we were a high priority for him. We weren't a platinum-selling band or the cool underground guys. We were that scene in America: "Oh, it's just that hardcore thing. Nu-metal is what's in."

PETE: But Tue, a European guy, flew to festivals to watch us live so he could not only pitch us, but know how to get our live sound down. Because hardcore is taken seriously everywhere in the world...except here.

1. THERE'S A FUCKING STIGMA ATTACHED TO HARDCORE!

LOU: We love commemorating our anniversaries because, on the one hand, we can't believe we've come this far, and, on the other, we don't know what the future hol

PETE: Yes, milestones. Some people take it like it's the end for us. No, it's not the end, it's just a celebration. Sort of a "Hey, we'll see you at the next one."

LOU: We're celebrating how long we've been around, but for the music industry, it's like, "Damn, these guys are old." How come all the so-called classic rock bands don't get treated that way? They're called "classic." Every release we come out with, people tell us how much they like our new album, and how fresh it sounds. We work hard to make these albums sound different and exciting. Then, a few months later, when we're trying to get on a tour, people are like, "Yeah, they're kind of an old band." An \ old band? I'll fucking kick the shit out of you. Performance-wise, I mean. A new album comes out from Sick of It All every couple of years, but in hardcore years, it's seems like a billion years later. There's a fucking stigma attached to hardcore! And it may have to do with how fast this shit moves, how fast the scene moves. It really is this youth movement. Then, there's how aggressive it is, and how much trouble there's been in the past. A lot of people would rather not deal with it.

PETE: Metal bands get this too, but they disappear for a while, come back, and EVERYONE's psyched they come back. We've never gone away.

LOU: We also still care about everything we do, and how we do it. We did that Revelation Records anniversary in L.A. They had everybody: Quicksand, Youth of Today, Bold, No for an Answer, Gorilla Biscuits. The day after we played, we heard people saying things like, "Did Sick of It All pay the soundman more money to sound better than everyone else?" Jordan from Revelation looked at these people and told them, "No, they're just a REAL band! They didn't break up twenty years ago; they're still going."

PETE: Almost every one of those bands was broken up before those anniversary shows. The others only play once in a while.

LOU: Of course, we started our set with old songs, but then we played a song that we wrote in 2006. Then another we wrote in 2010. As dumb as this sounds to some, I still love this music. I still listen to hardcore. I don't go to as many shows unless I know the band's really good, but I'll listen to a lot of new bands. Thank God I have friends who are still like, "Hey, you've gotta check this young band out." But a lot of my friends are in the "I'm only going to listen to old hardcore bands I already like" club. You know, "I've matured and moved on." I'm sorry, I don't get Radiohead. I never did. I don't get Mastodon. I don't get a lot of this shit. It doesn't appeal to me. It doesn't move me. It doesn't touch me like hardcore did and still does. I'm not putting those bands down; it's just not for me. I have friends who love Killing Time, and they love Youth of Today, but you try to play them something new, and then they're like, "Nah, I'm not into that anymore. I'm into this weird spacey shit."

PETE: What always gets to me is when the older scene people show up at the shows and they keep saying shit like, "Yo, I'm getting too old for this shit." You hear it a million times. Then just stay home! They're like, "I grew out of hardcore." Well, if you're here at our show, I guess you didn't. I mean, if you love Bad Brains, and you've loved them for decades, how the fuck could you ever say, "I'm not into this anymore"? Are they not incredible anymore? It's just strange to me.

LOU: We all spent so many Sundays going to CBGB and so many weekends going to shows and being a part of this community. Okay, these anniversaries or these other big events happen, and they're something special, so I understand that people come out of the woodwork. You can't go to every show because you've got a kid and a nine-to-five and things to do.

PETE: It's frustrating when we work hard to put together what we think are great tour packages and people don't come out because it's a weeknight or whatever. It's a little tough.

LOU: We could go to the West Coast with, say, Madball, and we'll do amazing in L.A. or San Francisco. Then you play one of those smaller towns, which we have to do to make the tour make financial sense, and we'll get like fifty or seventy-five people. Like

Reno, Nevada, which used to have a huge hardcore scene: we go there, Sick of It All and Madball, and there are seventy-five tickets sold. I get it to a degree, but I know there are plenty of people sitting at home who could come to these shows but are fighting their midlife crisis: "Is it still okay for me to go to a hardcore show at my age, or with my job, or with a family?"

PETE: Something tells me if it was Turnstile playing or Knocked Loose or one of the newer-generation bands, people would come out and not have those excuses. It's not like they don't like us too, but the younger crowd doesn't use those excuses to stay home.

LOU: We've taken the popular young band out with us, but there's no guarantee that their fans are going to stay to see you if you close the show. I've seen it a million times. Madball took Terror, who worship Madball, out on the road. On their first album, they have two dance parts that are stolen blatantly from Madball. They even admit it. They say it onstage, like, "Here's the second dance part we stole from Madball." They were playing in Detroit, one of Madball's strongholds, and when Terror ended their set, half the crowd left. The younger people didn't stay, and I'm like, "How could they not stay for Madball?!"

PETE: For a lot of the younger kids, hardcore is their identity, but they're not wholeheartedly invested in the scene. They like the cool young bands. I guess it's cool to go to school that week wearing their shirts and shit, but they don't get that we have to keep this thing alive, and how hard that is.

LOU: Plus everyone in America has a "fest" now. Those are the big hardcore events, but there's a weird dynamic with those a lot of the time. We played United Blood Fest in Virginia, named after an Agnostic Front song, so you figure people would know the history. It was in 2010 or 2011. There were the young bands, and they all had this old-school sound. I remember Armand turned to me and said, "These kids love the old-school sound; this is going to be a great show with our fans and all these young kids. It's going to be awesome." Bane and Sick of It All were the headliners. We were getting ready while Bane was on, and Armand said, "Let's see how Bane's doing, it's got to be awesome." There were fifteen hundred people there the whole day, going crazy. We go down to see Bane, and half the crowd had left the room. They were sitting at the merch area, or someplace else. We were like, "What the hell's going on here? This place is half empty now." Then we go upstairs and continue getting ready, and now there's even fewer people there. It was such a generational thing. When I was younger, I didn't go see Raw Deal and leave before fucking Circle Jerks went on. I wasn't even a huge Circle Jerks fan, but they had great songs, and live, their energy was amazing. Just as important, they were part of our history and were an important band. I made the joke when we came out onstage. I said, "Aw, did everybody's mommy and daddy come to pick them up already?" There were a lot of older people, and there were some young kids still there, but the young kids were the most annoying because they were just yelling for us to play songs off the first album.

PETE: The different generations in hardcore are so different from each other. Sometimes I wonder, *Do they only love those older songs, or is it a "keepin' it real" thing, where they have to prove they know old-school Sick of It All?*

LOU: I looked at them from the stage and told them, "You weren't even born when that shit came out." That's when I knew the whole nostalgia thing was in full swing. They wanted to live vicariously in that era, and it's like, just enjoy all the music. Fuck, I'm just being bitter, I guess. And don't get me started on all these reunions! These bands play a show or two for a thirty, forty dollar door price, and the first one's great, but then the crowd dwindles when they do it again and again. In Europe too: "Yeah, we're going to Europe to get some of that Sick of It All money." We would just look at them like, "We've been touring Europe for twenty-something fucking years. That's why we do so well over there. We put in the fucking work, plus, we're not fat, old, and out of shape. You guys couldn't make it through five songs doing what we do.

PETE: Yeah, we're just OLD. But the truth is, we don't feel old at all.

LOU: And again, we CARE about what we do: our sets, how hard-hitting the setlist is, and the sequence of songs. You don't just throw shit together. At that Rev reunion in California, Arthur from Gorilla Biscuits was up there trying to figure out why Craig sounded so good, but in the end, he was like, "Whatever, it sounds all right as it is." He didn't really give a shit how good the gear sounded, which means he didn't care that much about how the band sounded.

PETE: Part of it is that we consider ourselves entertainers. We put on a show, and know our crowd expects that of us. That's why we're still here, and why anyone still cares about us. Because we care about them.

LOU: When we did our twenty-fifth anniversary show at Webster Hall, and we had the confetti cannons, it was just for fun, a laugh. There were "certain people" who never stopped complaining because we took money out of our pockets to entertain the fans. "You might as well shred the money and throw that up in the air as confetti." But we fought for that because we thought we should. People really dug that. Look, a lot of it is perspective. I try not to look at all the bands who've opened for us over the years and wound up getting really big like, "Why them and not us?" Korn, Rancid, AFI—they're all great, and they deserve their success. But there are certain other bands I look at, and I'm like, "Why THEM and not US?!" I'll say this: their audience didn't grow up saying shit like, "You're a hardcore band, you shouldn't make money from this." The generations that came after us think, *you've been successful, that's fucking great*. Not to sound cliché, but, for us, it was a struggle. It took over a decade for us to not have to have day jobs. Some people think we should just feel lucky: "You have what every band wants. You guys make a living." It didn't just magically happen.

PETE: Bands like AF had it rough, but we were part of the first hardcore generation that had to deal with fucking "hardcore politics" and snobbery like in a high school lunchroom.

LOU: Nobody dared to tell AF or the Cro-Mags that they thought they were doing something wrong. No one was going to tell Murphy's Law that they shouldn't tour with the Beastie Boys because they thought they were selling out.

PETE: Because they would get a fucking punch in the face! Plus, it WAS punk rock to play with Beastie Boys in arenas. That was punk as fuck! No one looked at it as a money thing or anything other than a great opportunity.

LOU: People assumed they were probably getting paid dirt, and they got it immediately. They were happy for Murphy's Law. But when we were going to do certain things, we were almost being blamed for doing them.

PETE: *Oh, those guys just took another step towards ruining hardcore.* It was so great when the music was the most important thing, not what a band wore, or how many other great bands were around.

LOU: When Slayer came out and was faster and more evil than Metallica, people still loved Metallica. They didn't forget about them, or Motörhead, or anyone else that was great. It took *...And Justice for All* to bring out the people who would say things like, "Yeah, I hate all the people in my school who like Metallica, so I don't like Metallica anymore." That happens with hardcore too, but it seems as if it only takes six months, not years.

PETE: With hardcore, when the crossover was going on, all the hardcore people who had been metal people five minutes earlier felt like they had to pretend they never liked metal. Sure, they moved on to something different, but why act like your past never existed?

LOU: We've been addressing this for years: "What can we do to get the younger crowd to listen?" I wish people could get back to just being fans again. When Metallica put out *Ride the Lightning,* I didn't suddenly only want to hear the stuff off *Kill 'Em All.* I was excited for them to put out new albums. I wasn't so focused on what new band would dethrone them or anything like that.

PETE: We were avid fucking music fans. The more great bands, the better. We were into it on a level that other people don't usually get to. That mentality seems to have really changed. There were a lot of people like us, but younger people just aren't into music the way they used to be. Music fans have rebelled against the whole music business system. Did you see that Tower Records documentary? They thought they could charge whatever they wanted forever. It was like, "Okay, my favorite band is going to put out an album. Now it's delayed. It's delayed again, and then it's not even that good. You're overcharging me, almost twenty bucks for a CD that I don't even really like. There's one good song on it, and I had to wait an entire year for the fucking label or the band to get their shit together to put this thing out in the first place." People figured it out and were like "Fuck this!" With Fat, we were actually getting royalty checks for the work we put in, and then it just stopped.

LOU: Thanks, streaming services! It's a double-edged sword. Sure, now more people can get your music, but you don't get paid properly for it, and those services don't exactly help create real, hardcore music fans. Unless you ask them to play a band's full album for you, they're basically choosing for you, and their choices are usually terrible!

PETE: Fast-forward to nowadays: it's as if people just don't care. They can't seem to be bothered with music. Like Lou says onstage all the time, "Hey, motherfuckers, it's free! Why the fuck don't you know the new shit? It's fucking free." The "I don't have the money for it" excuse is out the window. Laziness, man.

LOU: There's definitely laziness, but also, kids' priorities have changed. Our dream has always been to play Madison Square Garden. You know who plays MSG now? Fucking gamers! That's who kids go to see at Madison Square Garden. Or it will be an orchestra playing the soundtrack to Pokémon or Final Fantasy, sold out at sixty bucks a ticket.

PETE: And it's full of Comic-Con nerds. My daughter and all her friends, their heroes are guys who play fucking Minecraft. They're in the corner of the screen playing the game. I talked to her about it, like, "This guy is just playing a video game," and she told me, "But I'm learning more about the game too," which was true.

LOU: He has millions of dollars and four Lamborghinis.

PETE: Yeah, he just bought a new green Lamborghini, then sold his green Lamborghini and got a purple one. The guy's twenty-one years old! I cannot understand music not being important in somebody's life.

LOU: It was our escape, and we identified with it. I don't know how gaming has taken so much away from that, but it has. Maybe it's the control kids have over it, holding the controller in their hands and succeeding or failing along with their friends. I remember when people started watching movies on their phones, and I would just be like, "I can't watch a movie on my phone." I can now, but I would rather have that big, loud, theater experience. Even when we're on flights, I'll still want to see the movie in the theater because watching on this little screen doesn't do it justice. I love to take my daughter to the movies. She loves the experience. We go, and she gets the kid's pack with the popcorn and the drink, and we laugh and watch the movie. But she could just as well watch it on her iPad. It doesn't matter to her.

PETE: The games are fun, but you don't really feel anything. Music can make you feel happy. It can make you feel cool. It can make you feel tough. Lucy sits there and laughs because the guy makes funny faces and acts like a goofball, but there's no soul-touching aspect to it.

LOU: It's like the casual music fans when we were younger. The guys who were really into sports would say, "I like some Metallica." They were never the "Fucking Metallica" people. A great song makes me want to check out all the other shit. I get sucked in.

PETE: Are we're basically saying we're just old now?

LOU: Nah, but shit's really different now. Remember when our parents couldn't really figure out what the fuck we were doing, or what we were into? We never thought we'd be those parents, EVER. But I mean, as far as trying to get the younger kids to care about what we do, I don't have the answer. I wish I did. I feel like we've tried so many things to regenerate the fanbase. Some things kinda work, but there's no secret potion, that's for sure. Plus, the challenges we deal with in America are way different than in Europe or the rest of the world. In the States, hardcore will always be in the music ghetto, but in Europe, it's treated like a legitimate genre. You can make money over there, but it's become harder to balance with how hard it's become here.

PETE: It's just really strange in the States nowadays. It's much more of a challenge to make it work on the road.

LOU: In the States, there's the whole nostalgia thing going on, this reliving-your-teenage-years thing, but I don't think we could keep going if people didn't like our new records. We could go to

Bogotá, Colombia, and open the show with the first song off our new album, and the place would go absolutely ape-shit.

PETE: Whereas in America, they'd be standing around waiting for us to play something from the first three albums. They keep up with us elsewhere, with all of our albums. They don't define hardcore strictly by what's "old-school." They're dedicated to the band as long as we're still good. And we do change the setlist in the States. We put more of the older songs in the set. What if your favorite band didn't play your favorite song?

LOU: It makes me wonder if any new hardcore band starting out could possibly wind up being around as long as we have, without much industry support and without being on the radio, fueled only by their fans. If we were starting out today, just doing what we love, could we survive?

PETE: I don't think so, but I'd rather be in this band than anything else. That's how we make it through the lean times.

LOU: Yup.

1. HE'S UNCLE FREDDY, AND THEN THERE'S UNCLE VINNIE, AND UNCLE DAVEY, AND UNCLE LOU....

LOU: My wife, Melissa, used to go to shows all the time. She was one of those kids who would sneak into CB's when she was underage. I've known her since she was a young kid. She just stuck around after shows, and we became really good friends. Then it changed years later. It was a little strange, I guess, but it didn't feel strange because we were such close friends. It was just a natural progression. We had similar taste in things and always had fun, laughing. It progressed from there.

MELISSA KOLLER (LOU'S WIFE): My cousin was babysitting me once, and there was a show she wanted to go to. I think I was twelve. I promise, it's not as controversial as it's sounding already. She wanted to go to this show. Her older brother had already exposed me to punk and some other stuff, but she had started to introduce me to New York hardcore. I wanted to go with her, and she was like, "There's no way you're coming to this show with me. I just won't go to the show." I was like, "No, no, no. We can go. My parents aren't going to be home until tomorrow. Just find a way to get me into the show." So, she found a way to get me into

CBGB, and we saw Black Train Jack. That was the first time I met Lou. Sick of It All was my favorite hardcore band, so, I kept in touch, not just with him, but with Pete too. When I got older and moved out of the house, that's when Lou and I started dating and became a couple. There was some apprehension at first. I mean, knowing him before dating him, there was total apprehension.

PETE: I actually met Mei-Ling at the gym. She had nothing to do with hardcore at all. What's crazy is that I lived on First Avenue between Fourth and Fifth Street for eighteen or nineteen years, and she lived on Fourth Street between First and Second Avenue, but somehow, I never ran into her. I'm sure that we crossed paths though. She was a Lower East Side hip-hop girl, and she would only go to dance clubs and stuff like that, but she knew the neighborhood. Now she always tells me stories like, "When we were little kids, we would run past CBGB and be scared because everyone looked so weird." Then one day at the gym, we smiled at one another and started talking. That was that.

MEI-LING KOLLER (PETE'S WIFE): I'm pretty sure when he smiled at me. He thought I knew who he was because of the band, but I didn't. We went to California Pizza Kitchen on our first date 'cause I'm easy. I remember taking some leftover pizza with us, and Pete gave it to a homeless person on the street. The guy asked, "What is this, pizza?" When we said yes, he threw it away! We were both like, "Fuck that guy!" That's some New York shit right there!

PETE: Mei loves music, all kinds of music. Early on, I asked her, "Hey, do you want to come with me to a show?" I took her to Warped Tour, and we were standing onstage watching Pennywise in front of probably fifteen thousand people. At first, she was like, "What the fuck is this?" But she took an interest in the music, and also the community aspect of it.

MEI-LING: I still called them concerts. "Oh, we're going to a concert? You're playing a concert?" I didn't realize other people called them shows. I even wound up in a band later on, and Pete was our bass player.

LOU: Melissa has gotten up and played bass with Murphy's Law. She never had her own band, but she can play instruments. She can play guitar, and she can play bass.

PETE: I would tell Mei, "Well, I didn't know how to play guitar that great when I started," and then I got her a bass from Gibson. We sat there and wrote some songs, and then she started a band called Skizo Nation. They even recorded something. Being in Sick of It All, we have lots of friends, so Mei's first show with Skizo Nation was opening for Rancid. Then they played with us, and then they played with the Bouncing Souls, and then they played with Agnostic Front. I was like, "Wow, that's pretty good." She's also my guitar tech when Lucy's on vacation. She has done three full tours already.

MEI-LING: I'm just happy I get to work for the band and be with Pete and Lucy doing something fun. I stay completely out of their way, and out of band business. If he asks my opinion about something, that's one thing, but I try not to be Yoko Ono.

LOU: Melissa and I talked about having kids when we moved in together. Then a year or so after moving in together, we got married, then we got a dog, and then she was so excited that she wanted to have a kid. I said, "All right, let's try it." Then we had Aurelia. I'm a go-with-the-flow kind of guy. She felt like we were ready, partly because we had a bunch of money saved up. I was confident, but being in a band, you know, it's feast or famine. We could tour for four years and be like, "Look at all this money!" and then the second we stop touring, the bank account just shrinks because you have no income. The decision to have a baby put some stress on us, but you don't want these types of decisions to be about money.

MELISSA: I had some health issues when I was in my early twenties and ended up having some major surgery. That surgery caused a lot of scar tissue internally, and I was told that I was going to have a hard time having kids. Now, I'm the type of person who, if you tell me I can't do something, I'm going to prove you wrong, so, WE'RE GOING TO HAVE A KID! We consciously made the decision to try to have our daughter. We ended up having to go through in vitro to have her because of all the health issues.

PETE: Mei and I tried to have a baby for around ten years after getting married, and nothing was happening. The doctors said there was nothing wrong with me and nothing wrong with her.

MEI-LING: All of my friends were having babies, so we tried too, but I had a miscarriage, and we stopped trying for a long time. The band actually took me on the road that first time to cheer me up because I was so sad. Pete didn't want me to stay home alone and depressed while he was on tour. After we stopped trying to have a baby, naturally, I found out I was pregnant with Lucy.

PETE: Being a father to Lucy is the greatest thing ever! I love being married, and I love having Lucy. We go to these places we've toured a million times over, but now it's new again. When we had three days off in Prague, it was great. Lucy got to see a real castle. All the teachers in Lucy's school are just like, "God, I wish I could go with you guys." She's been around the band her whole life. I have this really cool picture of her from the Czech Republic, and there are twenty thousand people in front of her, and she's just standing there at the edge of the stage looking out at them. When her friends see that, they're like, "Oh my God, that's crazy!" Little do they know, the whole time, in between songs, she'd be like, "Daddy, how many more songs? Are you almost done?" When she meets people in other bands, she's not fazed at all. But if it's her favorite YouTuber.... Band members are not celebrities compared to him. Those are her rock stars.

Lucy vs. Behemoth

LOU: Aurelia comes on tour once in a while. We had one weekend where we did three festivals, and Melissa and Aurelia came. There was one in the Czech Republic; the other two were in Germany. It went from ten thousand people at the first one, to twenty thousand people at the second, and we ended at Full Force, which is sixty thousand people. She'd just stand there onstage and watch. As I'm walking offstage, she grabs my hand and goes, "You did good today, Daddy. There were a lot more people today than usual." I have a great picture of that moment. It's a silhouette of me coming offstage with a towel.

The first show she came to, she was a year old. We opened up for Suicidal Tendencies in New Jersey, and it was great. Her friend Ella came too. She definitely loved playing with Ella more than seeing us, but when we played, she stood onstage and watched. She was amazed by the subwoofers vibrating the stage. She would feel her feet vibrating and stare at her feet. She liked Mike Muir though. When Mike was running around and doing all his crazy moves, she just stared at him. She was amazed by him. She came on the last Warped Tour we did, and she liked that. She didn't want to watch any band but Sick of It All unless they had females in the band. We saw every female-fronted band and every all-female band, even if it was only for a couple of songs, because she's a kid and wants to run around and play. I'd say, "Come on, I want to go see this band," and she would look; if there were no girls, she would be like, "I just don't want to see this band."

MELISSA: One of the things with me personally is always being supportive of what he does because, honestly, how many people can say they do what they love, or what they set out to do as a kid, and are following through with it? At the same time, I have my own career. I do things that are meaningful to me as a person and just always know that when we come home, then we're together. Being Aurelia's father is something that keeps Lou grounded. He's definitely a different person when she's in the room. She knows how to pull on his heartstrings, and I see him in her too. I can see the fire in her. They're best buds. Also, I think it's a great experience for her to see different places and what her dad does, to understand that you don't have to define your life by somebody else's definition of success. I think it's great to expose her to that, but, as a mom, I also want to be mindful of the fact that she's still a kid. There are things on the road that, in my opinion, children don't need to be exposed to. I'm also mindful of the fact that people go to the shows to have a good time, release some stress, and have a couple of drinks and go crazy, and they may not be as comfortable doing that around a child. I want to have a sense of balance in raising her.

PETE: Our girls are around it a lot, so they're used to it, and there are a lot of fun parts on the road for them. Lucy loves Davey from AFI, and she loves their music. She also loves Freddy from Madball because, once, when we were playing our set, Freddy and

Lucy sat on the side of the stage together, and Freddy played with her. He's a dad, so he knows the kid's probably bored. But she's never been like, "Wow, that's Freddy from Madball!" To her, he's Uncle Freddy, and then there's Uncle Vinnie, and Uncle Davey, and Uncle Lou. She has ten thousand uncles. It's cool that they aren't so impressed by who's in what band. They only see them as family.

LOU: I'm actually very shy. Everybody says, "You're not shy. You get up in front of all those people," but that's totally different for some reason. I mean, I'm nervous before I go on: *Is the crowd going to react tonight?* But as soon as I walk out there, it's like they're my friends. I might get embarrassed if I stumble or something, but I'll go up there and make fun of myself right away. With Aurelia, I can see that she gets stuff from both me and Melissa. She's started to show the shyness that I have. We'll be playing basketball and one of my neighbors will tell her, "Hey, you're really good. We have this girls' basketball team." Immediately she's like, "No, I don't want to do it." She says, "I don't want people looking at me." At her age, I might have said the same thing, but it's easier to deal with because I've been there myself.

MELISSA: When Lou's away on the road, I try to keep her going and lead by example. I'm like, "Yeah, sure you can miss somebody, but you have to keep doing the things that are important to you. There are tasks that need to be done, but we can still have fun. We're not going to sit at home and just wait for somebody to come home." I'm always trying to keep her on the move and keep her busy, of course, understanding that she's still going to miss her dad. When he's not on tour, he's with her 24/7, but when he's away, it does take a toll on her. I try not to make a big deal of it, but sometimes I do feel bad. He missed her kindergarten graduation; there are things he misses because of touring.

LOU: Balancing all that I do is a challenge, but you have to make it work. I love being home, but I have to go on tour because not only is it the way I make money, it's something I love to do. When I'm home, I love spending time with Aurelia. I love that I have extended time to spend with her. Some of Aurelia's friends' dads come home at 8:00 at night, see their kids for twenty minutes, and then put them to bed. That would suck for both of us. But there are those times on the road when all I want to do is be with her. We played this place in Oklahoma, and it sucked! You'd think this place would have been amazing because they had a record store selling punk and they had this underground club, but it was in the middle of nowhere. It's just so depressing. You get there, and nobody shows up. I was on the phone with Aurelia right when we were about to go on. She's bawling her eyes out: "Daddy, I miss you. Daddy, come home." It's a Wednesday night, and we're basically doing this show for gas money to get to the next town. It was our bridge between wherever we'd been and the West Coast. I hang up the phone. My daughter's crying. I go to get onstage, and there are fucking forty-five people standing at the back of the room. I'm thinking, Why the fuck are we here? I worked my ass off to try to get people going, and have some fun, but no, everybody hid in the shadows in the back. That was one of those nights where, in between songs, I was like, *Wow, I'm really questioning my life choices right now.*

PETE: It's funny because I was a bachelor dude, doing whatever I was doing. Now this is all I want to do. I want Lucy and Mei with me all the time because I have fun with them. I think I was born to be a dad. I really do. When I'm home, I'm home. I see all of our friends working so hard, and they can only see their kids for small amounts of time because they have to rush to sleep, to rush back to work. In the summer, maybe they have a week off. It sucks for them.

LOU: Now that Aurelia's a little older, she'll spend time with her friends and all that, but I still have all the time I want with her. I'm here. I get to pick my kid up every day after school. A lot of parents don't get to do that. Of course, they have much nicer houses! Also, as Pete mentioned, our kids get to see all these great places around the world. When Aurelia was little and we'd take her on tour, we'd go to Paris, and she'd say, "I want to move to Paris." The next day we'd be in London, and she'd be like, "I want to move to London!" Then Milan, and it's crazy. Now television has entered her life a lot more, and she tells me, "Daddy, take me to Hollywood." I'm like, "You don't want to go to Hollywood, it's a shithole!"

PETE: What does she want to see there? What does she think is so special about it?

LOU: She used to love these TV shows where all the kids go to L.A. High, and everybody is a singer. I'm like, "It's not really like that. Just go into Manhattan, and then we'll watch Fame." I'm actually a bit of a sucker for that Southern California lifestyle: the cars, skateboarding, that whole life.

PETE: Wherever it is, of course I want Lucy to have it better than I ever did, but I want to pass on certain things I've learned about life, you know? I have a problem with authority. None of us want to be working for someone who's going to belittle you or anything like that. You don't want to be in that position. But if you apply yourself to something you really love, then you don't ever have to take shit from anybody. But I also tell her that she doesn't have to follow her friends. Do what you like doing, and if someone makes fun of you for that, then they're not your friends. Fuck them.

LOU: I try to give Aurelia plenty of advice, but she doesn't listen to any of it. I tell her the same thing Pete tells Lucy: just do what you love.

PETE: I wish our kids could spend more time together. Lucy absolutely LOVES Aurelia.

LOU: Yeah, they love each other.

PETE: Anything we do: "Can we go get Aurelia?" I'm like, "But we can't. She lives in New Jersey." She'll have her birthday party and ask, "Can you pay for her to come down to Florida?"

LOUIS KOLLER SENIOR: Both Louie and Melissa, and Pete and Mei-Ling, have beautiful little daughters and have made us very happy and lucky grandparents. Without question, Melissa and Mei-Ling are good mothers. As far as Lou and Pete, I think that they are more like best friends to Aurelia and Lucy than they are fathers a lot of the time. Don't get me wrong; they are very good parents. When the girls were younger, they both suffered separation anxiety when their fathers would leave for a tour. There was a lot of crying by the girls and the need for consoling by their moms.

LOU: It sucks that we don't live closer. Growing up, we had a lot of cousins, and we were all maybe an hour away at the most from each other.

PETE: Any birthday, there were at least ten, eleven kids there.

LOU: We'd go to all of the cousin's birthday parties, and they'd come to ours. We'd go to family barbeques, then to this one's for Christmas, and that one's for whatever. Thanksgiving was always at our grandmother's house, and everybody would come to Queens. For Lucy and Aurelia, it sucks that we live so far apart, but when they get together, it's just nonstop. They see one another, and, in front of us, they're a little awkward. They're like, "Hi," and they hug each other, but then, bang: two seconds later, they're thick as thieves, going wild in the house.

PETE: It's amazing how kids relate to one another.

LOU: We went to a friend's wedding in Chicago. She said, "Bring your daughter because all my other friends are bringing their kids," so we went to the wedding, and there was one other little girl there Aurelia's age. She didn't speak a word of English, and Aurelia doesn't speak German. They just looked at each other, grabbed each other's hands, and took off running. They were playing, speaking their own languages to each other with their stuffed animals, having the time of their lives. Kids are awesome like that.

PETE: We were just in Europe, and we did a few days of rehearsal. Lucy was bored at first, but then the club owner brought his two kids. The kids didn't speak English, but they became immediate pals. Pretty cool.

LOU: Aurelia and Lucy have to do another tour together one of these days. The meeting place is usually my parents' house because it's almost in between us, a little closer to Florida, but close enough for me and Aurelia to fly down, and it makes our parents so happy. They regress ten years in age when their granddaughters are around them. The kids come in, and they just light up.

LOU: When Pete and I were kids, my dad would watch the news or sports all day. But the grandkids come in and every TV in the house is on Disney or Nickelodeon. I'll say, "Hey, let your grandpa watch the news." He'll be like, "No, no, it's okay." They're not even paying attention—they're just screaming and yelling—but my mother will say, "No, no, the house is always too quiet." They'd love for us to have more kids, but I can't afford it.

PETE: For us, it just didn't happen.

LOU: I kept saying, "All right, she's two, or she's three, now. This is the perfect time to have another one." But Melissa was just getting back into her career, and I was like, "It's getting late." To me, the cutoff is five years; otherwise the age difference is going to be way too much. From the age of three, I'd be like, "Do you want a little brother or sister?" At first, she'd say, "No brothers! I don't want a little brother." But because on *Peppa Pig* they call them "little BOTHERS," she'd say, "I don't want a little bother." Now she's just like, "I don't want any siblings because I don't want to share my toys, and I don't want to share my room." I remember my dad saying something about us being the last of the Koller line because neither of us have boys. I always tell Aurelia, "If you get married, keep your last name." She says she will.

PETE: Because we have such a famous last name, of course.

LOU: Now if she was in that other KOHLER family....

PETE: She could swim in that toilet money! You know something else that's weird? Both of our wives are a mix of Asian and Hispanic. It just worked out that way.

MELISSA: I'm a Mexipino. Mei and I are both half Asian and half Hispanic. It's such a weird dynamic. Plus, each of us has one girl.

LOU: Yeah, egg rolls and tacos and a lot of rice in there.

MELISSA: At the end of the day, I think Lou and Pete rely heavily on one another, even if there's not a conscious effort to rely on one another. I feel like because they know that the band means so much to the other, they keep it going. There's a peace of mind to it, and to have your brother on the road with you all the time, I just think there's a sense of comfort in that. The sense of family runs deep, but at the same time, that's your blood, and they're the two youngest out of the four boys. I think that if it had been any other way, if they had started a band independently of one another, neither one of them would've stuck it out as long as they have in Sick of It All.

MEI-LING: I just wish they got more credit for what they've done. I feel like they never get enough recognition for what they've accomplished. They hold it down, and they're brothers. There's no drama; they're just regular guys. They're friends who hang out acting silly all day. There are these two brothers in the band, but you know, it's really four brothers with Armand and Craig. It's definitely a family.

MELISSA: It's almost like a yin-and-yang scenario. It really is. I think they know what buttons to press and not press with one another. If they share a hotel room, Lou knows automatically that

Pete's going to turn the AC all the way up, even if it's going to hurt Lou's throat, and he's going to complain to me about it, but he's not going to complain to Pete. But, most importantly, seeing them as brothers in a family dynamic, they're both very present for their daughters, and, at the same time, have very different parenting approaches. But you can see that they both adore those little girls of theirs.

2. THE KIDS WILL HAVE THEIR SAY

AURELIA KOLLER (LOU'S DAUGHTER): I really like Sick of It All. The band is really cool, and they jump around a lot. They're also really loud, and I like loud stuff. My dad jumps around a lot onstage. I don't think he jumps around at home at all unless we're playing some kind of game. Also, he doesn't sing at home unless he's practicing. He does help me build tents though.

LUCY KOLLER (PETE'S DAUGHTER): I think my dad is so cool! I love watching him do his spins.

AURELIA: All of the tours I've been on were really, really fun, but I really liked Warped Tour. Once we got to go to Six Flags. We went on the Ferris wheel, and, when we got to the top, you could see everything: the stages and where everyone parked. I would sit at the merch booth with my water gun, and when people would pass by, I would squirt them! I would hide behind the table, peek my head up to see if someone was coming, and then squirt them in the face.

LUCY: The only thing I don't like about tours is that there are no showers on the bus.

AURELIA: A lot of times I get to sit on the drum riser with my friends and watch everybody go crazy.

LUCY: I like to play drums, but I hide behind Uncle Craig's bass speaker because I get shy.

AURELIA: We were in Germany once. The band had played a few songs, and as they were starting the next one, the wind started picking up, and it started raining really hard. Everybody started packing up and leaving. It was a huge crowd too. So, we got on the bus, and there was a big lightning storm. I saw a tent up on a hill where people were sleeping for the festival, and people were running out of the tent because lightning had hit it. We ran back onto the bus and stayed there with our friends until it stopped.

LUCY: When we're out on tour, Mommy and Daddy let me eat pizza almost every night, and lots of good candy. Oh, and I get to ride my scooter all day, and in the club during sound check.

AURELIA: I miss my dad while he's on tour. I miss him playing with me and skateboarding with me while my mom's at work. I wish I could go on tour with him more. The tours are really fun, and I get to go to really cool places I've never been to before.

3. YO! LOGAN TELLS ME YOU'RE IN A HARD ROCK BAND

LOU: I had a godson, and he would come to shows when he was really young. I didn't think he really cared or was impressed by what I did, but one day I went to pick him up at school, and all of his little friends came running. They were the troublemakers in the class. They all come up to me, and this chubby little kid comes up and says, "Yo! Logan tells me you're in a HARD ROCK band." That was the first time I knew he had told other kids what I did. Logan turns and tells him, "HardCORE. Not hard ROCK. Hardcore!" I thought it was the funniest thing in the world.

I was dating a girl, but we broke up and stayed friends. She got pregnant by someone else, and I helped her through the pregnancy because she really didn't have anybody. We kind of started dating again, and I was there when the baby was born. She was like, "You could be Logan's godfather." From the day he was born until he was ten years old, I was in his life almost every single day, and my mom raised him. My mom liked the girl, and she fell in love with the baby and raised him. Then, when he was ten, his mom had a different relationship and wanted to be a family unit, so she cut him off from all contact with my mother and me. It was because of the boyfriend, because he was a "proud Latino man." You know, this is MY family now; we don't need this other guy in his life. It was bullshit, but whatever.

I managed to stay in touch with him for many years, and, out of nowhere one day, he asked if he could come to see us play with Rancid. I eventually lost contact with him for years, and then, it was one of those strange things. It was the day after my daughter's birthday. Melissa and I were talking, and she asked, "Have you heard from Logan?" I said, "No, I haven't heard from him in a while. I'll check up on him." The next day, Melissa went online and said, "I searched his name on Facebook, and there are all these sad notes; please go check it out." I looked, and then I put his name in a Google search, and his obituary came up. He had passed away.

I think it was only two days later because he passed away the night of Aurelia's birthday. They'd already had him cremated. I didn't even get to go to the wake. Nobody told us. Nobody called us. It was really hard for me and my mother. It was heartbreaking for me because I loved him. He was like my own son. He would even call me Dad years later. But I think it was even harder on my mom because that was like her first grandchild that she raised.

PETE: He was part of our family. He was at my parents' house every single day for ten years. Lou and I took him to Disney once.

LOU: He loved it. That was one of his favorite vacations ever. Not to sound cliché, but he fell in with the wrong crowd. He moved out to Long Island and got into heroin. It was one of the hardest things I ever had to go through. I hadn't spoken to him in maybe a couple of years, and then he was gone. I kept asking myself, "Could I have helped him if I was in his life?" It's horrible.

PETE: Everybody asks themselves that in that kind of situation: "What could I have done?" It's almost impossible that you could have done anything for them.

LOU: One of my best friends went through that for years. She was addicted, and it took her years and years, and several tries at rehab. She gave me the practical answer that, no matter what I would've done for that kid, he would've tried to manipulate me to get money from me for drugs. I was like, "Maybe, but still. I would have liked to at least been there." Also, it happened on the happiest day of my life, my daughter's birthday. Now I have to remember that that's the night my godson took his fucking life at twenty fucking years old.

LOU: There were times after he left our house when I saw him because he had been left home alone for the weekend. He would call me up and let me know, "Um, I'm home by myself." If you're ten years old, what are you doing on your own? He'd let me know, "Well, I have money, and I have food stocked up, but my mom won't be home until Monday morning." I'd be like, "Right. I'll be right over," and I'd pick him up, and he'd hang out with me for the weekend. It's fucking tragic.

4. IT'S KIND OF LIKE RUSSIAN ROULETTE

LOU: Our mom was diagnosed with cancer for the second time. We thought she'd beaten it, and so did her doctors. Aurelia and I were down in South Carolina with her, and she was going for her final test after a lot of treatment. She started saying that she couldn't breathe. Her doctor kept saying, "Don't worry, it's not cancer. It can't be cancer. You beat cancer. There's no evidence of cancer." Then, after the last test, they told her that they needed to test her bone marrow. They test the bone marrow, and, sure enough, it's cancer. Usually, that's a death sentence. You've got three months to live. She had been getting chemo for about a year. It was working too. They even said, "It's not going to cure it. It'll slow it down. It might even reduce it." When she was diagnosed, it was pretty weird. She was always very healthy. She would go for two-mile walks. Then one year, when she was down in Florida on the beach with one of our brothers, she told him, "I have to turn back. I can't catch my breath." We started her on a year of tests. We were going through all these tests, and the doctor kept swearing to her, "It can't be cancer again." They tested her bone marrow as just a formality: "It's probably not what's bothering you, but we have to test it." I happened to be there, and she comes home: "It's cancer." It was bone marrow cancer.

PETE: She always had a healthy glow, tan skin. But then she got super pale. Almost like a weird, grayish look. She was like, "Look at my skin. There's something really not right." At first when they went in, they said, "This is a cocktail of chemo. It's going to work really slowly, or it's going to knock it out super quick." It knocked out like 70 percent of the cancer. They told her, "This is great." She kept going with that. Then, eventually, that mixture of drugs stopped working. Her bones hurt all the time. She was super tired. It was horrible. And it really sucks because none of us really live close by. I live six hours away, and that's the closest. I just wish they lived here.

LOU: When you spoke to her, especially after the first treatment stopped working, she'd say, "It's kind of like Russian roulette." She'll come home from the treatment and be completely ill. The next day, she'll wake up, and she'll feel fine for a few hours. Then, out of nowhere, she'll get completely ill again, then be completely fine again. She can't travel because of that. She wanted to come up for Aurelia's birthday, but she can't do that. The saddest thing is, she says things like, "I just don't think it's worth it anymore because I'm not living. I'm just existing." That really hurts. Even when we're down there with our daughters, the one thing that makes her the happiest, she can't enjoy it. The girls will say, "Let's play Go Fish, Grandma." She can play two hands of Go Fish, and then she's like, "I have to lie down." At one point, she looked at me and said, "I really wish you had your daughter ten years earlier. I feel so useless right now. There's so much I want to do with her." I know she didn't mean to hurt my feelings, but I'm sitting there thinking, *Gee, thanks*. But it's not about me. Aurelia sits there and helps her out, and I don't have to tell her anything. Last time we were down there, Aurelia and I would sleep in the same room, and when I'd wake up, she'd be gone. I'd hear her in the kitchen helping my mom, saying, "Okay, you have to take these two pills now, right, Grandma? Then these four...." She learned in one day what pills my mom had to take in the morning, and every day, she got up and helped her. It was super sad when we were flying into Paris. I called my mom from the airport. She said, "Say hello to Paris for me, I'll never see it again." I was like, "Oh, don't say that."

PETE: You don't want to agree that it's true, but she can't travel anymore.

LOU: We have a dear friend, Susan. She had just had her baby and found out she had cancer. I remember talking to her about it, and she was always so upset: "I want to see my son grow up. I want to spend time with him...." Then one day, out of the blue, I get a phone call from her. "I'm just calling to say goodbye." She was so normal about it, almost happy. I asked, "What do you mean, 'goodbye'?" She was like, "There's nothing more they can do. It's only a matter of days or weeks at the most." I was sitting on the other end of the phone trying to think of what to say. I couldn't wrap my head around how she came to peace with this. She said, "What else am I going to do? I know my son is going to be well taken care of. Yeah, I want to see him grow up, but you know what? He's going to be fine." I just couldn't hear what she was saying after that. I've spent too many years involved in hardcore. I'd just be like, "Fuck you, death!"

PETE: I can't imagine life without my parents. Everything artistic—drawing, music, all of that—comes from my mom. Especially drawing, because when Lou draws something, it's the same way my mom would draw it. If I draw something, it's the same way that she would draw it too. Really strange how that comes to be.

LOU: They both instilled important values in us, but I think what we learned more so from our mom is compassion. My mom would always say, "You never judge a person by the way they look. It's about their actions."

PETE: My father is the complete opposite of that.

LOU: She was a young girl when the Nazis invaded Paris and took over Poitiers, where she lived. She saw horrors done to her neighbors. Her family was harassed, and her sister was thrown in jail because she told German soldiers to fuck off when they were catcalling her. They thought they would never see her again. She saw all of that stuff. They would bring escaped prisoners of war to the farm Pete and I almost worked at, and then they would take them to a boat, which would go over the channel back to England. Seeing that ugliness made her very open-minded, when it could have made her the opposite.

PETE: To this day, if I'm watching a fight on TV, boxing or MMA, if it's a black guy and a white guy fighting, I'll say to Lucy, "The guy in the blue shorts or the guy in the green shorts" if she wants to know who I'm rooting for. If someone asks her, "What does that person look like?" she'll never respond with skin color. I actually have to tell Lucy—I don't say "dicks"—that 99.9 percent of people you meet in your life are absolute idiots.

LOU: Most people ARE dicks! When we were punks like that, we weren't ever like, "Fuck you, old lady!" We weren't those guys. We were the guys who got up on the subway and gave our seats to elderly people. I remember Armand and me being on the bus once going to Flushing, and these old people got on. We both got up to give them our seats. The lady looks at Armand's jacket, which had an Iron Maiden patch on it. She goes, "Iranian Mailman?" We just started laughing. "Well, you're close."

PETE: That goes back to our parents. We have manners. We actually have manners.

PART XX
A FEW OF OUR FAVORITE THINGS

LOU

FAVORITE FRONT PEOPLE
– IN NO PARTICULAR ORDER

This list could have been my favorite NYHC front people alone, but the ones here have all had a big impact on me:

JOHN BRANNON (NEGATIVE APPROACH)
The voice!!! John, along with Chris Notaro of the Crumbsuckers, was a big influence on the way I wanted to "sing." John had such a brutal voice without sounding like Cookie Monster.

FREDDIE MERCURY (QUEEN)
He could control a crowd with a look and cheeky grin. Classy. He made it seem so effortless, and it looked as if he enjoyed every moment onstage.

WENDY O. WILLIAMS (PLASMATICS)

Energy! Innovator of the wild abandon of early punk!

LEMMY (MOTÖRHEAD)

He was rock and roll. He was Chuck Berry, Elvis, and James Brown all rolled into one badass motherfucker, who was the epitome of cool. I used to tell people that Lemmy was the Frank Sinatra of heavy music, but he was the whole Rat Pack and more. And his voice.... To be that rough and still carry a melody and hit those notes.... I wish I could do that.

DEE SNIDER (TWISTED SISTER)

Here's a man who really commanded your attention, and not just by the way he looked, mind you. He would single you out if you were at their show just to be seen and not for the band or music. A high-energy performer with the gift of gab, and his Long Island, New York attitude, he made sure the whole bar, club, or arena was having a good time.

H.R. (BAD BRAINS)

At his peak, one of the most amazing, if not the best, front men in any genre of music. Intense, explosive, and powerful. His influence is undeniable! Nonstop from the first note to the last! H.R is untouchable.

JIMMY G. (MURPHY'S LAW)

Take everything I said about all the other front people on this list, wrap it up, and add one of the funniest, wildest, nicest guys you'll ever meet, and that's Jimmy G. He can take a cold, uninterested crowd, and, by the third song, turn them around with his charm and humor! His shows at CBGB weren't just shows; they were the best parties you'd ever been to, uniting everyone with his jokes, beer, and some of the hardest pits of that time. He is a born entertainer, and my favorite front man of all time.

FAVORITE METAL/HARD ROCK ALBUMS

Black Sabbath (Black Sabbath)
Master of Reality (Black Sabbath)
Arise (Sepultura)
2112 (Rush)
If You Want Blood, You've Got It (AC/DC)
Destroyer (KISS)
Van Halen (Van Halen)
Battle Hymns (Manowar)
Morbid Tales (Celtic Frost)
The Best of Sweet (Sweet)
Ride the Lightning (Metallica)
Jailbreak (Thin Lizzy)
Under the Blade (Twisted Sister)
British Steel (Judas Priest)
No Sleep 'til Hammersmith (Motörhead)

FAVORITE NON-PUNK, HARDCORE, OR METAL ALBUMS

Decemberunderground (AFI)
Meat Is Murder (The Smiths)
Disintegration (The Cure)
Greatest Hits/The No. 1's (Diana Ross and The Supremes)
The Good, the Bad and the Ugly (Ennio Morricone)
Diamond Life (Sade)
American IV: The Man Comes Around (Johnny Cash)
Presenting the Fabulous Ronettes Featuring Veronica (The Ronettes)
Plus, a ton of Motown, '60s/'70s girl groups, classic rock, etc.

FAVORITE PUNK/HARDCORE/OI! ALBUMS

Voice of a Generation (Blitz)
Out of Step (Minor Threat)
The ROIR Sessions (Bad Brains)
Rock for Light (Bad Brains)
Never Mind the Bollocks, Here's the Sex Pistols (Sex Pistols)
Brightside (Killing Time)
Hear Nothing See Nothing Say Nothing (Discharge)
City Baby Attacked by Rats (GBH)
Screams from the Gutter (Raw Power)
The Shape of Punk to Come (Refused)
Let's Start a War (The Exploited)
Suicidal Tendencies (Suicidal Tendencies)
The Age of Quarrel (Cro-Mags)
Strong Reaction (Pegboy)
Tied Down (Negative Approach)
Hold It Down (Madball)
Tell Us the Truth (Sham 69)
Youth Anthems for the New Order (Reagan Youth)
Progression Through Unlearning (Snapcase)
Just Can't Hate Enough (Sheer Terror)
New Hope for the Wretched (Plasmatics)
Murphy's Law (Murphy's Law)
We Are...The League (Anti-Nowhere League)
Don't Turn Away (Face to Face)
It's Alive (Ramones)
Victim in Pain (Agnostic Front)

FAVORITE GUITAR PLAYERS

Joan Jett
Stevie Ray Vaughan
Vinnie Stigma
Tom Morello
Randy Rhoads

FAVORITE METAL/HARD ROCK ALBUMS

Welcome to Hell (Venom)
Battle Hymns (Manowar)
Paranoid (Black Sabbath)
Sad Wings of Destiny (Judas Priest)
Ace of Spades (Motörhead)
Show No Mercy (Slayer)
Vulgar Display of Power (Pantera)
Holy Diver (Dio)
Ride the Lightning (Metallica)
Under the Blade (Twisted Sister)
Roots (Sepultura)
Favorite Punk/Hardcore Albums
I Against I (Bad Brains)
Victim in Pain (Agnostic Front)
City Baby Attacked by Rats (GBH)
My Rage (Rest in Pieces)
...And Out Come the Wolves (Rancid)
Demonstrating My Style (Madball)
New Hope for the Wretched (Plasmatics)
We Are...The League (Anti-Nowhere League)
The Age of Quarrel (Cro-Mags)
Murphy's Law (Murphy's Law)

FAVORITE NON-PUNK, HARDCORE, OR METAL ALBUMS

Scarred for Life (Rose Tattoo)
Legend (Bob Marley and The Wailers)
Follow the Leader (Eric B. & Rakim)
Paul's Boutique (Beastie Boys)
Youth (Matisyahu)

FAVORITE COMEDIANS

Eddie Murphy
Jerry Seinfeld
George Carlin
Rodney Dangerfield
Richard Pryor

WORST AIRPORTS
IN NO PARTICULAR ORDER, BUT THEY ALL SUCK IN THEIR OWN SPECIAL WAY!

JFK–NYC
Charles de Gaulle–Paris
LAX–Los Angeles
Heathrow–London

—ACKNOWLEDGMENTS—

PETE

For me, music is playing all the time, either on the radio or at a show or on my headphones, and it's always playing in my head. It might be other people's songs, or something trying to make its way out of my head as a new song. Some people say that a certain song helped them through tough times, or even saved their life. I am a true believer when it comes to this. Not only has it given me this extraordinary, wonderful life, but it has also given me the two most precious gifts I've ever been given: my wife Mei-Ling and my daughter Lucy. It has also allowed me to travel the earth, make lifelong friends, and show me all the amazing lands and cultures I would never have gotten to see otherwise. Music can make you feel good or it can make you feel sad. It can make you feel cool, and it can humble you and give you the strength to get the job done. If you're sad, you might put on The Cure, which could actually make you feel sadder, but for some strange reason, it makes you feel better. It's crazy but it's true. Music has every color in the spectrum. From Hatebreed to Louis Armstrong, AFI to The O'Jays, Sade to Slayer, Hector Lavoe to Discharge, Twisted Sister to Edith Piaf, Rancid to Alicia Keys...I love it all. Music has given me everything and IS everything to me. Me and Lou are living proof that dreams come true. It takes really hard work, but if you really want it, you can get it.
You can't stop Rock and Roll!

I would like to offer my deepest thanks and praise from the bottom of my heart to:

the love of my life Mei-Ling—the one who shows me what true love is. Lucy, Mom and Dad Koller, my "other" brothers Armand and Craig, Steve and Lori, Matt and Connie, Amarilyn Robles, Sick of it All road crew past and present—thank you for keeping the train rollin', Dave Stein, Jimmy Marino, Peter and Shabana Giannoulis, Chris and Arin DeBello, Rachel and Fozz, Stormy Shepherd, Marc, David, Snoop, Ute and all from M.A.D., Fat Mike, Jens Prueter, and Howie Abrams

Special thanks to all the fans and friends of Sick of It All: the only reason we keep playing is because of all of you. Thank you VERY, VERY much! And a very special thank you to Motörhead and Black Sabbath.

Long live New York Hardcore, and Long Live Rock and Roll!

I want to thank my family who always stands by me and helps me on my journey. Aurelia and Melissa for holding down the fort and always supporting me, my parents for always being worried for our future, but allowing us to find our own way, my brothers Steve and Matt for unknowingly starting us on our musical path, Armand and Craig who complete the family and stick it out through all the highs and lows—the good times and the cracked times that we have endured, our hard working crew members past and present for their dedication, camaraderie, and for keeping us moving and laughing, our friends who keep us grounded while boosting us ever higher, and especially you fans all around the world who found a connection within the noise and words to a bunch of kids from Queens, NY! I am forever grateful.

WE DEDICATE THIS BOOK TO Armand (The Hammer) Majidi and Craig "Ahead" Setari. Sick of It All is the sum of four equal parts. Now let's hear your side of the story!

Howie would like to thank: Jacob Hoye and all at Post Hill Press, Donna McLeer, Laurens Kusters, Louis Koller Senior and Josette Koller, Melissa Koller, Mei-Ling Koller, Aurelia Koller, Lucy Koller, Steven Koller, Craig Setari, Armand Majidi, Rich Cipriano, EK, Chris Carrabba, Gary Holt, Kurt Brecht, Barney Greenway, Iggor Cavalera, Marc M.A.D., Toby Morse, John "Devil" Turner, Squirm, Sick of it Al, Bill Florio, BJ Papas, Dr. R.B. Korbet, Joel Ricard, and of course, Lou and Pete for trusting me to help tell their story, and for the many years of Queens NYHC glory! Oh, and you're welcome for my lyrical contribution, "short" on "Injustice System."

THIS BOOK IS DEDICATED TO Julie and Nia for always being by my side!

—ABOUT THE AUTHORS—

Lou and Pete Koller were born and raised in Queens, New York. Together, they formed Sick of it All in 1986–the most popular and successful hardcore band in the world. They have released a dozen full-length albums on both independent and major labels, in addition to several EPs and singles. Lou currently resides in New Jersey and Pete makes his home in Florida.

New York City native Howie Abrams has been a fixture in the city's music and entertainment scene since the early 1980s. Having held high-level creative positions at companies such as In-Effect Records–which he co-founded in 1988–to Roadrunner Records, Jive Records, Zomba Music Publishing and Warner Music Group. Howie has discovered and helped guide the careers of numerous highly influential and successful artists. As an author, Abrams has created The Merciless Book of Metal Lists, Misfit Summer Camp: 20 Years on the Road with the Vans Warped Tour, Finding Joseph I: An Oral History of H.R. from Bad Brains, Hip-Hop Alphabet, Hip-Hop Alphabet 2 and most recently, The ABCs of Metallica.

SICKOFITALL.COM
Facebook.com/SickOfItAllNY
Twitter.com/SOIANYC
Instagram.com/SickOfItAllNYC